D0369000

WITHDRAWN

THE FOUR PILLARS *of*

HIGH PERFORMANCE

How Robust Organizations
Achieve Extraordinary Results

PAUL C. LIGHT

McGraw-Hill

New York   Chicago   San Francisco   Lisbon   London
Madrid   Mexico City   Milan   New Delhi
San Juan   Seoul   Singapore
Sydney   Toronto

The McGraw·Hill Companies

1 2 3 4 5 6 7 8 9 0 DOC/DOC 0 9 8 7 6 5 4

ISBN 0-07-144879-9

This publication is designed to provide accurate and authoritative information in regard to the subject matter covered. It is sold with the understanding that the publisher is not engaged in rendering legal, accounting, or other professional service. If legal advice or other expert assistance is required, the services of a competent professional person should be sought.

—*From a declaration of principles jointly adopted by a committee of the American Bar Association and a committee of publishers.*

McGraw-Hill books are available at special quantity discounts to use as premiums and sales promotions, or for use in corporate training programs. For more information, please write to the Director of Special Sales, McGraw-Hill Professional, Two Penn Plaza, New York, NY 10121-2298. Or contact your local bookstore.

 This book is printed on recycled, acid-free paper containing a minimum of 50% recycled, de-inked fiber.

Library of Congress Cataloging-in-Publication Data

Light, Paul Charles.
 The four pillars of high performance : how robust organizations achieve extraordinary results / Paul C. Light.
  p. cm.
 Includes bibliographical references.
 ISBN 0-07-144879-9
 1. Organizational change—Management. 2. Strategic planning. 3. Crisis management. I. Title.
 HD58.8.L54 2005
 658.4'06—dc22

2004026457

CONTENTS

FOREWORD   V

PREFACE   IX

CHAPTER 1
Uncertainty Rising   I

CHAPTER 2
In Search of Extraordinary Results   43

CHAPTER 3
The Four Pillars of High Performance   93

CHAPTER 4
How Robust Organizations Operate   129

CHAPTER 5
Lessons on Managing Change   203

BIBLIOGRAPHY   245

INDEX   259

FOREWORD

James Q. Wilson

Everyone wants organizational life to be rational. We prefer knowledge to ignorance and insight to superstition. To argue otherwise would seem to make us less than human.

Of course, much of life is ruled as much by emotion and ambition as by inquiry and thought. We are humans, shaped by passions and interests as well as by reason and detachment. We cannot be otherwise.

The real enemies of knowledge are not passions, ignorance, or superstition, but the special kind of tunnel vision that arises from old habits, organizational loyalties, and personal commitments. As a wily bureaucratic veteran once said, where you stand depends on where you sit.

Over the past 50 years, an extraordinary effort has been made to increase the reach of reason in shaping our public and organizational life. RAND has been the leader in this effort, bringing about, by its own achievements and by the example it has set for others, a remarkable transformation in the way public choices are made and organizations are run.

RAND was created by General Hap Arnold of the Army Air Corps as a new way of mobilizing talent for research. The goal was simple: to use smart people based in a relatively autonomous organization to think through air corps needs and problems. General Arnold's decision profoundly affected how the military would cope with the Cold War.

In 1948 RAND became its own nonprofit corporation. In the half century that has followed its creation, we have seen an explosion of organizations that share the RAND approach in some way. Today we call them think tanks. In 1948 there were scarcely any; now there are dozens. Some, like RAND, are nonpartisan; others are partisan. But whatever their political coloration, think tanks have largely replaced universities as the most influential way for bringing the ideas of gifted thinkers and the discipline of hard facts to policy choices.

The accomplishments of RAND are now legendary. When you see a satellite photograph of the weather or use the Global Positioning System (GPS) to find your way, you are using technology that was imagined by RAND over two decades before Buzz Aldrin set foot on the moon. In 1946 RAND researchers proposed a world-circling spaceship that would have military value, while aiding research and providing for long-range communications. For decades after that paper was written, RAND helped guide the satellite development system.

When you use a personal computer, you are using technology that was refined at RAND. RAND built one of the world's first computers, called the JOHNNIAC, after John von Neumann, the great mathematician and RAND consultant, who conceptualized the computer.

When you send an e-mail, you are using a method created by Paul Baran, a RAND researcher, over three decades ago. Baran was trying to solve the problem of making communications secure in the aftermath of an enemy attack. Telephone systems and military radios were vulnerable to any attack that demolished the central stations that controlled these systems. Baran invented a system that had no central stations and required no fixed route. Messages would be broken into little pieces, or packets, and each would follow whatever electronic route existed, being reassembled at the end into a coherent message. Today we call it the Internet.

RAND has also become talented at understanding the human dimensions of organizational life. As Paul Light argues in this book, RAND has produced hundreds of studies of how organizations work. Results of these studies include how to recruit, motivate, and reward talented employees; organize the supply chain to guarantee access to spare parts; find leading-edge equipment; and communicate through the fog and friction not only of war but also of the confining routines of daily life.

Truth can be spoken to power when both the truth speakers and the power holders recognize that, at least on important matters, new information changes behavior only when it is linked to a shared view of the goals of the organization and the needs of its culture.

Both RAND and RAND's sponsors have learned these lessons. RAND understands that though a sponsor, in RAND's opinion, may ask the wrong questions, RAND is ready to answer the question that was asked, and to do so promptly and clearly, even when it suggests new questions that ought to be asked later.

Sponsors understand that RAND represents an asset that no sponsor can create within itself—namely, an autonomous organization, committed to the public interest, that by its analyses will broaden the perspective and clarify the vision of the sponsor.

The number of these sponsors is today vastly larger than it was in 1946. In addition to serving the Air Force, RAND serves the Army; the Secretary of Defense; private firms working in such areas as insurance, civil justice, health care, and pharmaceuticals; and agencies and foundations concerned about education, labor, population, immigration, drug abuse, and criminal justice. These studies are done not only for American sponsors but also for many in Europe and the Middle East.

Taking on these new clients has meant taking on intellectual tasks that pose even greater challenges to objectivity than do military ones. Many of the most important domestic disputes are about matters that defy mathematical estimation. It is not easy to measure good health or a good education. Moreover, disputes about health or education or crime are driven by profound differences of opinion about the kind of world in which we wish to live. By contrast, differing views about military tactics are often arguments about means to a shared goal. Everyone wants a secure America. The issue, then, is how best and most economically to achieve that goal. Arguments about domestic issues, however, are often arguments about the kind of world in which we wish to live: Should drug use be opposed, tolerated, or made legal? What constitutes an educated person? These are not simply disputes about the means to a goal, but about the goal itself.

Just as everyone wants a secure America, most of us want to work in high-performing organizations. As RAND has learned, creating high performance is easier said than done. It takes careful analysis and persistence. Paul Light suggests in this book that RAND research reveals a set of central truths. High-performing organizations stay *alert* by measuring results, evaluating program success, and creating clear expectations for performance; they stay *agile* by giving their employees authority to make routine decisions on their own, reducing barriers between units, encouraging participatory management, and fostering open communications; they stay *adaptive* by regularly surveying their customers, investing in new ideas, and creating strong incentives for performance; and they stay *aligned* by saturating the organization with information and providing effective information technology.

These lessons come from Light's detailed analysis of what RAND has learned over the past half century about making organizations work. His book is based on the reading of hundreds of reports and talking at length with RAND researchers. As Light points out, RAND's findings on Pearl Harbor, the Cuban missile crisis, and other forms of surprise are just as relevant to private firms as they are to government, while its work on innovation in the housing, petroleum, mining, communication, and biotechnology industries is just as relevant to government as it is to IBM and Intel.

He argues that there are some simple, evidence-based principles for designing organizations that can survive and prosper in an uncertain world. Light calls such an organization the *robust organization*, meaning that an organization that selects the best plan for a range of possible futures will hedge against vulnerabilities and surprise and then adapt to changing circumstances by shaping the future to its liking. Doing so requires a kind of alertness, agility, adaptability, and alignment that is too often lacking in today's organizations. As RAND itself found in the mid-1990s, organizations cannot become more robust merely by wishing it so. They must take concrete steps toward enhancing their performance, starting with a simple willingness to confront their own assumptions about the future.

Paul Light is a skilled and imaginative political scientist who has published important works on social security reform, sustaining innovation, and the true size of government. His work at RAND did not involve any preconditions or post-research clearances. What you will read here is Light's best independent advice.

PREFACE

This book is for readers who want to know what their organizations can do to achieve and sustain high performance in a turbulent world. It is for executives who come to work wondering what, if anything, might really work in strengthening performance; senior managers who must implement the CEO's latest idea for doing more with less; middle managers who shudder at yet another e-mail promising reform and reengineering; frontline employees who are asked to reread their tattered copies of *Who Moved My Cheese* as their organizations prepare the next round of change; and investors who are looking for organizations that can sustain high performance through turbulent times.

I believe that any organization, no matter how moribund or demoralized, can create a burst of high performance by terrifying the workforce or rallying the troops for yet another run at innovation. The real challenge is to build organizations that produce results by hedging against the inevitable surprises and vulnerabilities that lurk in today's environment, while exploiting opportunities to shape the future to their advantage.

In a perfect world, organizations would not worry about surprise and vulnerability. There would be one future and one future only. It would be steady and predictable, a simple extension of the past. Opportunities would be easy to identify and pluck, markets easy to read and exploit, and performance easy to measure and reward. But this is far from a perfect world.

High performance requires more than a robust strategy that will succeed in a variety of scenarios. It also requires an organization that is among the first to sense a change in probabilities across the range of possible futures; among the fastest to deploy resources against threats, surprises, and opportunities; among the most creative in forging a presence in the evolving future; and among the very best in moving as a whole into whatever the ever-evolving future holds. In a word, such organizations are robust. They are alert to change, agile in deployment, adaptive in practice and product, and aligned in purpose.

This image of the robust organization emerges from real research on real organizations conducted by the RAND Corporation, the Santa Monica–based think tank that has produced thousands of studies over the past 50 years that deal directly or indirectly with improving organizational performance. RAND has a special standing in helping organizations improve, in part because its researchers have no loyalties to any particular organizational reform, in part because they are so resistant to the latest change fads, and in part because they are so committed to analysis, not hunch and anecdote, as the basis for understanding.

The fact that RAND researchers share an agreement on the core characteristics of high-performing organizations, let alone an agreement that reveals a discrete image of an organization that does particularly well in today's volatile world, suggests that there may actually be some evidence-based truths for guiding change. RAND researchers may be more likely to speak in mathematical equations than in metaphor, but I believe their research has produced a common vision of what constitutes high performance, as well as how to achieve and sustain it.

THE RAND KNOWLEDGE BASE

Even among think-tank scholars like me, RAND has always been something of an enigma. Always rated at or near the top in reputation and rigor, it has rarely been above the middle in visibility and media mentions.

Having been affiliated with the Brookings Institution for 20 years before I began the project on which this book is based, I knew almost nothing about RAND, and what I did know was just a little unsettling: As the nation's first organization to be called a think tank, RAND was the place where nuclear warfighters like Dr. Strangelove worked—thinking the unthinkable, designing new weapons, and inventing the mutual assured destruction that would prevent Armageddon during the Cold War.

Even RAND's name was a puzzle to me. Its name is actually an acronym for "research and development." As I learned, RAND started out under the wing of the Douglas Aircraft Corporation as Project RAND in 1945 and changed its name to the RAND Corporation when it broke off as an independent organization in 1948. Although it calls itself a corporation,

RAND has always been a tax-exempt nonprofit—it has no shareholders and does not distribute profits.

Much of my earlier thinking about RAND was shaped by Sylvia Nasar's biography of John Forbes Nash, *A Beautiful Mind*. Read the book and you will come to think of RAND as an almost quirky retreat where brilliant mathematicians such as Herman Kahn, John von Neumann, Thomas Schelling, and Albert Wohlstetter played practical jokes on each other while thinking about how the U.S. could fight and win a nuclear war.[1] Indeed, Nasar's chapter on Nash's four years in Santa Monica starts with the informal RAND hymn:

Oh, the RAND Corporation is the boon of the world;
They think all day for a fee.
They sit and play games about going up in flames,
For counters they use you and me, Honey Bee,
For counters they use you and me.

Nash was initially responsible for the mathematical proofs underpinning nuclear deterrence. "It was unthinkable that such destructive power would be unleashed," writes Nasar. "Therefore RAND insisted that it was necessary to ponder the possibility."[2]

RAND had changed dramatically by the time I arrived in 2000. Half of its research revenue had come to involve domestic and economic issues, and its staff had grown to 1600 researchers who covered a wide range of disciplines well beyond mathematics.[3] RAND was still thinking the unthinkable, but it was doing so about a range of new issues, such as the spread of global infectious disease, the aging of the Russian nuclear fleet, fighting the war on terrorism, the rising costs of obesity, and declining competition in the aircraft industry. More to the point of this book, RAND had developed a deep knowledge base on organizational life. Its research database contains 5914 reports with some relevance to management, including a recent study on how to manage the Air Force pilot shortage during a period of "boiling peace"; 4404 reports on planning, including a recent report on General Motors's product portfolio; 1784 reports on organization, including a study of how to manage a naval shipyard; and 197 reports on innovation, including an analysis of product development by DuPont, Marriott, and Procter & Gamble.

Most of these studies involve real organizations and real problems, including how to motivate employees, measure performance, move supplies, deploy resources, collect and connect information, reengineer hierarchies, improve quality, and enhance accountability. RAND's analysis of loosely net-worked organizations such as al Qaeda shows how organizations such as IBM and the Army can become more agile; its insights on how Volvo entered the sport utility market show how other organizations can adapt to new futures; its research on high-performing combat units such as the 3rd Army's 4th armored division in World War II shows how any organization can build more effective teams; its analysis of the Kosovo air war in 1999 holds lessons for any organization that wants to build a better command and control system; its research on helping move the Air Force into battle within 48 hours can help any organization develop its own agile support system; its analysis of the effort to cut school class size in California reminds all organizations to worry about the unintended effects created by honorable intentions; and its study of how Patriot Missile operators are recruited and trained should reassure every human resource officer that people really do matter to success, which is no small matter when every miss costs $91 million.

RAND has produced more than just thousands of reports, however. It has also produced collective experience about what matters most to organizational performance. Although it is not in their nature to operate beyond the envelope of a specific study, RAND's full- and part-time researchers do draw conclusions about organizational performance. "When I first came to RAND out of a highly technical mathematical economics program, I was very unused to things that violated the standard assumptions," RAND's Susan Gates says about her work. "But when you're forced to get out there, interact with these organizations, and see what really happens in terms of providing incentives and motivating workers, you see that your assumptions in your model aren't any good if they're not realistic."

These insights are based on evidence, not hunch, and on analysis, not dogma. RAND researchers are reluctant to draw hard-and-fast conclusions about anything, and always stick close to their data. As senior researcher James Quinlivan told me in one of the long interviews for this book, "We probably overchew our food before we swallow. You know, 25 chews before swallowing is safe; 100 chews looks a little obsessive."

Quinlivan is quick to add that RAND does not promote a single model of organizational performance. "When you ask consultants how they think about an organization, they will echo back a whole set of beliefs and learned theories that they've been taught by the business school they went to and the firm that they work for. I would expect the mean of their views to be at one spot, and the variance ought to be pretty small relative to talking to RAND. As an organization, RAND does not inculcate a RAND view. As much as you will hear back a common RAND view or repeated themes at RAND, we don't create it through an indoctrination course in your first two weeks."

Instead, RAND research is guided by three basic principles embedded in its organizational culture.

First, RAND has a well-deserved reputation for questioning the questions. As RAND explains on its website, "over the years RAND has acquired a reputation for answering a different question from what the client initially asked—and this has led to some of the institution's best-known successes." As Hosmer translates, "There are some officials who want help with the issues in their immediate in-box. That's perfectly legitimate, important work—that's one of the reasons clients pay the bills. At the same time, I think we have to be concerned about issues that have not reached the in-box as yet, to think about what officials should know that they don't know now."

Second, RAND has a long history of questioning its own answers through peer review and quality control. "Part of our culture says, 'Hey, let's share what we have,'" says Robert Tripp. "'Let's beat it down.' I've always been fortunate enough to have someone on my team who questions everything I do. But part of our culture is to make sure that we 'murder board' things, and we get divergent views. And to the extent we do, that make us better."

One reason peer review works so well at RAND is that the organization and its researchers have no stake, financial or intellectual, in any particular answer. As Susan Gates notes, "RAND isn't out there trying to sell its 'little-off-the-shelf-solution.'" It also works well because of a basic commitment to evidence. "My feeling is if you can't say it with numbers," says John Birkler, "your knowledge is meager or insufficient. So I try to be very quantitative and follow where the numbers lead me. And I think as long as I do that and do it in a competent and robust manner, I will be fully supported by the organization, no matter what conclusions I draw." According to Leland Joe, who authored the RAND study of high-performing combat units, "we are scientists, either physical or social. We try to make our stands based on some sort of evidence or analysis."

Third, RAND allows the evidence to speak, even when it unsettles the client. As James Q. Wilson said at RAND's 50th anniversary celebration, "The sponsor must learn that there is a price to be paid for getting honest advice. Sometimes the think tank will give you answers to your questions that you do not like. Sometimes it will tell you that you are asking the wrong questions. And often it will take longer than you would like to do either. But in exchange for these costs, the sponsor gets something of great value: a disinterested voice with broad knowledge that analyzes choices on the basis of knowledge, however imperfect, rather than on the basis of loyalty, however well deserved."[4]

PLAN OF THE BOOK

I started working on this book in 1999 when RAND asked me to take a look at what its researchers had learned over the past decade about managing public organizations. The more time I spent shuttling back and forth to RAND's headquarters in Santa Monica, California, however, the more I focused on what RAND had learned about how any organization can achieve and sustain high performance.

The lessons cannot be found on the RAND website or in a handful of reports, however. Rather, they emerge from unstructured interviews with more than 100 principal investigators, an Internet survey of another 126 researchers, and content analysis of several hundred reports. These reports deal with everything from strategic purchasing at Brystol-Myers Squibb to environmental management at Hewlett-Packard, from high-stakes accountability in education to product development at Volvo, from supply management at the Army to innovation in housing and biotechnology, from the impact of consolidation in the aircraft and shipbuilding industries to the use of networks by terrorist organizations, and from innovation management at Intel to quality control at the nation's human tissue repositories.

Although this book is based solely on the RAND knowledge base, the conclusions are mine. I conducted the interviews, designed and analyzed the Internet survey, and searched for common themes across the studies referenced in the bibliography to this book. RAND did not review this book prior to publication, nor did it affirm more general findings.

The first chapter, "Uncertainty Rising," asks what RAND has learned about the future by examining four critical sources of organizational vulnerability: (1) ignorance, (2) inflexibility, (3) indifference, and (4) inconsistency. The chapter then argues that uncertainty is not only rising but deepening as the world becomes more unpredictable and wild cards such as terrorism increase. It is one thing to be lethargic, stiff, complacent, and misaligned in a predictable world, and quite another to proceed in a world beset by revolutions in living things, materials and manufacturing, information, global commerce, revolutions themselves, and organizational strategy. The chapter concludes by exploring RAND's recommendations for uncertainty-sensitive planning.

The second chapter, "In Search of Extraordinary Results," asks what RAND has learned about addressing the vulnerabilities of uncertainty.

Drawing upon the Internet survey of 126 senior RAND researchers, the chapter uses a statistical winnowing process to identify and sort the most important predictors of high performance. Although the winnowing produces a final pool of seven powerful predictors, it also reveals the four underlying pillars that help organizations achieve extraordinary results: (1) alertness, (2) agility, (3) adaptability, and (4) alignment. Drawing upon the RAND knowledge base more broadly, the chapter ends with a set of lessons about what does and does not matter to organizational improvement.

The third chapter, "The Four Pillars of High Performance," asks what RAND has learned about the four underpinnings of high performance identified in the winnowing process. The chapter starts with a brief definition of what I call the robust organization, then examines the four pillars of robustness in detail. After exploring RAND's general agreement on how organizations can harden themselves against uncertainty, the chapter examines the benchmarks of robustness. It concludes with a history of RAND's recent transformation into a robust organization itself.

The fourth chapter, "How Robust Organizations Operate," asks what RAND knows about operating a robust organization. Simply asked, how do robust organizations create the alertness, agility, adaptability, and alignment essential to high performance? The chapter offers four answers:

1. Robust organizations think in futures (plural) tense. They plan against landscapes of possible futures; accept the inevitability of surprise; challenge their assumptions about the futures they face; reduce regret by adopting robust, adaptive plans, avoiding unintended consequences, and reducing vulnerability; and focus on the direct, indirect, and cascading effects of what they do. As such, they are highly alert.

2. *Robust organizations organize for lightening.* They recruit their workforces for maximum flexibility; train for agility by drawing the right lessons from the past, reducing the cost of learning, and cultivating corporateness; set just-beyond-possible goals; provide authority to act; and think lean about every aspect of work. As such they are highly agile.

3. *Robust organizations challenge the prevailing wisdom.* They create both the freedom to learn and the freedom to imagine; aggregate expertise by creating teams and networks; unbalance their scorecards by measuring in futures tense, using multiple measures to avoid complacency and cheating, being careful about what they

measure, and inviting intuition; and strengthen command and control to assure that investments are well spent. As such, they are highly adaptive.

4. *Robust organizations lead to mission.* They grow and groom their own leaders from within; lead in futures tense; communicate through images and stories; anticipate their adversaries through careful study and assessment; and ignore irrelevant issues that impede command. As such, they are tightly aligned.

The fifth and final chapter, "Lessons on Managing Change," asks what RAND has learned about managing change. Drawing upon RAND research on change management in public, business, and nonprofit organizations, the chapter argues that change is both possible and manageable. The chapter starts by asking about RAND's preferences for picking an organizational change, then examines RAND's six suggested steps for improving the odds of success: (1) create a sense of urgency, (2) remove the barriers to success, (3) recruit the champions, (4) build internal momentum, (5) prove that change works, and (6) keep experimenting. The chapter concludes with recommendations on how to manage the journey to robustness.

Readers are reminded once again that this book is based on my reading of the RAND knowledge base and my interpretations of what RAND and its researchers have learned. Having spent months reading and rereading the RAND literature, conducting second, third, and even fourth interviews with key researchers, and teaching two seminars for the RAND Graduate School, I think I know RAND almost as well as RAND does.

Readers should also remember that this book is built in part on interviews with researchers who generally steer clear of the business bookshelves. When they have time to read about organizational performance, they turn to the classics of supply chain management, advanced mathematical modeling, statistical process control, or health management, not the latest *New York Times* bestseller. To the extent that they share a common image of what constitutes a robust organization and how to build one, they confirm some basic truths about the importance of management and organization to successful outcomes.

Finally, readers should note that the book is based on a veritable mountain of reports, many of which did not focus on organizational characteristics at all. RAND's primary business is about policy analysis, not organizational design. Other researchers might have put this puzzle together differently.

I would not have written this book if I did not believe RAND and its researchers had something to say to today's organizations, however. They might not visit the business bookshelves, but they have clearly come to close agreement about what matters most to extraordinary performance in an increasingly turbulent world. If they believe it, perhaps we should, too.

ACKNOWLEDGMENTS

This book could not have been written without RAND's initial invitation to conduct an internal reconnaissance of its knowledge base under a traditional consulting agreement. Although I severed the relationship in 2002 to assure complete independence, RAND continued to provide maximum access and encouragement. I am particularly grateful to RAND's executive vice president, Michael Rich, and the dean of RAND's Pardee Graduate School, Robert Klitgaard, for their patience and friendship as I moved from interview to interview, and to RAND's president and chief executive officer, James Thomson, for his gracious embrace of the project.

I am also obviously grateful to the enormous gifts of time from all of the RAND researchers who sat through an interview or participated in the Internet survey. I am especially grateful to the researchers who took time for more than one interview along the way, including Beth Asch, Tora Bikson, John Birkler, Dominick Brewer, Frank Camm, Natalie Crawford, Paul Davis, John Dumond, James Dertouzous, James Dewar, Rick Eden, Susan Everingham, Susan Gates, Laura Hamilton, Bruce Hoffman, James Hosek, Stephen Hosmer, Leland Joe, Jacob Klerman, Robert Lempert, Robert Levine, Mark Lorell, Elizabeth McGlynn, Nancy Moore, Steven Popper, James Quinlivan, Marc Robbins, Albert Robbert, and Gregory Treverton.

I am also grateful to my family, the Brookings Institution, and my colleagues at New York University's Robert F. Wagner School of Public Service for their encouragement as I worked and reworked this material. I am particularly thankful for questions and comments from students in my "Designing Organizational Change" class as they read early drafts, and for the careful readings by my Wagner School dean, Ellen Schall, my New School colleague Mary Bryna Sanger, several anonymous RAND researchers, and former Treasury Secretary and Alcoa CEO Paul O'Neill, who gave the manuscript a close reading at the very end of the process. Finally, I would like to acknowledge Will Lippincott, who helped me place this book with McGraw-Hill, and the entire editorial and production team who brought the manuscript to the page, including editor Jeanne Glasser and editing supervisor Pattie Amoroso.

NOTES

1   Sylvia Nasar, *A Beautiful Mind*, New York: Simon & Schuster Touchstone, 1998.

2   Nasar, *A Beautiful Mind*, pp. 110-111.

3   These figures come from Martin J. Collins, *Planning for Modern War: RAND and the Air Force*, Dissertation submitted to the Faculty of the Graduate School of the University of Maryland, 1998, p. 266.

4   James Q. Wilson, "RAND at Fifty," address commemorating RAND's 50th anniversary, the Library of Congress, April 8, 1998, access at http://www.rand.org/about/history/jqwilson.html, June 9, 2004, p. 3.

UNCERTAINTY RISING

If you aren't accident-prone don't put all your eggs into one basket—if you are accident-prone, become less so.
                                        Albert Wohlstetter, 1954[1]

Rand and its researchers have always been interested in uncertainty and the vulnerability that goes with it. Uncertainty was the dominant theme of RAND's work for the Air Force in the 1940s, its research on urban development, national health insurance, and welfare reform in the 1960s and 1970s, and virtually everything it does today.

This focus was palpable at RAND during the Cold War. Just ask Paul Davis, one of RAND's leading thinkers in strategic and crisis planning. According to Davis

> The objective degree of uncertainty has always been quite substantial, and was much greater than people acknowledged. Think about the big events that were either surprising or should have been because we were poorly prepared for them: the Hungarian revolution, the Cuban missile crisis, the Prague spring, the near-miss of the 1973 Arab-Israeli war, Egypt's peace initiative (which came out of left field), the Iranian revolution, apparent Soviet military interest in Southwest Africa, the collapse of the Soviet Union, reunion of Germany, Iraq's invasion of Kuwait. Anyone who did strategic planning in that lengthy period *should* have recognized deep uncertainty, and *should* have been extremely humble. Even

those who were doing more narrowly military work such as assessing the military balance in Central Europe *should* have recognized that the likely outcome of war, if it occurred, depended fundamentally on a number of key factors not knowable in advance by peacetime planners.[2]

RAND has never been interested in uncertainty for curiosity's sake, however. From its founding, RAND and its researchers have tried to both plan and prepare for surprises, whether by inventing tools for exploring the future, designing operating plans that perform well across a range of scenarios, or hardening targets against surprise. The core question for this book is not whether organizations face many futures, or even whether many of today's organizations are vulnerable. Rather, it is how organizations can harden themselves to survive and prosper no matter what future shows up.

Albert Wohlstetter was working on a study of how to protect fuel tanks at U.S. bomber bases when he used the eggs-in-the-basket metaphor. After noting that fuel was obviously critical to operational capability, especially on an overseas airbase where it is difficult to replenish quickly, Wohlstetter calculated that fuel tanks were more vulnerable when empty rather than full, when above ground rather than below, and when concentrated in a tight cluster rather than widely separated. Merely increasing the number of fuel tanks, or baskets, did little to alter the probability of arriving at market with enough eggs unbroken. "However, if the probability of dropping a basket has been made very low, then increasing the number of baskets provides useful insurance against the unlucky event that one basket is dropped....In the case of fuel storage, this may be interpreted to mean that splitting the storage sites offers obvious insurance benefits only when the expected proportion surviving has been increased to a satisfactory level."[3]

The advice is just as pertinent to today's organizations as it was to the Air Force at the start of the Cold War. As this chapter will suggest, organizations can substitute a thousand products for fuel stocks and still find good reason to worry about vulnerability. Even if organizations are not accident prone, they should never put all of their eggs in one basket. If they are accident prone, they should become less so. The first piece of advice is all about strategy, while the second is about organizational design. Just as strategies should be robust across a range of possible futures, organizations should be robust enough to make those strategies possible.

STUDIES IN VULNERABILITY

Wohlstetter was not the only RAND researcher to worry about uncertainty. It is a theme in a growing list of industry studies, including the petroleum industry whose products once preoccupied Wohlstetter. According to RAND's study of new forces at work in refining, the industry has gone through two decades of consolidation (hedging), product development (shaping), and organizational change, changing from an industry once led by a half dozen majors to one split between super-majors and a vast array of mid-sized and boutique refiners focused largely on refining and marketing within specific regions.[4]

Along the way, the industry has become leaner as the majors have scaled back, shut down, or sold off their excess capacity; cut their research and development; and left the retail business. As the number of refining firms declined sharply, the majors focused on product segments or regions where they held a strong position. They also continued to cut costs, especially downstream in the refining process, while adopting nearly every change strategy in the book, including downsizing, restructuring, mergers and acquisitions, joint ventures, and divestiture, all aimed at increasing profitability. As one refining executive told D. J. Peterson and Sergej Mahnovski, "You have to have a strong heart and tough stomach to be in this business." Wohlstetter would almost certainly agree.

The only thing the petroleum industry did not and could not do is make the future more predictable, however. Even as it scrubbed its organizations, it became more vulnerable to the same trends that are shaping most industries—terrorism on the oil fields, changing consumer habits, stiffness in the supply chain they no longer control, and unpredictable government regulation.

Yet, none of the industry executives Peterson and Mahnovski interviewed predicted technological breakthroughs in the future, no doubt because they are so focused on the industry's recent troubles that they cannot think beyond the short-term. Moreover, as they write, "innovation in mature process industries tends to be more incremental. And, as in other industries with a fixed capital base, operating companies have little incentive to promote fundamentally new technologies that might result in the accelerated depreciation or scrapping of a substantial portion of their existing capital stock."

The problem is that the industry as a whole is no longer as adaptive as it once was. The federal government has cut back sharply on subsidies for research and development in both academic and industry settings, while the number of scientists and engineers engaged in crude oil production and refining research has fallen steadily. At the same time, the industry itself has scaled back, spun off, or entirely eliminated much of its own research and development capacity. For most of the majors, RAND reports, research and development is restricted to short-term, plant- or equipment-specific problem solving. Although other industries such as chemicals, transportation, and machinery cut back, too, the petroleum industry started from a much smaller base, which makes it even more vulnerable to surprise, especially with a regulatory environment that can change with the next election. Refineries are now operating at or near capacity, which simultaneously increases profitability while leaving little room to exploit the increased market segmentation created by government requirements.

Viewed as a whole, the petroleum industry has both strengths and vulnerabilities. Many of its organizations have worked hard to cut costs, streamline operations, and tighten product lines. But it is also easy to spot at least four sources of vulnerability that face organizations today. Many organizations are not paying attention to longer-range threats and opportunities (*ignorance*), creating the capability to move quickly to hedge against vulnerability or exploit new markets (*inflexibility*), investing in the research and development needed to bring new products to scale (*indifference*), or aligning the organization to move as whole toward a hoped-for future (*inconsistency*).

Four Sources of Vulnerability

▶ Ignorance

▶ Inflexibility

▶ Indifference

▶ Inconsistency

The petroleum industry is hardly alone in its predicament. RAND researchers have seen all four sources of vulnerability across the sectors. Name a product, industry, or organization, and it is either grappling with one or more of these four, recovering from an accident or surprise, or trying to figure out what went wrong with the perfect plan. This is not to say that all organizations are vulnerable in all four areas, many do well against one, two, or even three areas. But as the following discussion of each vulnerability suggests, many organizations are so busy confronting the present that they cannot see the shocks and opportunities just beyond tomorrow.

Ignorance

Organizational ignorance comes in many varieties. Some organizations are so focused on fighting present battles against their corporate or political adversaries that they forget the future entirely. Others focus on a single future without worrying about the uncertainty that surrounds them. Still others collect thousands of dots about the future, but fail to connect them. As RAND might note, it is what you don't know that can hurt you.

Roberta Wohlstetter made the point in her classic study of the surprise attack on Pearl Harbor. As Thomas Schelling writes in the foreword of her 1962 book, "It would be reassuring to believe that Pearl Harbor was just a colossal and extraordinary blunder. What is disquieting is that it was a supremely *ordinary* blunder....If we think of the entire U.S. government and its far-flung military and diplomatic establishment, it is not true that we were caught napping at the time of Pearl Harbor. Rarely has a government been more expectant. We just expected wrong. We were so busy thinking through some 'obvious' Japanese moves that we neglected to hedge against the choice they actually made."[5]

Wohlstetter's analysis could not be more relevant for today's organizations. In retrospect, the U.S. had ample warning, including the disappearance of the Japanese fleet and troop movements in the Far East. Having broken Japan's secret code, the U.S. had access to thousands of messages about intent, almost all of them clear and direct. Moreover, the U.S. had plenty of short-term information on the morning of December 7 that could have, and possibly should have, alerted U.S. forces to prepare for battle, including contact with a Japanese submarine at 6:53 a.m. just outside Pearl Harbor, or the famous radar contact with "something completely out of the ordinary" moving steadily toward Pearl Harbor at 7:02 a.m., only minutes before the attack.

These were not the only dots on the intelligence scorecard in the days leading up to Pearl Harbor, however. As Wohlstetter writes, "signals announcing the Pearl Harbor attack were always accompanied by competing or contradictory signals, by all sorts of information useful for anticipating this particular disaster." Referring to the "vast congeries of signs pointing in every direction" and huge volumes of information as *noise*, Wohlstetter writes that the Pearl Harbor signals were mixed in with an onslaught of information from Europe, where a war was already in full bloom, and in the Far East, where Japan was preparing to attack the Soviet Russia. "In short, we failed to anticipate Pearl Harbor not for want of the relevant materials, but because of a plethora of irrelevant ones." As she concludes, "There is a difference, then, between having a signal available somewhere in the heap of irrelevancies, and perceiving it as a warning; and there is also a difference between perceiving it as a warning, and acting or getting action on it."[6]

Wohlstetter's study is echoed in dozens of other RAND studies of surprise, including its more recent work on the German invasion of France, which produced what one historian has called a "strange victory."[7] On paper, the French military looked unbeatable in 1939. Its officer corps was battle-hardened from World War I, its defenses included the impenetrable Maginot Line, and its intelligence gathering was superb. "It was the greatest military in the world, or so they thought," RAND's Steven Popper says. "The French Army, by any estimate, looked invincible. In fact, the German Army's general staff were plotting a coup against Hitler in late 1939 because they thought it was absolutely insane to attack France with the German Army. There was just no way that it could succeed."

But according to the RAND researchers who have been working to improve organizational decision making, the French failed to see the changing world around them. Although the French were clearly aware of the German threat, particularly in the wake of the Polish conquest, they were prepared for every scenario but the one that took place. Assuming that the Ardennes Forest was impassable to heavy tanks, and that their soldiers were much better trained and disciplined than the Poles, the French bet that the German's *blitzkrieg*, or lightning-war, simply did not apply to them. In fact, the Ardennes turned out to be passable, and the German revolutionary approach to war did apply just as well to the West as to the East. Although French soldiers fought valiantly, they were soon overwhelmed by reality. Despite its smaller size and perceived weakness, the German Army overwhelmed the French within weeks.

As with so many successful organizations, the French were blinded by their almost religious faith that the past was prologue to all futures. As historian Ernest May writes, the French would have almost certainly earned a draw in the battle had the Germans behaved rationally and attacked through Belgium where the French had positioned their best units. But, like any agile adversary up against a powerful foe, the Germans did the unexpected. "It is very hard to compose a scenario that would end with Germany so quickly victorious if the Allies had anticipated—even as one possibility among several—a major fast-moving German offensive through the Ardennes....Germany's strange victory of 1940 traces back, above all, to the German general staff's having been right in presuming that the French high command would (a) dispatch nearly all first-line forces to Belgium, (b) not recognize for several days that this had been a mistake, and (c) have great difficulty adjusting to and coping with the newly discovered reality."[8]

Not every RAND study of surprise involves war, however, nor are all surprises inevitable. As we shall see, there are many ways to imagine alternative futures, not the least of which is to develop a scenario space of plausible realities. Volvo did just that in the late 1990s when it began debating entry into the sport utility market. Although the debate eventually produced several new vehicles, including the XC90, *Motor Trend* magazine's 2003 Sport Utility of the Year, the entry was anything but assured. Indeed, the deep uncertainties associated with entering a new market had created gridlock within the company. Some said that Volvo had to build an SUV to compete in a rapidly expanding market niche, while others felt that an SUV would compromise Volvo's brand identity as a manufacturer of premier passenger sedans.

At first Volvo's planning group tried to assess the options using its traditional planning methods. The only problem was that the marketing, finance, production, engineering, and design groups each brought a different vision of the future to the decision. As Lempert and Popper write, "each department rightly focused on different aspects of the problem. Marketing focused on price points, that is, relative price for different vehicles within a line, while finance focused on net revenues. The analysts working each spreadsheet thus gathered their own data, conducted their sensitivity analysis over the futures they understood, and then passed a small number of outputs along to their colleagues who used them as inputs to their own extensive calculations." Although the method had worked well for less radical product lines, it raised questions and concerns when applied to entirely new vehicle classes, in part because the various spreadsheets contained a set of implicit assumptions that were often in conflict with each other. Each division understood the weaknesses in their own models, but there was no way to analyze the interactions and little confidence in the overall results.

Volvo broke the stalemate in part by using a computer-assisted, decision-making system for identifying, then reconciling the competing visions of the future. The system, which was designed by Lempert, Popper, and Bankes, had two components: (1) a scenario generator that produced a wide range of futures relevant to the decision, and (2) exploratory-modeling software that played the scenarios out in a visual layout that allowed Volvo to question every assumption underpinning the future.[9]

As Volvo considered its strategy, it moved away from its initial product plan, which performed best under the optimistic assumptions that had provoked initial interest in an SUV. The analysis confirmed the benefits of adopting a new program plan that sacrificed some potential profit in the case of better-than-expected performance in return for stronger hedges against the chances that all would not go as planned. Although Volvo might have done very well in 2000 and 2001 with a much larger vehicle, the world had changed dramatically by the time the XC90 reached the market in late 2002. Not only was the SUV a financial success, it reinforced Volvo's strong brand identity as a premier car-maker. "Volvo may be late to the SUV party," *Motor Trend* raved after a test drive in late 2002, "but it's bringing something new—an SUV with a conscience. That thinking has jived with Volvo wagon buyers over the years, and there's every reason to believe it'll work with SUV buyers as well. We'd say that's a safe bet."[10] It was a robust bet as well.

Inflexibility

Volvo's success depended on more than alertness to alternative futures. It also required a relatively tight turning radius in actually implementing its decision. Having waited 10 years to enter the SUV market, Volvo had no time to spare in bringing its new design to market.

Organizational inflexibility is a challenge for almost every RAND client, from hospital emergency rooms to classical symphonies. But no where has it been more visible than in the Army supply system. "Victory is the beautiful, bright-colored flower," Winston Churchill once wrote. "Transport is the stem without which it could never have blossomed."

Churchill was not writing of the early days of World War II, during which survival depended so heavily on supplies ferried across the Atlantic in Liberty Ships, however. He was writing of Britain's River War in the Sudan, during which the British built a railroad along the Nile to ferry supplies for the decisive April 1898 battle that assured victory. The battle may excite the imagination, Churchill wrote of his experiences as an officer under Lord Kitchener, but the "long trailing line of communication is unnoticed."[11]

Armies still depend on largely unnoticed supply lines to this day, whether they are fighting for territory abroad or for customers back home. Build them lean, and the supplies will flow so smoothly that customers will never see an empty shelf; let them thicken, and the supplies will pile up in the ports of entry while customers wait.

The 1991 Gulf War is a case in point. Although the U.S. won a decisive victory over Saddam Hussein's forces, the Army came perilously close to the end of its supply tether at the end of the 100-hour war. According to legend, the U.S. Army sent 41,000 cargo containers full of supplies to Saudi Arabia in the five months preceding the war, of which 28,000 had to be opened just to find out what was inside.

Once upon a time, the U.S. could comfortably preposition its forces and huge piles of supplies in Europe anticipating an invasion from the East.

That all changed, however, with the fall of the Berlin Wall. The U.S. now keeps most of its forces and supplies in the continental United States awaiting orders to move. "Logistics is what makes power projection a reality," says the head of RAND's Velocity Management program, John Dumond. "To the degree that you have to move from a continental U.S. base, deploy to a new location, fight your war, and come back out, you can't afford to put big piles anywhere and everywhere you want. You don't know where you're going to fight."

The only problem is that big piles of supplies are hard to move. During the Gulf War, the U.S. Army moved enough food and water to keep its troops in action for 29 days, enough fuel to keep its tanks rolling for just over five days, and enough ammunition for 45 days. By the end of the war, the Army had 65 days of ammunition piled up in Saudi Arabia, most of which had to be shipped back home.

There were good reasons to order big piles, of course. The logistics process was so unreliable that commanders got in the habit of ordering the same item over and over just to make sure they actually received it. As of 1994, for example, it took 26 days on average to fill a supply order, be it for bullets, spare parts, tents, or weapons. But the average only tells part of the story. It took the Army supply system 20 days to fill half of the orders, another nine for three-quarters to be filled, another 35 days for 95 percent to be filled, and a final 55 days to reach 100 percent. It was no surprise that commanders began to hoard supplies such as tank engines—they could never be sure just where their request would be in the highly variable process.

RAND and the Army drew lessons from dozens of organizations as they built the define-measure-improve continuous improvement system, including Motorola, Penske, and Toyota, while measuring their performance against Fed-Ex and Wal-Mart. Although the Army's Velocity Management program took five years to implement, order-and-ship times plummeted. By 2000 it only took seven days on average to fill half of the orders in the pipeline, another four to hit 75 percent, and another 12 to reach 95 percent, and that was not just for high-priority items or particular posts. Everything speeded for everyone. By 2003 average shipping times were down to five days, roughly equivalent to the Amazon.com mark.

The effort reflected a simple change process that started with a clear statement of intent. As Dumond says, "You set up the vision and say, 'This is what I think you really want. You don't really want to have big piles of stock everywhere. You're forced to have big piles, but that's not really what you want.' Once you get beyond the vision, then you have to figure out how to get rid of the piles. If we can convince them that they don't want piles, that's only the first step. The next thing is how to make it happen. That's where we went from there."

The impetus for change involved a simple confrontation with reality. "Having big piles might have been perfectly fine if the Army had continued to plan for major wars in Europe or Korea because it can preposition huge piles," Dumond says. "It has big tanks and big forces, and can just put the big piles there. Our argument was that the world changed. The Army is no longer fighting the Cold War; it's over."

Inflexibility affects more than armies, however. Just as it can undermine success in the streets of a city, it can weaken performance in the aisles of a super-store, the production lines of a tractor factory, or the product development stream at a chemical company.

DuPont learned that lesson when it confronted a slowdown in innovation in the early 1990s. Attacked on the front page of the *Wall Street Journal* in early 1992 as a "black hole" of wasted research, the company clearly needed an overhaul. As its chief executive officer told the *Wall Street Journal*, the company had a host of structural problems—it took too long to convert research into products; it was doing little to improve its manufacturing process; and it had built an internal culture that placed a greater value on job security than performance.[12]

According to RAND's study of environmental research and development at the firm, it would have been easy to blame the chemical industry itself for the problems.[13] Of the 63 chemical product innovations between the 1930s and end of the 1980s, 40 came in the 1930s and 1940s, 20 in the 1950s and 1960s, and just three in the 1970s to the early 1980s.[14]

Yet, as one of the industry's leaders, DuPont was particularly vulnerable to criticism. Having spent roughly $13 billion on research and development during the 1980s, DuPont's 5000 research scientists had not brought a single blockbuster to market during the 1980s, and had stopped producing Orlon fabric because it could not keep up with manufacturing breakthroughs among its competitors.

Even DuPont's own managers were less than enthusiastic about the company—according to the *Wall Street Journal*, only 5 percent rated the company among the world's best in introducing new products. Having been one of the nation's most innovative companies, DuPont researchers had become obsessed with *big-bang innovation*, searching for another nylon to restore the company's prominence. "With new-product development faltering, DuPont has relied on 'tweaking' existing products into slightly improved versions," the *Wall Street Journal* explained in its 1992 assessment.

"Its Lycra spandex fiber, which was introduced more than 30 years ago to replace rubber in girdles, has been modified to dominate the active-wear market. And low-dose herbicides, invented in the mid-1970s, are selling well."

Ironically, DuPont's history of innovation created a security-conscious workforce and a self-perpetuating bureaucracy. As DuPont's vice chairman later said, "We were too bureaucratic, too slow, too set in our ways, and our costs were too high."[15]

DuPont began its war against inflexibility by cutting its workforce by a third, replacing its headquarters hierarchy with 21 separate business units, scrubbing its production process, and learning to recycle waste products. Having slashed operating costs, DuPont turned to innovation. According to RAND's 2003 case study of innovation and change management, DuPont started its research turnaround by teaching itself to innovate again. Building upon lessons learned from its industrial fibers division, DuPont created a Center for Creativity and Innovation, which built networks of facilitators across the company, ran problem-solving workshops, and provided seed grants of $5000 to $50,000 for ideas that could not be funded from traditional sources. (See the study team's briefing chart on DuPont's change strategy for the list of interventions.)

Improving Performance at Dupont

▶ Used leadership to signal and sustain change

▶ Used structured innovation processes

▶ Formed innovation board with senior staff

▶ Developed innovation agenda and 10-year plan

▶ Established center for creativity and innovation

▶ Exploited knowledge from across the organization

▶ Incorporated information from external sources

▶ Aligned incentives for technical staff with mission and goals

▶ Empowered innovation leaders with funding and authority

▶ Nurtured innovation networks

DuPont also created a corporate-level process for identifying and funding breakthrough projects and a new product development process to make faster decisions on smaller projects within each business line. It also adopted a corporate innovation agenda, a 10-year technology plan, and a new incentive structure to reward breakthrough research. In addition, it expanded its use of innovation audits to focus on corporate strengths and weaknesses.

By 1995 DuPont was back in the headlines with the highest earnings in its history. According to the *Wall Street Journal*, virtually every business line was hitting or exceeding targets, in part because it replaced its traditional hierarchy with a loosely coupled network of semi-autonomous business units, and in part because its research scientists began focusing on applied results. The headline said it all: "DuPont Emerges Slim and Trim from Restructuring: Chemical Giant Has Pared Costs and Employees in Three-Year Makeover."

More importantly, the changes endured. In 2003, for example, DuPont won the National Medal of Technology, which is the federal government's highest honor for technological innovation, for its work on the reduction and eventual replacement of ozone-depleting chlorofluorocarbons. It was the fourth time in little more than a decade that DuPont had received the award—the first came in 1990 for DuPont's work on high-performance polymers such as nylon, the second in 1993 for the development of environmentally friendly herbicides, and the third in 1996 for its discovery and development of Kelvar, which is used in bullet-proof vests and helmets. Having been pilloried in 1993 as an "environmental laggard" in *Fortune*'s inventory of corporate citizens, the 2003 award showed DuPont's rise as a national leader in proactive environmental management, a point echoed later in this book.[16]

Indifference

DuPont's journey was about more than saving money, of course. It was also about attacking the indifference that had set in over the years. Even as it remade its production process, DuPont pushed its scientists to confront the future through multi-generation roadmaps, which were further reviewed and debated by DuPont's technology council as part of a headquarters level strategic planning process. Although DuPont drew heavily on the best practices at General Electric and Motorola, its system was also tied to historical patterns of innovation unique to the chemical industry, which tends to innovate in 15- to 20-year cycles.

Many organizations do not look 15 to 20 weeks into the future, let alone years. Some simply refuse to challenge the *load-bearing assumptions* that underpin their strategic plans; others merely assume that the future will echo the immediate past; and others do not have the systems to plan across a range of futures.

Norwegian shipbuilder Kvaerner found out the hard way that the future often has a way of exposing weakness. At first glance, Kvaerner had every advantage when it took possession of the Philadelphia Naval Shipyard in 1997. After all, the Navy had already spent $320 million to close the 114-acre facility, while the city and state were ready to provide almost twice as much to rebuild the site.

Moreover, Kvaerner had a proven record of both innovation and performance in its market. According to RAND's case study of the decision, Kvaerner's shipbuilding division had a 1996 pretax profit of $1.03 billion. At a time when other shipbuilders were downsizing and consolidating, Kvaerner had decided to build around a simple philosophy.

> Under Kvaerner's team approach to shipbuilding, all its shipyards do what they know best—build the ship's hull and manage and integrate the outfitting of the ship. Nearly all the other components of the ship are manufactured and assembled by subcontractors and then delivered to the yard precisely when needed. Within the shipyard, teams of highly trained workers are provided with first-class facilities and organized around core processes, rather than trade skills. Outside the shipyard, Kvaerner relies on teams of suppliers, selected for their innovative ideas and desire to enter into a partnership with the firm, rather than their low bid offers.

As RAND's study team noted, Kvaerner's strengths were clear: "Essentially, Kvaerner's strategy for making money in the hyper-competitive shipbuilding industry involved using a highly trained workforce to build complex vessels with high profit margins." It invested in first-class facilities; built strong partnerships with local suppliers; and used its corporate size, which included 11 shipyards, worldwide locations, and a highly trained workforce; to exploit niche markets such as diesel-powered container ships.

This agility was not enough to guarantee success, however. In 1998 Kvaerner's chief executive was forced to resign as his company's stock plummeted. In 1999 Kvaerner put all of its shipyards up for sale. In 2001 Aker Maritime won control of Kvaerner after a takeover battle with Yukos Oil of Russia.

Kvaerner was felled in part by its staggering debt load, which ballooned in the 1990s when it purchased the Masa shipyard and Trafalgar House, the British construction conglomerate. Although the two purchases gave Kvaerner control of the world's largest shipyard and the Cunard Cruise Line, it also created a corporation with 80,000 employees in 100 countries. "We've long accepted that the mid-1990s expansion was too fast and too extensive," a company spokesman acknowledged in 2001. "We were too slow in selling the businesses we didn't want and the debt we created kept on growing."[17]

Agile as it was in buying companies and building ships, Kvaerner was a victim of its own blindness to a rapidly changing future. Unable to sell off its shipyards, Kvaerner became a tempting and relatively inexpensive target for takeover. Kvaerner is not the only organization to bet the company and lose.

The Russian military learned about urban combat the hard way in the streets of the Chechen capital city of Grozny. According to RAND's analysis of Russia's failed Chechen campaigns, the soldiers who entered the city in December 1994 did not expect a fight. After all, their enemy was a loosely organized force of under-equipped, under-trained freedom fighters. They should have known better, if only because the word *Grozny* means "terrible" or "menacing" in Russian. "Although the Russians eventually managed to take control of the city, the learning curve was steep, and the costs high," RAND's Olga Oliker concludes. "Moreover, the victory was short-lived. A rebel counter-offensive followed by a negotiated settlement ended the war in Chechnya in the fall of 1996."[18]

As if to prove that hubris is a hard habit to break, the Russian Army returned to Chechnya for a second lesson in 1998. Having concluded that it could not win an urban war, Russia proceeded to bomb the city into submission. But the rebels merely dug deeper bunkers and waited for another street fight, which they won again. Oliker argues that the failure to prepare for urban combat was hardly the only Russian error. "Hampered by poor training and supplies, decrepit equipment, and abysmal planning, the 1994-1996 war presented a stark picture of how much this once-great force had deteriorated. It also demonstrated how poorly Russian military organizational structures functioned when disparate forces were called upon to work together."

The Russians did not make the same mistakes when they returned to Grozny in 1999. They did a better job of sealing the city, improved their supply lines, streamlined their command structure, gave increased authority to junior officers to make battlefield decisions, brought more troops into battle, and strengthened communication between their ground and air forces. They also developed a more sophisticated battle plan for winning the war, and placed a premium on avoiding casualties.

As Oliker writes, however, the Russians were still drawn into bloody urban combat. "In 1994 the Russians had ignored all evidence that a Chechen resistance remained in Grozny. In 1999 they convinced themselves that weeks of aerial bombardment had driven the rebels out." In both cases the results were the same: heavy Russian casualties and a block-by-block battle to hold the city. Having put all their eggs in one basket of bombardment, the Russians had no contingency plans for another round of urban combat. Moreover, even though their forces had become more agile, their equipment was still old, spare parts were often unavailable, their forces could not fight effectively at night, and the new command structure quickly broke down as the urban warfare increased. As the U.S. would find out in Baghdad, the biggest mistake the Russians could have made was to assume a future that did not exist: "By believing that they could avoid urban battle by not preparing for it, the Russian military guaranteed that any fight, successful or otherwise, would have a very high cost."

Kvaerner and the Russian Army could both take adaptability lessons from the Intel Corporation, which uses a highly structured, but fluid product development process to maintain the leading edge in the computer chip industry. As RAND's study of environmental research and development suggests, Intel built a *technology treadmill* designed to exploit the exponential growth in the number of transistors per integrated circuit that has characterized the industry since the 1960s.[19] For its first three decades, Intel bet its future on rapid, incremental technological advances in processing speed. It did so in part by designing new chips and their manufacturing processes concurrently, and by employing two product development teams to leapfrog each other in a race to market. The result, according to RAND's four-member research team, is a complete retooling of production facilities every two years.[20]

Intel managed this process through a fluid, amoeba-like organization that supported the entire corporation as chips were designed, tested, and transferred to full-rate fabrication facilities. The virtual organization allowed Intel to move chips to market quickly, which RAND's study team suggests is particularly difficult given the capital intensity of fabrication and the experiential knowledge needed to increase production yield. As a result, "yields can be kept high, and most important, changes and new technologies can be diffused rapidly."

Incremental technological advances could only take Intel so far, however, especially in an industry where a single breakthrough can create an entirely new future. It is a point well illustrated by Intel's own decision to introduce an entirely new line of chips in 2005. "All of our microprocessor development going forward is now multi-core," Intel's president and chief operating officer said of the decision to put the equivalent of two brains on one chip. "The design paradigm has shifted at Intel."[21] Intel expects half of its chips to be at least dual-core by 2006.

In placing its bet on multi-core chips, Intel acknowledged the limits of its technological treadmill, especially given the need to reduce heat and power in the highly competitive laptop and consumer-electronics industry. Even though rapid incremental innovation kept Intel a step ahead of the competition on processing speed, it needed breakthrough innovation to stay alive for the future. This is not to suggest that Intel will abandon its old system once the new chips are established, however. There is a time for breakthroughs, and a time for technology treadmills. "We knew that we had to invest our way out of the downturn," Intel's CEO, Craig Barrett, said in 2004. "So continuing to invest in new products—$28 billion over the past three years—wasn't frightening. I have a cast-iron stomach. It was just the recognition of, that's the way the chip industry works, and that's what we had to do. It's a majority of self-preservation. Our whole product line turns over every year. About 80 to 90 percent of the revenue we have in December of each year comes from products that weren't there in January."[22]

As Intel's decision suggests, organizations cannot be indifferent to alternative futures for their current products and strategies. Unlike Kvaerner, which bet the entire company on a single shipbuilding future, or the Russian Army, which bet its second visit to Grozny on a single strategy, Intel adapted an entirely different future by abandoning a product that had taken its global dominance in its market.

Inconsistency

Intel's success depends upon more than breakthrough designs, however. It also depends on an organization-wide commitment to the new product line, especially among the researchers who spent the better part of two years developing the next generation of single-core chips.

RAND has seen more than its share of organizational incoherence over the years, whether embedded in resistance, confusion, or competing priorities. As RAND's Quinlivan says, the inconsistency is easy to spot. Just put a group of executives, managers, and frontline staff in a room and outline the new strategy.

> We gave a presentation to a defense agency out there. We had some very serious doubts that they could do what they proposed technically. I prepared this briefing for my boss to give. He was up front. Through the accident of the way the room was set up,

I was seated against a wall sort of perpendicular to the audience, which was seated by rank. The important guys were up front, middle managers were next, and all the guys in the back were the ones who had worked on the project.

Our guy started giving the presentation. We started pointing out the serious things we had a problem with. The guys in the front are shaking their heads, "No, that's not a problem; we've solved that." The guys in the back are shaking their heads, "Yeah, yeah, that's a problem, we haven't solved that." But the guys in the middle kept their heads exactly straight. They didn't nod at all. That's the role of middle management because you need a stationary point in the hierarchy to translate this into that. If the organization is lined up, you'd like to hear somebody at a lower level volunteering not just what they do, but how what they do matches up to something in one of the slogans at the other end. You know, "Quality is job one, right after we get this puppy off the line."

Inconsistency is a major theme of RAND's evaluation of the ongoing New American Schools initiative. Launched in 1991 at the urging of President George H. W. Bush, and funded with $130 million from some of America's top corporations, the New American Schools Development Corporation eventually picked 11 school systems for what it called *break-the-mold reform*, including Cincinnati, Memphis, Philadelphia, San Antonio, and Miami. Although each of the 11 systems adopted somewhat different reforms, all included a mix of curricular and organizational change. In San Antonio, for example, one school adopted the *Success For All* reading curriculum, another built a program around the Outward Bound expeditionary model, and still another embraced real-life problem solving via the Internet.

RAND was involved in evaluating every phase of the initiative, asking whether the reforms actually changed classroom activities, improved student performance, and produced the durable whole-school improvement.

The answers are troubling at best. The initial notion that whole-school reform would improve student performance was largely unsupported, nor was there strong evidence that innovation in one group of schools changed district-wide attitudes. Bluntly put, RAND reluctantly concluded that schools do not provide fertile ground for break-the-mold ideas, in part because teachers are so busy implementing other reforms that they have little time to concentrate on any single initiative, and in part because districts are reluctant to give individual schools enough autonomy to innovate.

There were other reasons for the uneven success of the New American Schools effort, not the least of which is the level of poverty among students. But as RAND's research team concludes, school capacity and district support have emerged as critical factors in improvement, or the lack thereof.[23] So did consistent leadership and clear communication.

> Without strong principal leadership, without teachers who support the designs and have a strong sense of teacher efficacy, without district leadership and support, and without clear communication and provision of materials and staff support on the part of design teams, implementation is likely to lag far behind. These are sobering and important lessons for any efforts at school reform. They underscore the basic inequality among schools in terms of capacity to undertake reform and point to the need for development of leadership and staff capacity as the precursor to reform, not necessary the result of it.

RAND's research group also came to wonder whether high-stakes accountability based on annual testing could co-exist with comprehensive whole-school reform. Indeed, it is entirely possible that the testing regimes embedded in the *No Child Left Behind Act* might actually discourage schools from adopting the "rich and varied" programs that challenge students toward the kind of in-depth learning experiences that do not necessarily produce high test scores. Far better to teach to the test than take the risk that a school will be put on the failure list.

Although some of the problems are unique to public schools, RAND's findings apply to virtually any organization bent on transformation, especially under extreme financial and/or political pressure to show immediate progress. Organizations that rush to reform will almost always be disappointed. RAND's Robert Chapman found similar problems in the federal government's failed effort to help Chrysler, Ford, and General Motors develop a new generation of environmentally-friendly, high-mileage cars. At first glance, the effort should have succeeded: It was built around a formal partnership between government and the Big Three fueled by $2 billion in funding and full access to the federal research laboratories. It also had the Clinton administration's complete support. Launched in a 1993 Rose Garden ceremony, the partnership promised to leapfrog the competition by a decade by developing an 80-mile-per-gallon, five-passenger, easily recyclable, affordable family car.

Eight years later the partnership was dead. Chrysler, General Motors, and Ford were well behind Honda and Toyota in the race to produce clean cars, and the federal government had switched its bet to hydrogen fuel cells.

Although all three U.S. manufacturers had met their part of the deal by developing concept cars by 2000, the National Academy of Sciences concluded that "no reasonable amount of funding" would achieve the 80-mile-per-gallon goal: "While the bulk of the requirements (e.g., performance, comfort, cargo space, utility, and safety) can be met, the combination of 80 mpg and affordability appears out of reach."

Chapman saw the problems coming in an otherwise hopeful 1998 report titled *The Machine that Could*, a play on a best-selling book about Toyota's lean production system.[24] Although there was much to admire in the Partnership, including progress made on hybrid engines and lightweight materials, he reports that there was very little true invention under the Partnership and plenty of hubris.

Some of the inconsistency came from the government, where 20 separate laboratories split the research funding from 12 different appropriation accounts, six in the House of Representatives and six in the Senate. Agencies not only had strong self-interest in defending their slice of the budget, the federal government itself was "a less-than-perfect partner" for industry. Moreover, the risk in undertaking a multiyear, technically challenging Partnership with the government comes from both political and bureaucratic constraints. "If the duration spans several election cycles, interminable reviews and suspended budget decisions could disrupt program schedules and disillusion the industry partners."

Some of the inconsistency came from Chrysler, Ford, and General Motors. As Chapman also reports, the automobile industry had 100 years of experience and strong preferences for established technologies, meaning steel, internal combustion engines, and gasoline. Unfortunately, steel, internal combustion engines, and gasoline were not necessarily part of the high-mileage future.

The federal government and the carmakers also had cumbersome bureaucracies that made decision making difficult. Although younger engineers clearly understood that core technologies needed to change, the older engineers at the top often took a defensive stance, if only because they could "remember, and readily recite, all the earlier innovations that were disappointments . . ."

However, most of the inconsistency came from the nature of the partnership itself. The partnership itself was entirely voluntary, and had few measures of success and no independent capital to invest in particularly promising areas. More importantly, it was never quite clear just how committed the partners were to each other, nor how breakthrough innovation could come from a linear budgeting system and a risk-averse planning process. As a result, the partnership often behaved more like a Model T than the Toyota Prius, the gasoline-electric hybrid that entered the market in

1997 at 60-miles-to-the-gallon, and eventually became *Motor Trend's* 2004 car of the year.

Procter & Gamble learned its own lessons about consistency toward the end of a decade-long drought in new product development. Although it invested heavily in research and development during the drought, its efforts were widely dispersed and poorly coordinated. It needed to move new products more quickly to the market, and send a clear and consistent message down through the organization that innovation was the only way Procter & Gamble could survive in an increasingly brutal marketplace.

The company clearly understood that the message had to come from the top, and picked its chief technology officer, Gordon Brunner, to rebuild the product development process. According to RAND's history of the effort, Brunner started by creating an Innovation Leadership Team as a de facto venture-capital board. With $225 million to invest in new ideas, the team provides seed funding and technical assistance to both existing and new business lines. Brunner also took a more aggressive stance toward improving information flows under a new program called *Connect and Develop*. According to RAND, the program was designed to make the connection between "what's needed" and "what's possible," whether through the company's intranet and "smart" report systems for knowledge sharing, its global technology programs, committees of practice, or "connection-making" conferences.[25]

The company also adopted a more structured process for managing later-stage projects, using a *go/no-go, stage-gate approach* that subjects each idea to both laboratory testing and extensive market research before a the commitment to wider field tests and eventual commercialization. By 2002, 16 new brands had entered "learning markets," and six had crossed over to national markets. By 2004 Procter & Gamble ranked third on *Fortune* magazine's list of most innovative companies, first on employee talent, second on use of company assets, third on quality of management, and third on quality of products and services.[26]

Consistency does not mean constraint, however. "We totally changed our systems for innovating and manufacturing products," Procter & Gamble's CEO, A.G. Lafley, explained in 2004. "We need a much lower cost system. We began working with local suppliers....The P&G of five or six years ago depended on 8000 scientists and engineers for the vast majority of innovation. The P&G we're trying to unleash today asks all 100,000-plus of us to be innovators. We actively solicit good ideas, and if the concept is promising we put it into development."[27]

Nor does consistency mean isolation. Procter & Gamble developed its new Swiffer duster in collaboration with Japan's Unicharm Corporation, the

GLAD Press'n Seal plastic storage bag with Clorox, and Prilosec antacid through a joint venture with AstraZeneca. "I'm a big believer that we sometimes need help in solving problems," Lafley explained. "So I have set a goal to get half of our innovation from the outside. We're in the 20 percent range now, up from 10 percent three or four years ago. We have even worked with competitors. The competitors were nervous, and people in my company were anxious, too. But my point of view was, wherever they come from, you've got to get the people with the idea, the technology, and the ability to execute the idea in the marketplace together."[28]

The merger of Astra and Zeneca also reflected a desire for greater agility, albeit in the form of increased research and development spending. "R&D has been getting more expensive, and you do need to be big enough to afford the different technologies that will keep you competitive," AstraZeneca's CEO, Tom McKillop, said of the Astra and Zeneca merger. "But beyond a certain point you risk running a less efficient R&D business. You need speed *and* creativity. Those aren't attributes that you normally associate with big companies."[29]

Improving Performance at Procter & Gamble

▶ Innovations

- Established "key customer" liaisons
- Implemented model of "connect and develop"
- Funded "communities of practice" across organizations

▶ Change management

- Structured process to develop new brands
- Invested and supported internal collaboration, new ventures
- Experimented in the marketplace
- Established innovation leadership team
- Supported change through sustained leadership
- Provided reward and recognition for innovators
- Focused incentives on quality of work more than money

RAND has seen similar turnarounds in federal agencies, too, whether at the Food and Drug Administration, where a new drug review process cut approval times in half, the Veterans Health Administration, where new performance measures have improved patient care, or the Customs Service, where modernization has improved customer satisfaction and revenue collection simultaneously. In all three cases, the message was essentially the same: Successful change demands consistency from the very top of the organization to the bottom.

THE NEW UNCERTAINTY

Vulnerability is not a guarantee of failure. After all, all organizations are vulnerable to one degree or another. There are always unknowns outside, and always a bit of stiffness, complacency, and misalignment inside.

Moreover, even highly vulnerable organizations can produce extraordinary results on occasion. They might not pay much attention to the future, but could still have the right product for the right time; they might not be able to move quickly into new markets, but might be in an old market that suddenly heats up; they might not be particularly innovative, but might have a product that everyone needs; and they might not be well aligned, but still be able to produce the occasional breakthrough.

Organizations tolerate vulnerability at their own risk, however. It is one thing to build an army for a single enemy on well-known terrain, for example, and quite another to prepare for what the Air Force calls a *boiling peace* against many adversaries anywhere in the world. "Up until about 1986, we knew exactly what we needed to do," Frank Camm says of U.S. military planning. "We ran the same training script over and over. We knew exactly where all the Soviet forces were. We had a pretty good idea of where they were going and a pretty good idea of what their goals were in the first five days of combat. And we were set up to deal with that, and we practiced it over and over again. That just doesn't exist right now."

The U.S. military is not the only institution facing an uncertain future, however. Name an industry, and the story is the same: Uncertainty is not only rising, its character appears to be shifting.

Puzzles and Mysteries

Although the Cold War was clearly a frightening time, much of the uncertainty in the 1950s and 1960s consisted of statistical uncertainty, which can be defined as variation observed in repeatable phenomena such as defect rates, resupply time, or product development cycles.[30] Repeat the activity enough times, and the chances of getting the same outcome can be expressed in clear statistical probabilities such as the Six Sigma goal of only 3.4 defects per million (or 99.9997 percent perfect). As the authors of *The Six Sigma Way* suggest, there is still enough statistical uncertainty out there to justify action:

> Six Sigma initiatives have tallied billions of dollars in savings, dramatic increases in speed, strong new customer relationships—in short, remarkable results and rave reviews. Are these results for real? And is it really possible for you and your business to achieve some of the same gains? The answer is "yes." It can happen to any type of business and, contrary to many people's fears, you don't have to have an in-depth background in statistical analysis.[31]

Even as organizations attack these statistical results, which some label as risk, they must also deal with state-of-the-world volatility. Unlike statistical uncertainty, which can be measured through quantitative methods, state-of-the-world flux resides in phenomena that are by definition immeasurable. They are often also unobservable.

The two are roughly analogous to puzzles and mysteries. Like statistical uncertainty, a puzzle can almost always be solved with existing information—indeed, the answers are often provided at the bottom of the page or back of the book. Some answers might involve little more than a good guess, but the answer is out there somewhere.

Like state-of-the-world uncertainty, mysteries are sometimes unsolvable even with massive amounts of information. By definition, as RAND's Gregory Treverton writes, puzzles only arise after an event has occurred. "The missiles have been built, with warheads and accuracy that may remain unknown even though they are knowable. War plans have been framed, and the attack started, though it may still come as a surprise."[32] In contrast, many of the most interesting mysteries are not only unknowable at this time, but their eventual answer is a mix of hope and fear. "We often care most about events we hope to influence, or we hope to influence them because we care about them."

The two types lead to very different organizational actions—statistical uncertainty leads toward clear effort to reduce variation, while state-of-the-world concerns should generate efforts to increase organizational responsiveness to threats and opportunities. "In peacetime, the main kind of uncertainty is statistical, which assumes that each individual component has a failure mode, and they all depend on one another," Camm explains. "There's this diffuse noise in the system, but if you look at it from a macro level, the noise is pretty constrained around a small band of variation. So you can develop good ways to estimate the performance of the system as a whole."

In wartime the models begin to change, if only because there is an obvious change in the state of the world. "In peacetime, you don't actually test the software and the hardware that's used to defend against electronic attack," Camm continues. "Otherwise, you shut down your radio stations. As a result, you never see any failures in that equipment during peacetime. When you go to war, there are failures all over the place. Not only that, the failures all occur at the same time because you never actually tested them during peacetime."

Even wartime volatility can be contained, however, if the war remains the same. But as the U.S. Army discovered early in the Iraq War, tank treads had a disturbing tendency to wear out. "We had this parameter that said tank treads last this long in combat. That was one parameter. The other parameter said tank treads are going to spend this much time on the road." The more time the tanks spent on the road protecting convoys to and from Baghdad, the more the statistical uncertainty changed into state-of-the-world uncertainty. Every prediction said the tanks would be off the roads immediately after Saddam's palaces fell, but the world would not comply.

State-of-the-world change clearly comes in different sizes, including what James Dewar, the director of RAND's Center for Longer-Range Global Policy and the Future Human Condition, calls *deep uncertainty*. "There are a lot of times when we know how the system works but we don't know what numbers to plug in," Dewar explains. "And then there are times when we don't even know how the system works. There, you've got deep uncertainty."

Deep uncertainty is not necessarily unmanageable. Indeed, RAND's Robert Lempert, Steven Popper, and Steven Bankes maintain that humans often do well when they confront deep uncertainty in their own lives, especially if the intuition about the system in question works reasonably well. However, intuition and what-if thinking often fail when humans confront novel situations or extensive amounts of information. "In such situations," the three authors write in *Shaping the Next One Hundred Years*, "humans rapidly lose the ability to track long casual links or the competing forces that may drive the future along one path or another." Hence, RAND's concern with developing decision tools that help humans develop plans that do well across multiple futures.

The question for the moment is not whether humans and organizations can harden themselves against assorted levels of change, however. Rather, it is whether uncertainty has risen to the point where it deserves special attention in organizational design. If the level and mix of uncertainty has remained relatively constant over the past 50 years, for example, perhaps organizations can just accept occasional vulnerabilities based on ignorance, inflexibility, indifference, and inconsistency as a normal cost of doing business. If, however, the level is rising and the mix is changing toward greater state-of-the-world conditions, then organizations might consider a *robustness audit* to see just how tough they are.

Sources of Uncertainty

There is considerable debate within RAND about both the level and mix of uncertainty today. Some researchers such as Paul Davis believe that today's turbulence is not altogether unfamiliar. "I guess when all is said and done, I believe that deep uncertainty has been with us forever and what's new is that some of us have been trying to confront it analytically, rather than wish it away out of a desire to use clever mathematics. Now because there had been no war for decades, many people *believed* that things were predictable and stable, but do you really believe that if war had occurred, it would have looked exactly like the script?"

Yet Davis is willing to add that there are new deep uncertainties that have created their own turbulence, including terrorism, global economic and social unrest, and the revolutions discussed below. "Probably no deeper than some old ones (can't be much deeper than the uncertainties of the 1930s), but different and deep enough." (See Paul Davis's briefing slide on what organizations should do about deep uncertainty.)

What to Do About Deep Uncertainty

1. Recognize it (no denial, whether created by bureaucracy or wishful thinking)

2. Deal with it (no paralysis or hand-wringing)

3. Plan for it, looking both to opportunity-taking as well as dealing with negatives

Other RAND researchers believe that the Cold War was not as unpredictable as it now seems. "They had a pretty good idea of how to do things," Dewar says of planners in the 1950s. "They didn't have deep uncertainty. They had deep fear. The only uncertainty they had really was how fast they could play in the measures-counter-measures game. And they had a very clear path, a very clear vision, and a clear understanding of how the system worked. And so for 50 years, from 1947 to 1987, they didn't have to do strategic planning the way we have to now. Nothing was changing." The Cold War was very dangerous, Dewar suggests, but it was hardly a surprise:

- The enemy was not uncertain; it was the communist bloc, led by the Soviet Union.
- The threat was not ambiguous; it was the very survival of the nation under the shadow of a massive nuclear attack.
- The resources were not highly uncertain; the threat was so dire that the necessary funds would be provided regardless of other claims and claimants.
- The locale of conflict was clear enough; it was Central Europe, where the prize of two World Wars was left divided between the Cold War adversaries.

Finally, Dewar suggests that the standard scenario for war was so consistent that it bordered on truth: "It was a Warsaw Pact invasion of Western Europe, escalating to the use of nuclear weapons, first in Europe and then in the heartlands of the two superpowers."[33] There are great risks in comparing uncertainties over time, however. "Think about the world in 1800 compared to the world in 1900," Steven Popper recommends. "Think about what a world-class sailing vessel was like in 1800 versus 1900, or ground transportation, or manufacturing, or power."

Yet, as Popper notes, there is a different tone to what is experienced today. "Americans may have been operating under uncertainty in a bunch of different areas, but they were optimistic. They always assumed there would be a way to figure things out. Maybe what has happened in part is that people have become more frightened. They have less reason now to believe that all problems ultimately are solvable."

Indeed, there are at least six revolutions that have made organizational life much more uncertain than ever before: (1) the revolution in living things, (2) the revolution in materials and manufacturing, (3) the revolution in information, (4) the revolution in global commerce, (5) the revolution in revolutions, and (6) the revolution in organizational strategy.

The Six Revolutions

1. The Revolution in Living Things

2. The Revolution in Materials and Manufacturing

3. The Revolution in Information

4. The Revolution in Global Commerce

5. The Revolution in Revolutions

6. The Revolution in Strategy

The Revolution in Living Things This revolution has been underway for decades, driven in part by federal funding and in part by private ingenuity. But it is clearly accelerating as scientists continue to explore the genetic structure of life itself. According to a variety of RAND reports, advances in biotechnology could have at least two significant impacts by 2015.

First, the revolution could produce a dramatic increase in both the quality and length of human life through better disease control, custom drugs, genetic therapy, prosthetics, bionic implants, and new treatment therapies that may well convert life-threatening diseases such as cancer into chronic conditions. The range of possibilities is stunning both for its potential impact, but also for the speed of progress. It may soon become commonplace to manufacture custom replacement parts for the skeleton to reverse engineer new bones—after all, it is already possible to engineer skin for burn treatment, and cartilage manufacturing is in clinical testing.

Second, the revolution could launch an entirely new industry built about the use of genetic engineering to improve the human species. "These will be very controversial developments—among the most controversial in the entire history of mankind," RAND's team writes of the global technology revolution. But with or without government support, they predict at least some narrow attempts such as gene therapy for genetic diseases and cloning by rogue researchers. RAND issued the report in 2001 only three years before South Korean researchers cloned the first human embryo.

The Revolution in Materials and Manufacturing This revolution is affecting all facets of the economy, including new construction composites, rapid prototyping systems, self-assembling products, smart fabrics, nanofab-ricated computer chips, and molecular manufacturing. It has even changed running shoes—Adidas now sells an *intelligent shoe* that adjusts heal compression to match terrain. "What we have, basically, is the first footwear product that can change its characteristics in real time," the lead engineer on the project says.[34]

The *Adidas 1* was only one of many breakthroughs that RAND researchers imagine by 2015. Alongside smart materials that respond to weather, deliver medicines, monitor vital signs, and protect wounds, they see the emergence of agile manufacturing systems that command hundreds of production lines from a single locale. They also see increasing use of nano-technology, including *quantum dots* that could guide drugs through the human body and nano-satellites through space, self-assembling products, and a host of other technological wild cards that could transform global technology overnight.

Viewed as a whole, the revolution in materials and manufacturing could have at least four impacts. First, it could accelerate the pace of the creative destruction of entire industries, as consumer expectations change with each new breakthrough. In turn the acceleration would impose great pressure on societies to adjust through agile education and training. National economies may well rise and fall on the basis of what happens in the first year or two of grade school.

Second, the revolution will absolutely encourage greater multidisci-plinary, multi-industry collaboration as engineers turn to biologists for help in developing new applications for nano-technology and smart materials, while nano-scaling existing technologies such as heart pacemakers. Not all of the applications are biological, however. RAND researchers even imag-ine a world in which smart roads and bridges repair themselves.

Third, leadership in the revolution will depend on government investment, international property rights and protections, the structure of corporate research and development, and, perhaps most importantly, the willingness of organizations to embrace radical change in the way they perceive technology. Just as the digital divide splits older and younger Amer-icans today, the nano-divide may well leave many companies behind.[35]

Finally, some organizations will be able to exploit the revolution by mor-phing established technologies into new applications—e.g., by taking the best shoe, roofing tile, airbag, paint, washing machine, air conditioner, or heart stint and making it smart. The basic product will not be new per se, but the per-formance will be different enough to justify separate patents and protections.

The Revolution in Information This revolution is largely driven by technology. Looking at the future course of the revolution in 2003, the authors of RAND's *Global Course of the Information Revolution* expect the exponential growth in computer power to continue unabated for at least another 10 to 15 years, or to the foreseeable limits of silicon technology, with very strong synergies between info-, bio-, nano-, and material technology.[36] They also expect product development to accelerate, allowing information systems to react more quickly and comprehensively to changes in their environment, with display products such as computer screens and handheld devices a major source of breakthrough innovation, including what RAND's team describes as electronic paper that can be rolled or folded. Finally, they expect information services to grow, with entertainment at the leading edge.

In turn these advances could have impacts across at least five areas of the economy and society. First, the revolution will continue to reshape the workforce. Information work and information workers will occupy an increasing fraction of economic activity, freeing organizations to relocate, outsource, and offshore their workforces without moving a single employee—how long will it be before India begins to subcontract back to the U.S. in search of specialized skills? Although information-driven changes in business operations have quickened in the past decade, they are furthest along in the U.S., Europe, and Asia. Most organizations still have extraordinary opportunities to exploit technology, products, and services for enhanced performance and profit.

Second, the information revolution is changing political and social boundaries. Both for good and ill, governments can no longer control the flow of information. Thus, even as the revolution in living things raises many questions of privacy, fears of Big Brother are fading with information anarchy. Governments can still isolate their societies from international communication, but not easily and only at a high price.

Third, the revolution may create an entirely new source of international conflict between information winners and losers. "Extreme losers in the information revolution could become 'failed states,'" write the RAND authors. "Such failed states could become breeding grounds for terrorists, who could threaten U.S. interests."

Fourth, and perhaps most important for organizational design, the future course of the revolution involves a number of wild cards that are absolutely unknowable, whether in the form of new materials that create an entirely new generation of chips, cyber-combat by governments, terrorists, and plain old fashioned hackers, which undermine reliability and consumer confidence, or a large-scale regional conflict that paralyzes or destroys essential nodes in the revolution. As hard as the computer industry has worked behind the scenes to calm tensions between India and Pakistan over nuclear testing, the conflict may eventually blossom into a war that could change the course of the information revolution in a nanosecond.

The Revolution in Global Commerce Globalization remains a key driver of state-of-the-world uncertainty, whether in the form of infectious diseases or breakthrough innovation. Whether measured by the flow of goods and services, direct investment, the decline in real earnings among less-skilled workers, or the movement of people, globalization continues to redefine national borders as anachronisms of a bygone time.

Despite a certain amount of what my Brookings Institution colleagues, Gary Burtless and Robert Litan, describe as *globalphobia*, there seems to be no way to stop either the integrating and disintegrating effects of this revolution.[37] On the one hand, globalization integrates the world by reducing distances and providing easy access to markets of all kinds. On the other hand, it disintegrates by increasing inequalities between nations and citizens, increasing the potential for terrorism both within and across borders.

The effects are easy to illustrate in the workplace, where employers and employees face increased pressure to compete. According to RAND's study of the future of work, globalization interacts with an aging population and technological change to produce at least four potential impacts:

1. Employees will work in more decentralized, specialized firms, and employer-employee relationships will become less standardized and more individualized.

2. Slower labor force growth will encourage employers to adopt approaches to facilitate greater labor force participation among women, the elderly, and people with disabilities.

3. Greater emphasis will be placed on retraining and lifelong learning as the U.S. workforce tries to stay competitive in the global marketplace and respond to technological changes.

4. Future productivity growth will support rising wages and may affect the wage distribution; the tie between employment and access to fringe benefits will be weakened.

It is not yet clear just who will emerge victorious in these trends—highly-skilled workers who can trade their abilities in an international labor market, highly-agile employers that shift jobs from bidder to bidder regardless of borders, temporary employment services that create virtual homes for workers, or variations on labor/management partnerships based on at least some stability from year to year. What is clear is that globalization creates an uncertain climate for identifying essential jobs. Given the revolution in revolutions described just below, organizations that outsource all of their institutional capacity can easily find themselves with no capacity at all.

The Revolution in Revolutions The revolution in revolutions began well before the September 11, 2001 terrorist attacks on New York City and Washington, D.C., but has clearly accelerated in the months and years since. "Who would have predicted on September 10, 2001, that the next major U.S. military operation would have been weeks away; in Afghanistan; against the Taliban rulers and their 'Arab guests; with special operations forces on horseback calling in air strikes; with the underachieving Northern Alliance as the main ally and land force; and in response to the devastation of lower Manhattan?" RAND's David Gompert writes. "As hard as guessing the who, where, when, and why of the next contingency in today's security environment is trying to figure out how the environment will change over time."

One only needs to page through RAND's work on how terrorism is changing to understand how the revolution in revolutions is changing organizational life. Even as terrorists become more opportunistic, their weapons are becoming more ordinary. "On the low end of the technological spectrum, terrorists continue to rely on fertilizer bombs," Bruce Hoffman writes in introducing a long list of examples that includes the 1995 Oklahoma City bombing. "Fertilizer is perhaps the most cost-effective of weapons, costing on average 1 percent of the comparable amount of plastic explosives.... Moreover, unlike plastic explosives and other military ordinance, fertilizer and at least two of its most common bomb-making counterparts—diesel fuel and icing sugar—are easily available commercially and completely legal to purchase and store."

Hoffman's colleague, Theodore Karasik, worries about an even more sinister threat that he calls "toxic warfare." As he explains, "toxic weapons are made from materials that are usually readily (and legally) available in connection with industrial operations." The list includes irritants, choking agents, industrial gases, fertilizers, oxidizers, chemical asphyxiants, and pesticides, not to mention toxic waste such as refuse, sewage, and medical waste. Although chemical plants are the most obvious places to look for toxic materials, ingredients can be found just about anywhere, including garden-supply warehouses, college laboratories, glass and mirror plants, pesticide plants, and illegal chemical and toxic waste sites. Millions of tons of toxic waste are transported each year by criminal networks, Karasik notes, often to conflict-ridden countries such as Somalia.

Toxic weapons are hardly an imaginary threat. To the contrary, Karasik offers a long list of recent examples. In 1986 the Sri Lankan rebels poisoned several tons of tea with potassium cyanide in an effort to cripple the nation's export industry; in 1992 Kurdish rebels also used potassium cyanide to poison water tanks outside a Turkish army base; in 2000 and 2001, Columbian rebels attacked police stations in Cajibio, Puerto Liera, and Huila with sulfuric acid, ammonia, and what appeared to be chlorine. The learning curve is clearly increasing, as is the terror that goes with it.

International corporations recognize the risks embedded in this revolution. According to a 2004 RAND worldwide survey of 88 security and risk management professions at major corporations, 36 percent of the companies represented expect terrorists to attack their organization or staff, a 50 percent increase since 2003 when 24 expressed similar concern. In addition 66 percent said that terrorism is now a significant threat to their organizations, and four out of five believe the threat will go up in the next two years. Terrorism now rates as the number one threat to businesses, eclipsing fraud, industrial espionage, and cyber-crime, all three of which appear to be more like puzzles than mysteries.[38]

The Revolution in Strategy   The final revolution involves basic changes in how organizations attack their markets through what John Arquilla and David Ronfeldt call *swarming*. As they define the term, swarming involves a "deliberately structured, coordinated, strategic way to strike from all directions at the same time." It works best, they argue, when designed around the use of myriad, small, dispersed, networked pods organized in clusters to carry out their attacks.

As Arquilla and Ronfeldt readily admit, there is nothing new about swarming. It was used by the Athenian Navy to defeat the Persians in the battle of Salamis in 480 BC. But their work suggests that swarming is ideally suited for the information age, if only because it depends on tight coordination for its signature act: the *sustainable pulsing* of force against an adversary. (See Arquilla and Ronfeldt's briefing slide on the key elements of swarming.)

Key Elements of Swarming

▶ Autonomous or semi-autonomous units engaging in a convergent assault on a common target

▶ Amorphous but coordinated strike from all directions—sustainable pulsing of force or fire

▶ Many small, dispersed, Internet-worked maneuver elements

▶ Integrated surveillance sensors

▶ Attacks intended to disrupt adversary's cohesion

Humans are hardly the only living things to swarm—bees, wolves, mosquitoes, and viruses all use swarming to survive and prosper. Armies are not the only organizations to swarm, either—businesses, social activists, drug cartels, and even football teams also use swarming to overwhelm small and large opponents alike by *flooding the zone* with pressure.

Although wars will still be fought with huge armies and large maneuvers, swarming is becoming the preferred method for both social and military revolution. From 1994 to 1998, for example, Zapatista rebels in Mexico used swarming to mount a revolution in the southern state of Chiapas. Although their revolution started on January 1, 1994, as a traditional military contest between relatively large units (500 to 700 fighters) on each side, the Zapatista forces were no match against the Mexican army. Having failed to provoke a national uprising through massed battle, the rebels soon dispersed to squads of 12 to 16 fighters for what became widely dispersed skirmishes that could have lasted for decades in the dense rain forests of Chiapas.[39]

The rebels also opened a second virtual front in the war by calling upon a loose network of human rights groups such as Amnesty International, Physicians for Human Rights, the Jesuit Refugee Service, and Food First to come to their cause through the Internet. What began as a war of bullets soon became a war of e-mails, faxes, and telephone calls that produced international attention, divided the Mexican government against itself, panicked investors and creditors alike, and rallied public support. Although the Mexican army could have continued fighting, the information *netwar*, as RAND's Arquilla and David Ronfeldt call it, brought the government to the negotiating table only 12 days into the conflict, and again each time the war flared back up.

As the study suggests, *netwarriors* can put strong pressure on government and private institutions alike without the use of violence. The successful use of netwars by other organizations also suggests two significant impacts on the targets. First, as we shall see later in this book, it takes a networked organization to defeat a networked organization, and second, building such an organization requires significant organizational and technological investment. Communication systems must be both hardened and redundant, tools for decoying the adversary are essential, authority must be greatly decentralized, yet all nodes of the network must be able to work together under central command to create the swarm.

Planning on Uncertainty

If there is one thing RAND knows about the future, it is that it is likely to be different from the past. The question, therefore, is how to plan and prepare for it.

Traditional short-term planning would be perfect for the task if only the future would behave. Unfortunately it often behaves very differently, a point well illustrated in Warren Walker's study of the 1995 decision to restrict growth at Amsterdam's Schiphol airport. At the time, the decision to restrict growth to 44 million passengers embraced the most optimistic assumptions about future demand, and the most pessimistic assumptions about noise.

The only weakness in the plan is that the assumptions were based on a past that did not include the growth of hub-and-spoke networks in Europe, the code-sharing alliance between Northwest Airlines and KLM, and further competition in the airline industry under the European Union. As air traffic soared from barely 20 million in 1995 to just under 40 million by 2000, the government's limits began to press on the airport. By 1999 the noise limits had been breached; by 2000 the airport was planning to increase passenger load to 55 million within six years. As if to prove the new plans were wrong, the 2001 recession knocked traffic back under 40 million, while the 2003 merger of Air France and KLM threatened even greater uncertainty.[40]

Testing Assumptions

Persistent problems with picking the right assumptions have led RAND and its researchers to invent a variety of tools for planning under uncertainty.

RAND most certainly did *not* invent strategic planning, but it has adapted traditional planning in ways that make it much more responsive to uncertainty. Over the years it has become just as adept at testing plans as creating them, and at breaking assumptions as making them.

Much of the adapting followed the end of the Cold War. But even before the Soviet Union collapsed, RAND was already starting to move away from traditional planning, which was also beginning to collapse.

It is nearly impossible to pinpoint the pivot point in RAND's thinking. Indeed, Paul Davis says that there was no pivot point at all. "Instead, a few of us pursued uncertainty-sensitive analysis pretty much independently," he remembers. James Dewar's assumption-based planning got its start in 1987, for example, when the Army asked him to look 30 years into the future at changing missions. "Even in the fairly stable geopolitical world of 1987, the idea of coming up with a 'most-likely' world in 30 years seemed like a stretch," Dewar remembers of the Army 21 project. "So we received permission to think about an alternative to the 'most-likely' world approach." RAND started by exploring the Army's vision of the future, then built one scenario each for the failure of the four most significant, load-bearing assumptions that underpinned the vision.

One of the scenarios was built around the Army's longstanding assumption that the Soviet Union would remain the Army's adversary far into the future. Under the scenario, which was called *Gorbachev Works*, RAND broke the Army's assumption by imagining that Gorbachev's *glasnost* and *perestroika* reforms would actually succeed in changing the future. Although the scenario did not include the fall of the Berlin Wall, it did include a rapprochement between East and West Germany, which rendered most of the Army's plan for blocking a Soviet invasion instantly obsolete.[41] As Dewar writes, RAND's draft report reached the Army literally the week the colonel in charge of the effort cleaned out his desk. "With the fall of the Berlin Wall two years later, the Army again came calling and asked if we could resurrect the planning 'methodology' we had developed in 1987....We did."

Assumption-based planning is only one of many *uncertainty-sensitive planning* methods that help organizations think in futures tense. Over the years RAND has developed tools for creating portfolios of possible futures (exploratory analysis and longer-range policy analysis), which inform plans that perform well across those futures (robust adaptive decision making), which in turn again, help organizations develop the capability to make robust, adaptive plans possible (capabilities-based planning). Although each has its own specialized methodology, all share a common set of principles about how organizations should confront uncertainty.

Having seen their share of plans implode at the end of the Cold War, RAND researchers uniformly rejected the notion that planning should be based on a handful of fixed scenarios of the future. Not only does the future change quickly, organizations often come to view the chosen scenario as truth, which is exactly the wrong way to plan on uncertainty. Rather, as Davis maintains, organizations are better off creating a scenario space filled with possible futures that can be compared to each other as Volvo did.

Exploring Scenarios

RAND researchers argue that uncertainty is a natural product of complex systems in which thousands of assumptions interact to shape the future. As such, the system itself is not constant—it includes human beings and organizations that think, behave, and adapt to events in myriad ways. As Davis suggests, uncertainty is not only ubiquitous and large but impossible to reduce by merely working hard. "So what do we do about this burden? Do we just wring our hands? In a phrase, we should get on with business— learning to plan in a way that includes the expectation of surprises and the need for adaptations."

Having seen organizations cling to their plans long after the future has rendered them obsolete, RAND researchers put their faith in adaptability. Instead of a linear process that produces *the* plan, RAND tends to view planning as a process that emphasizes learning and change rather than a final decision. As such, the process produces insights, knowledge, and ideas that can be used as circumstances change. Just as there is no such thing as one best estimate of the future, there is no one best plan for moving forward.

This is not to suggest that organizations should never make plans. But even as they make choices and set goals, organizations must constantly challenge their own prevailing wisdom about the path they have taken. This requires the courage to identify serious alternatives to the way they currently do business, adopting needed changes without having to first lose a war, and developing the capacity to deal with a wide range of contingencies.[42] As this book argues, they must also design their organizations to be equally responsive to the plans they have made. It hardly makes sense to build a robust, adaptive plan that does well against many futures if the organization can only do what it has always done.

RAND has also moved steadily away from *predict-then-act thinking*, which combines the search for rational decisions with methods for reducing statistical uncertainty. Designed to find the optimal solution to a predicted future, these tools have proven invaluable under conditions of well-understood realities.

However, predict-then-act thinking creates its own vulnerability as uncertainty deepens. According to Lempert and Popper, the approach encourages organizations to underestimate ambiguity, while conveying an "unjustified level of accuracy" about important value judgments. "Seasoned human decision makers, especially those who rise to lead large organizations, often understand quite well the limitations of predict-then-act analysis," they write. "At best, predict-then-act analyses provide one ingredient in a stew of information from which decision makers craft the narratives they ultimately use to debate and communicate their choices." Given the statistical elegance embedded in predict-then-act analysis, and the multiple futures generated by an increasingly uncertain future, decision makers have ample opportunity to confuse what is true with what they wish to be true.[43]

Robust, adaptive decision making is one way out of the trap. Whereas predict-then-act analysis often generates just one hoped-for future, robust decision making produces hundreds, even thousands, of possible futures, then measures the strengths and weaknesses of competing plans against each other before picking the one that does best across the range of possibilities. Because robust decision making is only possible with the kinds of computing power produced by the revolution in information described above, the computer must be up and running at all stages of the process.

The key, as in most of RAND's uncertainty-sensitivity planning, is to reject the notion that any one future can capture all the unknowns ahead. "The set of plausible futures expressed in the scenarios should be as diverse as possible to provide sufficient challenges against which to test near-term policies," Lempert and Popper suggest. "These scenarios can be constructed to represent many different types of information about the future." In turn decision makers should adopt robust strategies that will apply across a range of possible futures, and then adapt to new information as it arrives. As organizations adapt to new information, performance should rise accordingly.

All plans do not require the same level of robustness, however. Nor is predict-then-act analysis obsolete. RAND still uses traditional analysis tools to study everything from supply chains to early childhood.

Yet, no matter what the plan, be it short-term or longer-term, organizations have ample incentive to reduce their vulnerability to uncertainty. Although RAND's Gregory Treverton does not think uncertainty can rise much further than it already has, he does argue that the harder question is whether its consequences will increase. "On that score," he writes, "we ain't seen nothing yet—and don't want to." Thus, they are in a remarkably stable environment, and are unaffected by the revolutions described above. Organizations need at least some robustness to survive—some may need a little;

others may need a great deal. As this book contends, organizations cannot adopt robust, adaptive plans unless they can make them happen.

Preparing for uncertainty therefore requires at least some consideration of organizational capabilities, which Davis describes as capabilities-based planning. Davis' technique is designed to match an organization's operating plan to the specific building blocks needed for success. The goal, says Davis, "is to provide capabilities suitable for a wide range of modern-day challenges while working within an economic framework that necessitates choice. Its implementation should emphasize flexibility, adaptability, and robustness of capability (as distinct from planning some particular threat and set of assumptions." Again it does not make sense to plan for a robust, adaptive future if the organization does not have the building blocks needed to respond. If the organization itself is not robust and adaptive, it may be far better perhaps to simply pretend that there is a single future, and sleep well at night until the surprise comes calling.

CONCLUSION

No one knows whether the five revolutions described above will add up to what some futurists call the *Singularity*, an astrophysical term that refers to the center of a black hole where Albert Einstein's rules no longer hold. What is clear is that the pace of change appears to be accelerating as biology, technology, globalization, and information merge together to create an onslaught of both potential and peril.[44]

Measured by both the velocity and variety of change, most organizations already recognize that they live in uncertain times. Hence, "tried-and-true compass-setting" tools such as strategic planning, benchmarking, and mission and vision statements topped Bain & Company's annual survey of management tools in 2002. Of the companies surveyed, 80 percent said they had used all three tools in 2002, up from 70 percent in 2000.

Even if they set the right course, however, many organizations are poorly designed to respond to the changes that they face, whether because of ignorance, inflexibility, indifference, or inconsistency. Although they may have survived, even prospered, with pockets of vulnerability in the past, the question is whether they can survive at all facing the revolutions described above, and what they can do to improve the odds of success. Instead of launching another planning process, benchmarking the competition, or writing a better vision statement, perhaps they should think about the next surprise. "Unless it's suppressed, there's going to be some breakthrough in either electrical propulsion for cars or fuel cells," RAND's Robert Roll warns the car industry. "Or China will all of a sudden have two cars per household and we'll be drowning in greenhouse emissions. Circumstances are going to force a change on the automobile industry. The question is how to get ahead of it."

Getting ahead of the next surprise is easier said than done, of course. Unfortunately, there is little hard research on how organizations can structure themselves to improve the odds of success under conditions of uncertainty. There are plenty of lists of how innovative, built-to-last, good-to-great, or just plain excellent organizations behave, but few that provide guidance on the underlying scaffolding needed to innovate, improve, or sustain excellence, and even fewer that ask what matters most to high performance. As a result organizations often try to do every good thing at once, adopting fad after fad in search of something, anything, that works.

The next chapter is designed to temper that pressure by asking what matters most to high performance. The first step toward improvement is knowing what to change and what to leave alone, what to nurture and what to ignore.

NOTES

1 Albert Wohlstetter, F. S. Hoffman, and M. E. Arnsten, *Measures to Protect Air Base Fuel Stocks*, RM-1394, October 21, 1954; accessed at http://www.rand.org/publications/classics/wohlstetter/RM1398/RM1398.html, June 10, 2004.

2 This quote is drawn from a March e-mail exchange with Davis; his emphasis.

3 Wohlstetter, et al., "Measures to Protect Airbase Bulk Fuel Stocks," p. 2.

4 There is so much RAND literature cited in this report I decided it is better to provide a bibliographic inventory at the end of the book rather than clutter each page with footnote after footnote.

5 Thomas C. Schelling, "Forward," in Roberta Wohlstetter, *Pearl Harbor: Warning and Decision*, Palo Alto, CA:Stanford, 1962, p. vii.

6 Wohlstetter, *Pearl Harbor*, pp. 388-389.

7 Ernest R. May, *Strange Victory: Hitler's Conquest of France*, New York:Hill and Wang, 2000.

8 Ernest May, *Strange Victory*, p. 452.

9 The software engine, called Computer Assisted Reasoning System (CARS™), was designed by Evolving Logic, a company headed by Bankes, Lempert, and Popper, and was used to apply the company's robust adaptive decision-making methodology to Volvo's problem.

10 "First Drive: 2003 Volvo XC90: SUV Now Stands for Swedish Utility Vehicle," *Motor Trend*, October 2002, access at http://www.motortrend.com/roadtests/suv/112_0210_volvo/index.html.

11 Winston Churchill, *The River War: An Account of the Reconquest of the Soudan*, Carroll and Graf, 2000, pp. 162-163, originally published in 1902.

12 Scott McMurray, "Changing a Culture: DuPont Tries to Make Its Research Wizardry Serve the Bottom Line," *Wall Street Journal*, March 27, 1992, p. A1.

13 The study of DuPont, Intel, Monsanto, and Xerox, was conducted by Susan A. Resetar, Beth E. Lachman, Robert J. Lempert, Monica M. Pinto, and is cited in the bibliography at the end of the book.

14 RAND's study team cites Nathan Rosenberg, *Exploring the Black Box: Technology, Economics, and History*, Cambridge, 1994, on these numbers.

15 James P. Miller, "DuPont Emerges Slim and Trim from Restructuring—Chemical Giant Has Pared Costs and Employees in Three-Year Makeover," *Wall Street Journal*, April 6, 1995, p. B3.

16 Faye Rice, "Who Scores Best on the Environment," *Fortune*, July 26, 1993.

17 Edward Harris, "Norway's Kvaerner, Once a Global Player, Faces a Scaled-Down Future," *Wall Street Journal*, October 29, 2001, p. A19.

18 Olga Oliker's study, *Russia's Chechen Wars, 1994-2000*, is cited in the bibliography at the end of the book..

19 See Intel's description of Moore's Law at http://www.intel.com/research/silicon/mooreslaw.htm.

20 The study was conducted by Susan A. Resetar, Beth E. Lachman, Robert J. Lempert, Monica M. Pinto, and is cited in the bibliography at the end of the book.

21 Don Clark, "Intel Bets on a New Design Strategy," *Wall Street Journal*, May 14, 2004, p. B2.

22 Ellen Florian, "Special CEOs on Innovation," *Fortune*, March 8, 2004, p. 89, accessed on http://www.nexis.com July 17, 2004.

23 The conclusion emerged from a series of reports conducted over the life of the New American Schools experiment.

24 James P. Womack, Daniel T. Jones, and Daniel Roos, *The Machine that Changed the World: The Story of Lean Production*, New York:Harper Perennial, 1990.

25 RAND references N. Sakkab, "Connect & Develop Replaces Research & Develop at P&G," which was presented at the Industrial Research Institute Semi-Annual Meeting, Washington, D.C., 2000.

26 Ann Harrington, "Who's Up and Who's Down; How Companies Rank in Their Industries," *Fortune*, March 8, 2004.

27 Quoted in Ellen Florian, "Special: CEOs on Innovation," *Fortune*, March 8, 2004, p. 89, accessed at http://www.nexis.com, July 17, 2004.

28 Florian, "CEOs on Innovation."

29 Janet Guyon, "No Innovation Can Replace Direct Discussions," *Fortune*, July 26, 2004, p. 167, accessed at http://www.nexis.com, July 17, 2004. (The article was available on Nexis before its publication date.)

30 I draw here on James S. Hodges, *Onward through the Fog: Uncertainty and Management in Systems Analysis and Design*, RAND, July 1990.

31 Peter S. Pande, Robert P. Neuman, and Roland R. Cavanagh, *The Six Sigma Way: How GE, Motorola, and Other Top Companies Are Honing Their Performance*, New York:McGraw Hill, 2000, p. ix.

32 Gregory F. Treverton, *Reshaping National Intelligence for an Age of Information*, New York:Cambridge, 2003, pp. 11-13.

33 This list comes from Carl H. Builder and James A. Dewar, "A Time for Planning? If Not Now, When?" *Parameters*, Summer, 1994, p. 8.

34 Michael Marriott, "Designing a Smarter Shoe," *New York Times*, May 6, 2004, p. G1.

35 Nano-scaling and nano-divide are my term, not RAND's.

36 The study was authored by Richard O. Hundley, Robert H. Anderson, Tora K. Bikson, and C. Richard Neu, and is referenced in the bibliography.

37 Gary Burtless and Robert Litan: *Globalphobia: Open Trade and Its Critics*, Washington, D.C.:Brookings, 2003.

38 The survey was conducted by RAND Europe in collaboration with Janusian Security Risk Management. The results were published in the *Financial Times*, May 10, 2004.

39 RAND's report on the Zapatista netwar was coauthored with Graham E. Fuller and Melissa Fuller, and is referenced in the bibliography.

40 Graham Dunn, "Schiphol to Remain Prominent in Air France-KLM Tie-Up," *Air Transport Intelligence*, March 19, 2004.

41 The Army built much of its strategy on the high probability that a Soviet invasion would come through the Fulda Gap, which would open the corridor for the shortest run through Frankfurt to the Rhine.

42 These suggestions come from Paul Davis and Zalmay Khalilzad's report, *A Composite Approach to Air Force Planning*, cited in the bibliography.

43 The quotes are taken from Lempert and Popper's draft chapter, "High Performance Government for an Uncertain World," in R. Klitgaard, ed., *High-Performance Public Service*, RAND, forthcoming, 2005.

44 See James John Bell, "Exploring the 'Singularity,'" The Futurist, vol. 37, no. 3, May 2003, for an introduction to contemporary thinking on the issue.

IN SEARCH OF
EXTRAORDINARY
RESULTS

RAND and its researchers have never been interested in uncertainty for uncertainty's sake. Convinced that uncertainty is a central challenge to organizational performance, they have spent more than a half century looking for ways to both "harden" organizations against turbulence and increase the odds of high performance during peace and war.

Indeed, a RAND researcher named Paul Baran imagined the first version of today's Internet as a way to insulate military communications against the chaos of nuclear war. "At the time, the nation's long-distance communications networks were indeed extremely vulnerable and unable to withstand a nuclear attack," write Katie Hafner and Matthew Lyon in their best-selling history of the Internet, *Where Wizards Stay Up Late*. "Yet the president's ability to call for, or call off, the launch of American missiles (called minimal essential communication), relied heavily on the nation's vulnerable communications systems."[1]

According to Baran, who began working on the problem in 1959, the Air Force had two options for solving the problem: a *decentralized* communications network with regional hubs that would collect and distribute information, or a *distributed* network with no hubs at all.

Baran clearly favored a distributed network composed of autonomous "nodes" that would be capable of receiving, routing, and transmitting information to the final destination through any available path. "Many of the things I thought possible would tend to sound like utter nonsense, or impractical, depending on the generosity of spirit in those brought up in an earlier world," he told Hafner and Lyon 30 years later. Baran remembers talking with other researchers outside of RAND about the human brain, which often reroutes information around damaged cells, thinking, "Well, gee, you know, the brain seems to have some of the properties that one would need for real stability."[2]

The only way to design such a system would be to break each communication into short, fixed-length pieces that could be addressed to another station and routed through the network to their ultimate destination. That meant digital, not analog, technology, as digital technology allowed information to be moved from one place to another in packets, which were then reassembled. "By dividing each message into parts," Hafner and Lyons write, "you could flood the network with what [Baran] called 'message blocks,' all racing over different paths to their destination. Upon their arrival, a receiving computer would reassemble the message bits into readable form."[3]

Although Baran eventually convinced the Air Force to pursue the idea, American Telephone & Telegraph (AT&T) was unimpressed. "After I heard the melodic refrain of 'bullshit' often enough, I was motivated to go away and write a series of detailed memoranda papers to show, for example, that algorithms were possible that allowed a short message to contain all the information it needed to find its own way through the network."[4] Five years after starting the project, Baran finally hit the wall when the newly created Defense Communications Agency was put in charge of the effort. Concluding that the new agency would "screw it up," Baran moved on to other work.

Baran's idea lived on, of course. With funding from the Defense Department's Advanced Research Projects Agency (ARPA), Baran's "packet-switching" system was eventually built in 1967. Called ARPANET, it had seven nodes, the first at UCLA and the seventh at RAND. By the 1980s, ARPANET had become the Internet, and the rest, as they say, is history.

LOST IN CHANGE

Today's organizations have never been more interested in hardening themselves against uncertainty, especially at the top. According to ongoing studies of executive turnover at the world's 2500 largest companies, executives must either deliver or depart. Writing in the spring 2003 issue of *strategy+business*, a team of Booz Allen Hamilton researchers concluded that involuntary, performance-related turnover had reached a record high in 2002, accounting for nearly two out of five departures.[5] Firings were up, patience was down, and hiring an outsider was no longer the guarantee of success that it once had been.

Although the deliver-or-depart pressure subsided slightly with the economic recovery, almost a third of executive separations were still involuntary. As the Booz Allen team concluded in 2004, "Companies remain focused on firing overcompensated, underperforming chiefs—the rate of CEO dismissals increased by 170 percent from 1995 to 2003." Unfortunately for CEOs, the departures bore almost no relationship to performance, creating even more pressure for change. "At some juncture, the prospect of forced dismissal will seem so likely that it will hang like a cloud of misery over a chief executive, undermining his or her ability to perform," the Booz Allen study argued. "Concerned about their mortality, CEOs will try to get even more done quickly, emphasizing quick fixes at the expense of company transformation."[6] The problem is not too little change, but too much.

RAND might argue that the best way to counter the pressure is to ask what matters most to high performance, which is exactly how its five-member team developed the organizational blueprint for a state-of-the-art human tissue bank.[7] Recognizing that progress in the fight against cancer depends on access to a network of high-performing organizations, the team began looking for best practices at 12 of the nation's leading tissue banks. Although some of these banks were operated by federal agencies, such as the National Cancer Institute, some by universities, such as Duke University, and some by private firms, such as Ardais Corporation and Genomics Collaborative, Inc., all of them shared a common demand for organizational capacity, including the technology to register and track specimens (bioinformatics), storage facilities, inventory control, shipping procedures, and quality assurance systems.

The one thing tissue banks do not share is national standards for collecting and storing specimens, which can undermine confidence in the resulting research. In a market in which samples must match protein for protein, banks must be more alike than different, especially when it comes to collecting, identifying, and storing tissue. Hence, RAND has recommended a new kind of bank built around a network of geographically dispersed organizations that follow the same protocols covering all facets of the process.

The list of best practices includes everything from sample collection to freezer maintenance and backup; there are nine recommendations on sample collection, nine on processing and annotation, five on storage and distribution, five on information management, six on identifying consumer/user needs, five on business planning and operations, six on privacy and ethical systems, five on intellectual property and legal issues, and two on public relations, marketing, and education.

On sample collection and processing, for example, the team urges standard operating procedures for collecting all samples, clear guidelines for processing each sample within one hour of collection, bar codes for tracking individual shipments both to and from each tissue bank, a quality assurance process for ensuring compliance, around-the-clock monitoring of storage conditions, and frequent employee training. On business planning and communications, it recommends close contact with collection staff at all sites, continuous review of new technologies for improving performance, a cost-accounting system for tracking each stage of the process, a marketing plan for increasing access, and outreach to donors and researchers alike on the benefits of a standardized system. In a sentence, high-performing tissue banks must be alert to changing research demand, agile in collecting and distributing samples, adaptable to new technologies and research, and aligned around a core set of operating procedures that assure quality.

It is impossible to implement these best practices without some minimal organizational capacity, however. Tissue banks cannot create standard operating procedures without at least some business planning, expand their donor networks without a communication plan, track their operating costs without a decent accounting package, track their samples without scanning technology, or learn new languages without training.

As RAND's team notes, all of the existing banks follow at least some of the best practices, but none follow all 52. Ardais is a leader in quality assurance, for example, but it is not at the top in creating broad networks of academic and community medical centers, whereas Genomics Collaborative is a leader in setting high ethical standards on everything from informed consent to patient confidentiality, but it is not at the top in reviewing researcher submissions and credentials.

The question for this chapter is not whether RAND has learned a great deal about designing a high-performing tissue bank, however, but whether there is a set of core organizational characteristics that can make high performance more likely. It is one thing to compile a long list of best practices, and quite another to identify the underlying infrastructure that is needed if an organization is to succeed in a rapidly changing environment. Of all the things that organizations can do to improve performance, which matter most in producing the high performance that RAND has observed over the years?

This chapter uses a statistical winnowing process to provide a first set of answers. If the voluminous literature on organizational change is right, high-performing organizations are practically perfect in every way. They have clear goals, adequate funding, strategic plans, flat hierarchies, talented leaders, rigorous metrics, powerful incentives, a focus on results, and tight management systems.

But as the rest of this chapter suggests, these characteristics do not demonstrate equal statistical power in explaining success. When characteristics are tested against one another through an ever-tougher set of statistical tests, some turn out to be surprisingly weak, while others show surprisingly strong staying power as the winnowing progresses. Moreover, as this chapter shows, RAND researchers share some clear agreements on what matters most for predicting high performance in the organizations they know best.

Designing Organizations

This book is also based on the idea that organizations can reduce their vulnerability to ignorance, inflexibility, indifference, and inconsistency through basic changes in their structures and operating systems. If a running shoe can be designed to adapt, why not an organization? If an automobile can be built to crouch or pounce, why not an organization? Simply stated, organizations can be designed for high performance in a turbulent world.

This conclusion is clear in a recent RAND study of innovation and change in six government and business organizations.[8] The project was designed to look at a particular kind of organization—one that has sustained innovation over five or more years; that has a complex, geographically distributed mission, multiple partners and stakeholders, and predictable leadership change; and that faces severe consequences from failure.

After considering hundreds of candidates, the RAND team chose the U.S. Customs Service, DuPont, the U.S. Food and Drug Administration (FDA), Marriott, Procter & Gamble, and the U.S. Veterans Health Administration (VHA) for its study. According to the team, the six organizations shared a variety of common characteristics, including highly committed leadership, strong incentives for innovation, pliable organizational structures, performance measurement systems, and maximum access to training and technology:

- All six clarified their mission statement and revised their business model at the start of their effort to become more innovative.
- All six implemented performance measures and evaluated innovation in the context of goals and measures.
- All six routinely gathered new information from external sources and integrated it into their business operations.

There was plenty of variation in characteristics, however. As RAND's study of innovation and change shows, Marriott was an excellent example of the effective use of information and performance measures to stimulate improvement and innovation, whereas DuPont and Procter & Gamble provided useful examples of the role of senior leadership in guiding and sustaining innovation.

Moreover, looking down the long list of characteristics, there was more than enough variation to frustrate the search for a silver bullet. While all six organizations aligned resources with priorities, for example, only two (Marriott and the VHA) used a balanced score of financial and nonfinancial measures to track performance, and only one (Marriott) used a core-competency model for investing in innovation.

Similarly, while all six built trusting relationships with users, only four (Customs, the FDA, Marriott, and the VHA) streamlined their organizational structures through consolidation, only three (Customs, Marriott and Procter & Gamble) led the effort from headquarters, and just two (Customs and the VHA) flattened their hierarchies.

Whereas five of the six (the FDA being the exception) diffused ongoing innovation throughout the organization, only three (DuPont, Marriott, and Procter & Gamble) monitored employee attitudes and morale, only three (Customs, DuPont, and Procter & Gamble) added resources to pay for innovation, and only three (the FDA, Procter & Gamble, and the VHA) used promotion to reward star performers.

Finally, whereas five of the six (excluding only the FDA) created incentives for motivating employees, only two (Marriott and Procter & Gamble) used internal competition to drive organization-wide improvement, and only one (Marriott) used integrated screening, training, and mentoring to retain hard-to-recruit, nontraditional employees.

As we shall see later, some of the characteristics turn out to be situational, others are luxuries, and still others just do not matter. DuPont, Marriott, and Procter & Gamble did not consolidate in part because they had greater incentives to flatten and decentralize; Customs, the FDA, and the VHA did not create innovation-investment funds in part because Congress controls the purse strings and rarely provided unrestricted funding; and the three government agencies did not regularly track employee attitudes and morale because that is just the way it is done when the workforce advances on automatic pilot. The question is never whether a given organization can improve, but where it should begin.

RAND Preferences

This book is also based on the notion that RAND and its researchers have developed important insights into what is important for high performance. At least some of these insights were collected through an Internet survey of 126 senior RAND researchers during the summer and fall of 2002. Of the 300 researchers invited to participate in the survey, 160 visited the password-protected Internet website and were asked how much they knew about how organizations work. Of the 160, 126 said that they had learned either a great deal or a fair amount and were allowed to continue.

The final sample was both educated and experienced. All of the participants had an advanced degree, two-thirds had a doctorate, and three-fifths were over 45 years of age. The sample also represented a wide range of research interests—62 percent said that their work focused on defense and national security, 25 percent said science and technology, 24 percent said health, 17 percent said international policy, 14 percent said education, 9 percent said social policy, 8 percent said labor, 6 percent said justice, 6 percent said transportation, 4 percent said environment and energy, 4 percent said child policy, 2 percent said population, and 18 percent said "other," all of which adds up to two research areas per participant.

The sample also drew upon a deep reservoir of organizational information—98 percent of the participants said that they had gained their organizational knowledge through their own observations and experiences, 74 percent by doing research on questions involving organizational performance, 70 percent by reading the literature, and 66 percent by solving organizational problems for clients.

As a group, the participants initially agreed that high-performing organizations should do it all. Asked to think about all the high-performing organizations they knew, not any organization in particular, 92 percent said that the words *innovative* and *resilient* described those organizations very or somewhat well, 87 percent said the same about the word *disciplined*, 79 percent about *rigorous*, and 71 percent about *entrepreneurial*.

However, when pushed to identify the most important features of high-performing organizations, the participants coalesced around innovation and resilience. Overall, 38 percent said that organizations should be innovative, 21 percent said that they should be resilient, 19 percent said disciplined, 16 percent said rigorous, and just 3 percent said entrepreneurial.

The group had the same initial opinions about the leaders of high-performing organizations. Asked to think about the leaders of the high-performing organizations that they knew, 96 percent said that it was very or somewhat important for those leaders to be *decisive* and *honest*, 86 percent said the same thing about being *innovative*, 71 percent said the same thing about being *trusting*, and 63 percent said the same thing about being *charismatic*. In other words, leaders should be "all of the above."

Yet, when pressed to identify the most important characteristic of leadership, 66 percent said that leaders of high-performing organizations should be honest and trusting, 21 percent said that they should be decisive,

9 percent said that they should be innovative, and just 4 percent said that they should be charismatic.

When the two sets of preferences are combined, a majority of the RAND participants favored organizations that were innovative, resilient, or disciplined and leaders who were honest, decisive, and trusting. Overall, 63 percent of the participants put innovative/resilient/disciplined organizations together with trusting/honest leaders, 20 percent put innovative/resilient/disciplined organizations with decisive leaders, and just 10 percent put innovative organizations together with innovative leaders.

Translated into a simple recommendation, these researchers might urge organizations to put their faith in innovation and resilience at the middle and bottom, and to ensure trust, honesty, and decisiveness at the top.

Some RAND researchers believe that these particular characteristics apply to any professional organization, be it a think tank, a law firm, or a consulting company. As senior researcher Tora Bikson said about her experience at RAND:

> I suspect we believe that innovation does and should come from the interactions among the researchers—and we probably wouldn't buy a top-down innovation no matter how charismatic its proponent. What we do want is honesty and transparency—kind of like having a level playing field for the intellectual marketplace (fairness, no hidden deals or agendas, no pressure to tune the research to woo particular clients, and so on). Maybe honesty is all the more salient in the climate of corporate scandals, although RAND doesn't offer the kind of big bucks temptation to be found in parts of the for-profit world. Of course it doesn't hurt if the top guy is likeable.[9]

Paul Davis agreed: "We do not have 'political whining' in the hallways, nor any discussion of 'how we sold out on that one, but we did what we had to do.' Instead, the self-image is that we're quintessentially straight-shooters. Although it's also very nice if the top managers are very smart, innovative, etc., integrity and competence come first." James Dertouzos seconded the need for honesty at the core of a professional research enterprise: "Most RAND researchers believe that organizational performance is mostly about the sum of individual contributions. If that is the case, then good leadership is really mostly about hiring, motivating, and retaining a high-quality workforce and creating a healthy work environment that encourages risk taking, allows a large degree of autonomous decision making, and provides the resources and support so that individuals can be successful. Honesty and trust are essential."

Even as they talked about RAND's own culture, many researchers also viewed the combination of innovation and honesty as essential for high performance more generally. "The RAND culture tries to use analysis to deflate the influence of personal charisma, so it is possible that there would be a natural lack of affinity for charismatic leadership," Frank Camm wrote. "RAND also tries to develop recommendations that work whether people involved in them are exceptionally good or not—the 'no heroes' approach; RAND tries to counter the common belief in the Defense Department, for example, that good people can make any process work—that is, that the best solution to any problem is to hand it to your best person and not worry the process details."

John Dumond offered a similar explanation to me about companies that have used quality management to rise to the top:

> They recognized the need to get buy-in and ideas from all the workers. They set up "quality councils" of leaders who were honest, and made use of "quality circles" of employees to generate ideas for improvement. Our efforts with the Defense logistics community have mirrored these ideas—an important coalition at the top, filled with honest leaders and fed by process and site improvement teams with ideas for change. The Army leaders we encountered were willing to see how poor the performance was—being honest—because they knew that the organization had to start somewhere. It's rarely the single individual that possesses all the wisdom, skill, and knowledge to move an organization from mediocre to high performing. One person might bring tremendous domain knowledge, but lack leadership skills; another might have management skills, but lack other talents.

Finally, at least some senior researchers view the findings as being characteristic of high-performing organizations. "I personally don't want all organizations to behave that way," Davis said of the innovative/honest combination:

> I think that definitely makes sense for organizations in which innovation is crucial—high-tech companies, research and development

companies (military and non-military), etc. The military is a more interesting example. To the extent that our military is becoming a "high-tech company," it is experimenting with making lower-level decision makers much more autonomous. That's a radical switch from what has worked for militaries since Roman times when the hierarchical organization was founded, and I think the jury is still out on its long-term survival as an organizational concept. That model also fits with the general "learning organization" concept in the business world—another instance where the jury is still out."

Although the rest of this chapter deals with the characteristics of the single organizations identified by each of the 126 respondents, it is important to note that RAND does not deal with just any organization or problem in its work. Given RAND's history of questioning the questions, its client base tends to be composed of organizations that worry about the future. Therefore, the winnowing process described here is less about organizations in general, and more about the kind of organizations that RAND researchers get to know well.

A WINNOWING STRATEGY

My winnowing strategy was built around a relatively simple notion. After asking the 126 researchers about their personal histories at RAND and their views of high-performing organizations in general, I asked the participants to think about the one organization they knew best, regardless of its performance.[10] The question produced a list of 126 organizations, including government agencies such as the Air Force, Army Recruiting Command, and Centers for Medicare and Medicaid Services; businesses such as AK Steel, CIGNA, Hughes Aircraft, and State Farm Insurance; and nonprofit organizations such as the University of Minnesota Medical School and RAND itself. Two-fifths of the organizations had budgets over $500 million, three-quarters were more than 30 years old, and three-quarters had more than 1000 employees.

I then asked each participant to rank the performance of the chosen organization on a seven-point scale from exemplary to extremely poor. The result was that 13 percent of the participants rated their one organization as exemplary, 37 percent as very good, 44 percent as somewhat good, neither good nor poor, or somewhat poor, and 7 percent as very or extremely poor.

Finally, I asked each participant 37 questions covering nine different areas of organizational performance: (1) demographics, including age, size, and sector; (2) strategy, including mission, funding, and measurement; (3) trajectory, including shocks, growth, and change; (4) environment, including uncertainty, turbulence, and competition; (5) internal structure, including layering, delegation, and funding for new ideas; (6) leadership, including style, communication, and political skill; (7) management systems, including planning, budgeting, and evaluation; (8) resources, including information, technology, and training; and (9) incentives. Did the organization have a clear mission? Did it regularly survey its customers? Had it been through a recent change in its mission? How turbulent was its environment? Did it delegate authority for routine decisions? Did it have charismatic leaders? Did it give employees enough information? And did it set strong incentives for performance?

It would have been easy to end the winnowing by simply asking how the high-performing organizations scored on each of the 37 questions. However, as the following list suggests, the questions produced a long list of "Mary Poppins–like," "practically perfect" characteristics that reveal little about what matters most for high performance:

- 100 percent had a clear mission.
- 95 percent gave their staff authority to make routine decisions on their own.
- 92 percent always or often provided access to the information needed for high performance.
- 90 percent had few barriers between organizational subunits.
- 90 percent had very or somewhat strong incentives for high performance.
- 88 percent had sufficient revenue to achieve their mission.
- 88 percent always or often provided the technological equipment needed for high performance.
- 87 percent had very or somewhat clear incentives for high performance.
- 85 percent had leaders who fostered open communication.
- 84 percent had the budgetary flexibility to invest in new ideas.
- 84 percent had budgets under $500 million per year.
- 82 percent always or often had enough employees to achieve high performance.
- 82 percent had fewer than 10,000 employees.
- 81 percent measured the results of what they did.

- 79 percent had effective information technology.
- 77 percent had leaders who were charismatic.
- 77 percent had leaders with a participatory style of management.
- 77 percent always or often provided access to training for high performance.
- 76 percent had few layers of management between the top and the bottom of the organization.
- 75 percent had leaders with good political skills.
- 74 percent operated in a turbulent environment.
- 74 percent had an effective budget and accounting system.
- 71 percent operated in a competitive environment.
- 70 percent regularly surveyed their customers and clients about their performance.
- 69 percent operated in an uncertain environment.
- 69 percent were more than 30 years old.
- 66 percent had experienced significant growth in funding or staffing over the past five years.
- 66 percent had experienced significant growth in revenue or staffing.
- 66 percent had an effective planning system.
- 64 percent had effective information technology.
- 63 percent were nonprofit agencies.
- 60 percent had experienced a significant growth in demand.
- 58 percent had an effective program evaluation system.
- 37 percent had hit a significant shock or crisis, such as a budget cutback.
- 30 percent operated in a hostile environment.
- 23 percent had experienced a significant change in their mission.

The question, however, is not how high-performing organizations are alike, but whether and how they differ from poor performers, and what poor performers can do to improve. The answer involves three rounds of a statistical winnowing process designed to test the true strength of each characteristic in actually predicting high performance.

Before turning to the results, readers should note that several characteristics were left out of the competition. For starters, there was no characteristic describing the organizations' products or industries. The problem here was that a nuanced product or industry measure would divide the sample into such tiny parts that statistical comparisons would be useless.

In addition, there was no separate characteristic describing the quality of the workforce. Such a characteristic would be useless unless it was divided by levels of the organization—for example, board, senior leadership, middle-level managers, middle-level employees, and frontline employees—and this would have added enormous length to an already formidable survey. Moreover, the quality of the workforce is covered indirectly through a number of other characteristics, including delegation of authority; barriers between units; leadership style; access to information, training, and technology; and incentives for high performance, all of which measure how the workforce is managed regardless of where it begins.

Finally, there was no measure of public support, reputation, or profit against which to assess the performance ratings. It is entirely possible, for example, that public support for organizations such as NASA, the University of Minnesota Medical School, or RAND itself might influence their performance. It is also possible that high performers are much better at managing change than their peers. Given the range of characteristics already in the field, the difficulties of assessing public support and change management from a distance, and the need to keep the survey to a manageable length, these characteristics were left on the cutting room floor.

The First Round of Winnowing

The first round of winnowing set a relatively low bar for survival. Characteristics could remain in the pool by merely showing a significant one-on-one *association* with performance.

For example, organizations that measured results, gave their employees authority to make routine decisions on their own, embraced participatory leadership, and had effective program evaluation systems were much more likely to be rated as high performers than their peers, which is why all four of these characteristics survived the first round of winnowing. In turn, organizations that had experienced a change in mission, operated in competitive and/or turbulent environments, and had charismatic leaders were no more likely to be rated as high performers than their peers, which is why these four characteristics were winnowed out.

Given the low bar for survival, it is no surprise that so many characteristics remained in the pool.[11] Converted from characteristics into recommendations for action, the 29 survivors should be familiar to anyone who has paged through the business best-seller list, and could easily provide the outline for a book on the essential elements of high performance.

The First Round of Winnowing: Strong Associations with Performance

Demographics

▶ Act small (budget).

▶ Stay lean (employment).

▶ Avoid government.

▶ Go nonprofit.

Strategy

▶ Sharpen the mission.

▶ Generate sufficient revenue.

▶ Measure results.

▶ Survey customers regularly.

Trajectory

▶ Avoid shocks and crises.

▶ Grow the organization.

▶ Increase demand.

Environment

▶ Avoid hostile markets.

Internal Structure

▶ Flatten the hierarchy.

▶ Delegate authority for routine decisions.

▶ Reduce the barriers between units.

▶ Invest in new ideas.

Leadership

- Embrace participation.
- Manage the political world.
- Foster open communication.

Internal Systems

- Strengthen the planning system.
- Strengthen the budget and accounting system.
- Strengthen information technology.
- Strengthen program evaluation.

Resources

- Increase access to information.
- Increase access to technology.
- Deploy enough employees to do the job.
- Increase access to training.

Incentives

- Create strong incentives for high performance.
- Create clear incentives for high performance.

Such a book would do little to resolve the confusion about what matters most for high performance, however. Those who like operations management would find ample comfort in the call for measurement and strong incentives; those who prefer employee empowerment would find support in the call for delegation and participatory management; and those who want greater accountability would be energized by the call to saturate the organization with information.

More importantly, such a book would discourage the learning that is essential to higher performance. "I'm surprised that big, successful companies don't actually try to learn from their own mistakes more," Shan Cretin says:

> When something doesn't work, heads will roll and people are removed. It's almost like the traces of the real evidence about the failure are no longer accessible. It's clear in the experimental work that you can learn a lot by looking at what didn't work. If you have a theory that fails, you have evidence that you had something wrong and you can go back and try to tease out what didn't work and try something different the next time around.

Since the winnowing process was designed to help organizations set a course toward high performance, it seems reasonable to remove characteristics that organizations simply cannot change. Although being a government organization reduces the likelihood of high performance and being nonprofit increases them, neither characteristic is particularly pliable. There are big, cumbersome, mediocre organizations in every sector, and there are at least some agile, innovative, well-aligned organizations in government.

This is not to suggest that sector is irrelevant. Just 35 percent of the government organizations were rated as exemplary or very good, compared to 55 percent of the businesses and 63 percent of the nonprofit organizations.

As RAND's own work on lean manufacturing in the aircraft industry suggests, even private firms that work for government face serious barriers to high performance. First, these private firms produce fewer copies of their core product, raising the risk associated with error—the United States builds just one nuclear aircraft at a time, and each one takes more than six years to build, for example. Second, private contractors do not pay the cost of failure—the government pays for the development of the system, thereby lowering the risk, and the disciplining effect, of loss. Third, private firms face an array of obstacles en route to an actual contract—government is hardly a paragon of efficiency in actually making budget decisions, and it often changes its mind on what it wants. Finally, the market has virtually nothing to do with price—instead, prices are based on a manufacturer's costs, allowing for a reasonable profit.

Yet, even though being in government reduces the likelihood of high performance, government agencies have little choice about their location. Much as a government agency might long for the agility of a private business, it is still part of government; much as a private business might long for the security of government, it must still compete for market share; and much as a nonprofit organization might long for the security of government and the access to capital of a private business, it still exists in between the two. The challenge in any organization, therefore, is to get as close to robustness as its sector will allow.

It also seems reasonable to remove organizational growth and demand from the pool. Although growth was positively correlated with high performance in the first round and emerged as a strong contender in the second, growth may be more a consequence of high performance than a cause of it. On the one hand, growing organizations are more likely to generate the financial slack needed for innovation and strong incentives. On the other hand, high performance could be causing the growth. Given the ambiguity of the relationship, it is better to disqualify the characteristic and keep the winnowing clean.

The Second Round of Winnowing

The second round of winnowing created a much tougher test for identifying the most important characteristics of high performance. Having passed a relatively weak challenge in round one, a characteristic could remain in the pool through round two only by showing a strong *predictive relationship* with performance when pitted against the other surviving characteristics in its category.[12]

Within the leadership category, for example, embracing participation and fostering open communication emerged as statistically significant predictors of organizational performance, which is how the two survived, whereas managing the political world faded into insignificance and was removed from the pool. Within the resources category, providing access to information also emerged as a significant predictor of performance, whereas providing access to technology, enough employees, and training showed little predictive power and were removed.

This much more aggressive winnowing removed 16 characteristics from the pool, leaving just 13 survivors: sharpening the mission, measuring results, surveying customers regularly, delegating authority, breaking down internal barriers, investing in new ideas, embracing participatory leadership, fostering open communication, staying on the technological edge, focusing on results, saturating the organization with information, and creating strong and clear incentives for performance.

The Second Round of Winnowing: Strong Predictive Relationships with Performance

Strategy

▶ Sharpen the mission.

▶ Measure results.

▶ Survey customers regularly.

Internal Structure

▶ Delegate authority for routine decisions.

▶ Reduce the barriers between units.

▶ Invest in new ideas.

Leadership

▶ Embrace participatory management.

▶ Foster open communication.

Internal Systems

▶ Strengthen information technology.

▶ Strengthen program evaluation.

Resources

▶ Increase access to information.

Incentives

▶ Create strong incentives for high performance.

▶ Create clear incentives for high performance.

A number of well-regarded characteristics left the pool in round two, including organizational size, generating sufficient funding for the mission, flattening the hierarchy, managing the political world, and strengthening the budget and accounting system. Although avoiding shocks and crises did not survive the winnowing as a predictor of high performance, RAND's own work on managing change suggests that shocks and crises, whether real or imagined, are essential to creating urgency for change. As RAND's Mark Lorell argues, urgency gave the armed services ample reason to cooperate in designing a Joint Strike Fighter that would serve the Air Force, Navy, and Marine Corps. "There were two clarifying issues. One, if there is a war and you screw up this fighter, you're going to die. Two, the Defense leadership went to the services and said, 'You will not get another airplane unless you make this thing work together. And if you don't, it's going to get cancelled and you will have no new airplane.'"

The Third Round of Winnowing

The third and final round of winnowing was designed to reduce the pool of characteristics to the smallest number possible by pitting the 13 survivors against one another to see which ones showed the strongest predictive relationship with performance.

Two caveats are worth exploring before moving on to the results. First, the statistical winnowing process covers only one part of the RAND knowledge base, the experiential knowledge of the 126 researchers who answered the Internet survey. It does not include the 31 researchers who were not allowed to complete the survey because they did not indicate enough knowledge of how organizations work, nor does it include the researchers who never responded to the survey at all.

Second, despite this caveat, the level of agreement in the third round is surprisingly high, particularly for a group of researchers who maintain that there is no such thing as a common model for high-performing organizations. In overall impact, the 13 third-round contestants explained more than two-thirds of the variation in the ratings of high performance. As analyses go, this one is impressive indeed. Much as RAND researchers may forswear a common vision of high performance, the statistical analysis suggests otherwise. These 126 respondents clearly shared a solid agreement on what matters most for high performance.

Caveats noted, the final winnowing produced seven significant predictors of performance. Statistically speaking, providing access to information emerged as the strongest predictor of high performance, followed by investing in new ideas, setting strong individual incentives for performance, having a clear mission, delegating authority, fostering open communication, and measuring results.[13] The other six characteristics simply faded into the statistical background as insignificant contributors.

The Third Round of Winnowing: Strongest Predictive Relationships with Performance

Strategy
- ▶ Sharpen the mission.
- ▶ Measure results.

Internal Structure
- ▶ Delegate authority for routine decisions.
- ▶ Invest in new ideas.

Leadership
- ▶ Foster open communication.

Resources
- ▶ Increase access to information.

Incentives
- ▶ Set strong incentives for performance.

Readers might wonder why strong characteristics such as surveying clients and customers, reducing barriers between units, participatory management, and so forth failed to survive. The answer, statistically speaking, is that their relationships with performance were simply eclipsed by the greater predictive power of the seven survivors. It is entirely possible, for example, that measuring results picked up much of the predictive power embedded in surveying customers. It is also possible that delegating authority reduced the impact of reducing barriers between units, and that fostering open communication and providing access to information worked together to knock out participatory management and information technology.

The Organizational Infrastructure of High Performance

The third round of winnowing produced more than the seven most powerful predictors of performance in the survey. It also revealed four statistically significant factors that underpin the 13 characteristics that entered the round.[14]

The first factor focused on the three characteristics that address organizational ignorance—measuring results, strengthening program evaluation, and setting clear incentives for high performance. The second factor centered on the three characteristics that reduce organizational inflexibility—delegating authority for routine decisions, embracing participatory leadership, and fostering open communication. The third factor converged on the three characteristics that confront organizational indifference—surveying customers regularly, investing in new ideas, and setting strong incentives for high performance. And the fourth factor focused on characteristics that counter inconsistency—reducing the barriers between units, strengthening information technology, and increasing access to information. One final characteristic, sharpening the mission, was found in all four factors, confirming that organizational purpose is the centerpiece for both addressing vulnerability and producing value.

These factors also describe the core elements, or infrastructure, of high-performing organizations: alertness, agility, adaptability, and alignment. Like Baran's Internet, high-performing organizations must be alert to changing circumstances, agile in addressing vulnerabilities and opportunities, adaptable in taking alternative paths to their destination, and aligned around a clear purpose. As such, the factors describe the four pillars of extraordinary performance highlighted in the title of this book and discussed in much greater detail in the next chapter.

The Four Pillars of High Performance

▶ Alertness

▶ Agility

▶ Adaptability

▶ Alignment

LESSONS FROM THE WINNOWING

Beyond providing a list of what matters most to high performance, the winnowing process provided 10 lessons on organizational design. Some of these challenge the conventional wisdom about how to improve performance, others echo findings from other research on how organizations can go from good to great, and still others reflect the RAND preferences for innovative, resilient, and disciplined organizations led by honest and trusting leaders.

However, as a group, the lessons suggest that the most important starting point for improvement is simple self-awareness. Organizations hardly need a "vulnerability audit" to ask themselves about the clarity of their mission, their commitment to measuring results, or their readiness to delegate authority or share information. As such, the Super Seven act as a guide to self-assessment, particularly for organizations that worry about increasing uncertainty.

RAND's work on managing environmental issues helps make the case for this kind of self-assessment. Having studied environmental management at leading private firms such as Walt Disney and Hewlett-Packard, RAND urges organizations to handle shocks and crises the way they handle most other threats to performance: one step at a time.

Yet RAND also notes the common strengths among proactive businesses firms. They motivate their employees to be not only creative but dogged in their determination to change the status quo for the better. Toward this mission-driven end, they design measurement systems that hold the organization accountable, make decisions that are compatible with the organization's broad goals, create incentives that are compatible with the organization's broader norms about compensation and advancement, expect individual failures to occur when employees push hard enough for real change, and limit the damage from such failures, while helping employees learn from their failures rather than punishing them for failing. More to the point, these winning companies "communicate continuously, internally and with key stakeholders, to sustain trust and commitment."

The 10 lessons presented below reflect my interpretations, and mine alone, of what RAND and its researchers have learned about what organizations do and do not need to achieve and sustain high performance. The first five items on the list offer cautionary advice regarding the conventional wisdom about what organizations need. At least by my reading of the winnowing results and the RAND knowledge base, high performance is not always accidental, and does not require charisma or a particular organizational structure. Nor are high-performing organizations always efficient or neat.

The second five items on the list involve minimal requirements and strong preferences. Again by my reading, RAND and its researchers believe that organizations must have a combination of "minimal viability" and competition to build momentum toward high performance, even as they saturate their organizations with the information and delegation to keep themselves alert, agile, adaptive, and aligned. They also believe that high performance is worthless unless there is an important mission to be served. Organizations do not exist to be pretty or nice—rather they exist to achieve a valued end.[15]

Ten Lessons on Organizational Design

1. Poor performance is not always accidental.

2. High performance is not always neat.

3. High performance is not always efficient.

4. High performance does not reside in hierarchy (or the lack thereof).

5. High performance does not require charisma.

6. High performance requires "minimal viability."

7. High performance requires at least minimal competition.

8. High performance thrives on information.

9. High performance thrives on delegation.

10. High performance starts and ends with mission.

Lesson 1: Poor Performance Is Not Always Accidental

Hard as this may be to accept, some organizations are designed to fail. Some start out with the best of intentions, but are quickly sidetracked by quick profits and the *built-to-flip*, quick sale philosophy that brought down so many high-tech firms in the early 2000s.[16] Although there are good reasons to create throw-away, *built-not-to-last* organizations, including what Jim Collins calls the "company as a disposable injection device" and the "company as a platform for genius," such organizations often absorb capital and creativity that would be better invested in longer-term performance.

Other organizations start out with no goal other than to survive, no matter what their performance. They may have the political muscle to ensure government subsidies ad infinitum, the regional monopolies to guarantee a market in spite of their performance, or enough fans to keep them going for one losing season after another. As my colleague Stanford University professor Terry Moe has written, many government organizations reflect an amalgam of choices that lead almost inexorably to disaster: "Just as policy can get watered down through compromise, so can structure—and it almost always does. . . . In the economic system, organizations are generally designed by participants who want them to succeed. In the political system, public bureaucracies are designed in no small measure by participants who explicitly want them to fail."[17]

Still other organizations have such murky missions that it is impossible to know whether they have succeeded or not. "You've got a military command structure in the Army, and you've got people who are very disciplined," James Dertouzos said of the organization he described in my Internet survey. "The particular command structure I picked has a fairly decent performance outcome and a fairly obvious mission, and it's pretty easy to evaluate whether their people are making it or not. Other organizations have much more fuzzy outputs."

Indeed, failure may actually be a sign of organizational success. This is certainly the lesson from James Quinlivan's short report on *coup-proofing*. Sometimes the goal is an organization that does not work very well, especially if the leader in charge is not particularly popular. As Quinlivan explains, "in order to coup-proof at the top, you at least have to have some degree of self-knowledge that, 'Man, a lot of people in this country don't love me. I'm not here through acclamation, and however we rig the next referendum, we've got to have a lot of checks and balances in place so that I don't end with a sudden loud noise from behind.'"

Imagine that you wanted to create a coup-proof government, Quinlivan suggests. What would you do? The answer would be to exploit family, ethnic, and religious loyalties; create parallel militaries that counterbalance the regular armed services; establish security agencies that watch everyone, including other security agencies; build an expert, or professional, military that is completely dependent on you for its well-being and livelihood; and find the money to support all of the above. As a result, your best units would be assigned to protect the leader, not the country. As Quinlivan likes to remind his audiences, "first-rate leaders pick first-rate people, second-rate leaders pick third-rate, third-rate pick fourth-rate, and so on." (See Quinlivan's briefing slide on the consequences of coup-proofing themselves.)

The Consequences of Coup-Proofing

▶ The military appears stronger than its actual capability.

▶ Inefficiencies in application of military power.

▶ Limits imposed on regular military.

  • Burdens of frontline service shifted to least-favored elements.

  • Relative weakness of common knowledge in regular military.

  • Those most likely to meet foreign enemies are the least capable.

Ironically, coup-proofing a government actually reduces its fighting ability. The special troops get the best weapons, the highest pay, and the deepest training, while regular troops get whatever is left. Moreover, as Quinlivan concludes, "units of the parallel military, armed with the best weapons, may not be readily available for military operations against external enemies. . . . The net effect is to present a more formidable force in the pages of military publications than can be brought to real battlefields."

Moreover, poor performance may involve flaws that flow from an organization's lack of faith in itself. This is clearly the case in the long-troubled Los Angeles Police Department (LAPD). According to RAND's 2003 study, the LAPD needed a new vision of police professionalism that put the emphasis on *corporateness*, meaning a sense of unity and purpose; *responsibility*, meaning a sense of service to society; and *expertise*, meaning basic policing and communication skills.[18] Blaming much of the department's trouble on a failure to "communicate clearly and consistently to its own officers what is expected of them," RAND's research team maintains that training is the key to future agility.

Current LAPD recruit training is based on a mid-twentieth-century military model. Like basic combat training, it seeks to tear down recruits and reconstruct them as LAPD officers. While this is certainly a transformation, the methods employed are more akin to information transmission than to transformative learning. Yet the ultimate goal of academy training is to produce a graduate similar to the product of a transformative educational process—an individual who is skilled in synthesis and evaluation and in making informed personal judgments.

One path to a new professionalism is through problem-based learning, in which students are placed in the active role of problem solvers confronted with real-world situations. Just like many business, law, public policy, and medical schools today, as well as the Royal Canadian Mounted Police, the LAPD could use problem-based learning to forge a common sense of mission among teams of recruits, even as it provides the basic skills and sense of social responsibility that are essential to a profession. Until it does so, the allegations of abuse that sparked the LA riots will continue.

Lesson 2: High Performance Is Not Always Neat

RAND researchers have seen more than their fair share of dysfunctional organizations, some of which have already been described. However, as RAND's Frank Camm suggests, organizations can be neat and orderly and still not be high performing. Asked how long it takes him to tell if an organization is working well, Camm answered, "It takes me a long time. Some people I know will go in, look around. Everything's clean and orderly, and they'll say 'This place works great.' Well, maybe. It's not immediately clear to me."

Camm then told me a story about how the French food-services company Sodexho runs mess halls for the Marine Corps under a nearly $900 million contract:

> The contractor said, "What you're going to see is that, right now, every mess hall is completely orderly and completely under control. In another three months after we show up, you're going to see that things are working at the edge of chaos. The reason for that is if you want to have fresh food for people, you prepare it just before it's served."
>
> You go into a place that looks like it's going nuts and say, "This is really out of control. It must be awful here." In fact, it's a good thing, because again it's a pull thing instead of a push thing. I have a hard time going into an organization. To me, what

I find myself doing is judging it by the quality of the people I talk to. If they seem to know what they're doing, that's good.

In fact, the Marine Corps picked Sodexho in part because it was an innovator in not being predictable. It had become an industry leader in providing food services to universities and businesses because of its *cook/chill system*, in which food is cooked to the just-done point, then chilled for storage and reheated just in time to be served. Sodexho does not cook/chill just any food, however. It has also become an innovator in developing recipes that taste better using its semi-automated system.

The notion that high performance is not always neat extends across a host of RAND studies. The U.S. and the North Atlantic Treaty Organization (NATO) clearly proved the case in the air war over Kosovo, which began on March 24, 1999. Although the war eventually stopped the ethnic cleansing in Kosovo, the end came too late for thousands of Kosovars and was the product of what RAND generously calls a "disjointed war."[19]

In theory, Operation Allied Freedom was a joint operation between the U.S. and other NATO countries. In principle, joint operations provide a range of options for the kind of swarming described earlier in this book—after all, joint operations bring more troops and more capability to bear on targets.

In reality, however, the operation was often anything but joint. The U.S. decided early, and unilaterally, that ground forces would not be used in the war, thereby giving Serbian president Slobodan Milosevic the opportunity to accelerate the ethnic cleansing. Knowing that his adversaries would never attack on land, Milosevic concealed his air defenses, dispersed his troops, hid his tanks, and stalled for time.

In the meantime the senior leadership of the operation, which was headed by U.S. Army General Wesley Clark, fought early and often about the choice of targets—fixed targets such as bridges and factories versus moving targets such as troops and vehicles. As RAND's research team writes, these types of disagreements are hardly unusual in battle. However, the lack of a land option created enormous tactical problems in both targeting and hitting Serbian forces. Only a small number of air strikes flown during the war actually hit Serbian forces, and an even smaller percentage of those air strikes actually killed any Serbian forces or destroyed any equipment. "NATO's air effort against fixed military and infrastructure targets was far more successful," writes the RAND research team. "But even here, command and control and various air defense assets survived the bombing in relatively good shape, despite being priority targets."

If Milosevic thought that these problems would bring the war to an end, he was mistaken. His decision to drive 700,000 refugees into Macedonia and Albania outraged the international community and led to even heavier bombing of industrial, communication, and petroleum targets, which led in turn to his surrender on June 3, 1999, and his eventual removal from office by the Serbian people. It was a victory for NATO, but it was far from neat.

These and other cases lead RAND researchers such as Quinlivan to conclude that organizations can be highly flawed and poorly managed and do just fine. "Does it require a well-managed organization to be an effective organization?" asks Quinlivan. His answer:

> No, it doesn't. Some of these positive signs are just tributes to good management, rather than predictors of whether they are effective. You can get a lot of people that have wonderful collective self-esteem and mutual respect, but they just aren't very good at what they do. It's sort of a third-place team, but a friendly third-place team. Sometimes you can find organizations that are genuinely unpleasant yet genuinely good at what they do. I suspect the French Foreign Legion might fall in that category.

There are consequences to being nasty, however:

> You can make it so bad that you hemorrhage people, so you never have the skill level you need to do the job. If you fail in that way, the organization is going to fail. . . . If your management failures actually break the critical tools for effectiveness, then you can't succeed. If you've got a benign enough environment, or if you've got nasty enough tools, you can still be effective even though your management style is brutal. To my mind, being brutal is a failure of management as well. The clenched-fist style of management is really a failure to me.

Quinlivan's colleague Susan Gates agrees. "There are a number of ways for an organization to achieve success," she says.

> Your employees could be really unhappy, but the organization could still be doing well in terms of meeting its goals. If you'd walked into Enron a few years ago, you might have thought it was very successful. Employees were very happy; their stock options were worth so much, but that doesn't mean the organization was doing very well. You're asking what it means to be high performing, but from whose perspective?

Lesson 3: High Performance Is Not Always Efficient

Organizations that plan against multiple futures are not necessarily the most efficient organizations in their industries. They tend to keep something extra in reserve, they develop and often execute contingency plans against futures that do not come to pass, and they invest heavily in the kind of multiskilled workforce that can change directions quickly. Betting the company on a single future is far easier, and is admirably efficient if and when that future actually arrives.

The inefficiencies can reside in a variety of corners, from the planning department to the supply chain. According to Christopher Hanks, a logistician who defined a *loggie* as someone who thinks of aircraft as 10,000 spare parts flying in formation, a high-performing organization has to be able to "rapidly apply resources where the needs arise, rapidly apply resources, the right kinds of resources, people and money and stuff in a capacity to be able to respond to variability and the demands being placed on the organization." As he says, organizations have to keep something in reserve at all times.

> In the end there will always be a need for some level of inventory to protect you against some of the variability that you just will not be able to wring out, and no matter what level of spares you carry, unless you spend a lot of money, you are always going to face situations in which you have a back order: You have a user who's demanded something and the supply logistic system just can't give it to him. It's not on the shelf, it's not even repaired yet or we don't have any, we have to go buy one because one of these has never failed before. You know most things are always going to happen.

Other RAND researchers make the same point. "Effective organizations are not necessarily efficient," says Leland Joe, echoing Quinlivan. "In complex situations, where decisions are poorly defined or understood, or when there is great uncertainty as to the situation, efficient organizational structures do not always work well." Joe draws on his studies of high-performing combat units to make the case:

> In a military context, the planning and execution of large-scale air and/or ground operations is characterized by uncertainty and complexity in addition to actions by adversaries. The military characterizes these effects as the fog and friction of war. An effective organization in this context is characterized by widely shared information (situational awareness) and collaborative planning and

execution (synchronization). These capabilities support a *fault-tolerant approach* to performance, allowing organizations to quickly adapt to changing conditions. This attribute is not necessarily efficient.

In other words, some waste and inefficiency may be essential to the fault tolerance that is needed if an organization is to survive and prosper. An experimental physicist by training, Joe rightly notes that "organizational design and operation is all a question of trade-offs. No two high-performing organizations are alike, and managers need to tailor solutions according to the individuals, the environment, and the mission to be accomplished." (See Joe's briefing slide on measuring high performance.)

Measuring High Performance

▶ No two high-performing organizations are alike. There is no cookbook.

▶ Efficiency should not be confused with effectiveness.

▶ High performance is elusive and transient. Maintaining it requires continuous monitoring and adjustment.

▶ Adjustments require a combination of structure, procedures, and equipment.

Efficiency and effectiveness are not mutually exclusive, however. Boeing created both effectiveness and efficiency in the design of the 777 by using computer-aided design tools such as the Computer-Aided Three-Dimension Interactive Application (CATIA) system, developed by Dassault Systemes and IBM. As Joe writes, cross-functional design teams were able to use roughly 2000 CATIA workstations located across the country to both share information and test components in parallel, which helped eliminate 65 percent of change orders.[20]

Faced with trade-offs between the two, many RAND researchers are willing to put the emphasis on effectiveness first, even if that produces higher levels of inefficiency. Although RAND also places considerable weight on lean thinking and on its philosophy of reducing redundancy wherever possible, its long experience with war fighting suggests that reserves do matter, even if they are never used.

Lesson 4: High Performance Does Not Reside in Hierarchy (or the Lack Thereof)

At least for those who worry about the height and width of organizations, round two also produced another stunning defeat: Pitted against other structural characteristics, the number of management layers between the top and bottom of an organization had no significant bearing on organizational performance. RAND does not believe in an ideal organizational form, whether it be flat or tall, wide or thin, centralized or decentralized. It supports whatever form might be appropriate for the given task.

In military health care, for example, RAND's Susan Hosek and Gary Cecchine find that a relatively flat organization structure provides better performance than a highly centralized pyramid.

> Decentralization appears to be more efficient, for two reasons: (1) any economies of scale in management within a centralized organization are apparently offset by the inefficiencies of centrally directing a large, geographically dispersed organization, and (2) local knowledge is critical for effective management of health care. Thus, operating units are established to manage local market areas. These local units report through regional managers to corporate headquarters; at each level, six to eight units report to a single manager.

Decentralization comes at a price, however. According to Hosek and Cecchine,

> Decentralized assignment of responsibility is accompanied by strong accountability for outcomes that are clearly specified in advance and evaluated afterward. In the managed-care organizations we visited, accountability is achieved through a standard annual business planning process. Performance is assessed using a limited number of key outcomes. Overall business success is measured by profit (or net revenue for nonprofit organizations). . . . Beyond the financial bottom line, intermediate outcomes include the key factors in profitability (such as enrollment or pharmaceutical costs) and quality measures including patient satisfaction.

Thus metrics, not centralization, create accountability.

The same holds true for environmental management, where private firms tend to use whatever form is most appropriate to their situation.

"Proactive firms centralize environmental activities only if they are not closely related to their core activities, or if a uniform corporate environmental practice is cost-effective," a RAND research team reports. Otherwise, they deploy environmental managers throughout the organization. However, they centralize when it comes time to audit the organization's progress. "They draw on centralized data systems compatible with the corporate information architecture but draw auditors from throughout the corporation to enhance transfer of lessons learned between the divisions." The team points to DuPont and Olin as examples.

> DuPont and Olin sought to place financial and management responsibility with the business unit that creates a problem. When relevant state and local regulations varied, it was often better to place these responsibilities with local units. But this had to be balanced against the visibility and control of costs and funding and the consistent application of policy that central assignment of responsibility supports. On balance, DuPont and Olin chose to centralize remediation responsibilities. Taking responsibility away from the active product units allowed them to focus on the environmental issues that were relevant to current and future production. That said, to ensure that its 19 individual business units maintained some awareness that remediation costs money, DuPont taxed these business units to cover 35 percent of ongoing remediation costs.

At least for these two firms, centralization was the best way to send the signal that environmental management was central to their mission.

It is difficult to overstate RAND's lack of support for any one organizational form. As former RAND researchers Francis Fukuyama and Abram Shulsky wrote in their 1996 study of virtual companies, there are benefits and costs associated with all organizational structures, be they hierarchical, flat, or networked.

> Decentralization is not an end in itself; there are certain functions performed in organizations that are better performed by centralized authority than on a distributed basis. Centralized organizations generally can move more quickly and decisively than decentralized, and they can achieve scale economies more readily; on the other hand, they may adapt more slowly to changed circumstances, and problems at the "center" may tend to paralyze activity through the organization.

The choice of organizational form requires an assessment of the costs and benefits. There are times when centralization is essential, and other times when dispersion offers the highest returns. (See a modified version of Fukuyama and Shulsky's briefing slide on centralization versus decentralization.)

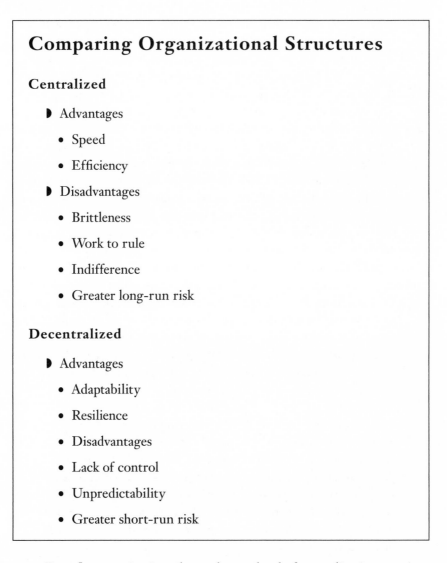

Comparing Organizational Structures

Centralized

▶ Advantages

  • Speed

  • Efficiency

▶ Disadvantages

  • Brittleness

  • Work to rule

  • Indifference

  • Greater long-run risk

Decentralized

▶ Advantages

  • Adaptability

  • Resilience

  • Disadvantages

  • Lack of control

  • Unpredictability

  • Greater short-run risk

Even flat organizations demand some level of centralization, particularly if they are to manage information effectively. "Despite talk about modern computer technology being necessarily democratizing," Fukuyama and Shulsky write, "a number of important productivity-enhancing applications of information technology over the past decide or two have involved highly centralized data systems that are successful because all their parts conform to a single architecture dictated from the top."

Given the need to choose between centralization and decentralization, the winnowing process suggests that high performance is built around relatively porous organizational structures. RAND researchers appear to be convinced, for example, that high-performing organizations should push authority down to the lowest level and across all units. This does not mean that the RAND researchers believe in organizational anarchy—indeed, the RAND knowledge base contains ample support for strengthening command and control. Yet, I believe the RAND researchers also understand that wars get fought by the troops, patients get treated by the nurses and paraprofessionals, kids get taught by the teachers and teacher's aides, and mines are drilled by the miners.

They also appear to believe that reducing the barriers between units improves the odds of high performance, whether in combat units, emergency rooms, nuclear submarines, or high-tech companies. Removing barriers does more than improve the flow of information, as discussed immediately below, however. It also produces better problem solving and service.

Collaboration certainly had a salutary effect in Ventura County's effort to reduce juvenile delinquency, for example. According to a RAND evaluation of the South Oxnard Challenge Project, collaboration among probation officers, the county health department, police and juvenile courts, the city recreation division, local nonprofit organizations, and private providers was the key to a one-stop solution to the problem of increasing juvenile crime.

As the RAND evaluators note, the program was designed to create an entirely different environment for diverting juvenile offenders from a life of crime:

> The environment was much different from that of a typical probation office—there were no metal detectors, bulletproof glass, interview rooms, or probation officers wearing "gear" as part of their daily attire. Although police officers wore their guns, they were not in uniform, and probation officers only wore their bulletproof vests when they were conducting searches. . . . Some youth were so attracted to the program that they "hung out" there daily.

This environment also permitted maximum collaboration among providers. Instead of referring youths to outside providers, all interventions were handled on-site. Not only did staff gain faster access to information, but families had a greater opportunity to engage. Although the program was expensive, which ultimately led to its untimely demise in 2001, the team approach gave juveniles greater access to services and the opportunity to succeed. As a result, the collaboration created a sum that was greater than the parts.

Lesson 5: High Performance Does Not Require Charisma

Given the unrelenting pressure to find gifted leaders today, charismatic leadership may have been the most significant characteristic to leave the pool in the first round. Charismatic leaders were only slightly more likely to show up in exemplary and very good organizations than in the rest of the field, and were just as likely to be found in very poor organizations as in somewhat good organizations. Ultimately, it was the lack of variation across most of the ratings that produced the defeat—simply put, having a charismatic leader did not increase an organization's likelihood of high performance by enough for that characteristic to advance beyond the first round of winnowing.

Simply put, charismatic leaders are nice to have around but are not essential to success. "There are too many examples where a program or intervention is successful when a dynamic, charismatic leader is involved, and the exact same program fails in another setting without the same kind of leadership," says Susan Everingham. "And the only difference that you can see between them is one of them had somebody standing at the podium with that special quality. . . . I've personally come to believe that charisma can be a very important ingredient for organizational success."

When pressed on just what that special quality might be, however, Everingham says, "Charisma alone isn't going to do it. I think you can be influential in this world without having an appealing personality, but it's easier if people automatically want to listen to you because you're charismatic. If you're the opposite of charismatic, if you're abrasive in some way, then people just won't listen. Even if you are right, even if you are clear, they're not going to want to hear you."

However, other RAND researchers saw charisma as a negative. "I've never seen charisma playing a role in these things," Robbins says of logistics reform. "Maybe Jack Welch is a charismatic leader or Lee Iaccoca. They're the kind of people who can pick up an organization and carry it, but I've never seen that work in logistics. Maybe it would work in a combat unit or a division where you really have to lead people into combat. With logistics, it's more of a collaborative enterprise. No one can really throw his weight around, even four-star generals."

Camm agrees. "What you need to lead these efforts is not people who lead people, but people who know how to do strategic thinking. You don't even want the same people any more. When you go in and talk to officers that way, they say, 'Well, I don't want to do strategic thinking. I'm a leader, I lead people.'" As Camm concludes, charisma and decisiveness have their place in organizational life. "They are important once the proper direction has been set, but they can be quite damaging if the leaders pursue the wrong goals, which happens too often."

Albert Robert offers a variation of the point: "It's not essential, but it certainly makes it easier to influence people and get them to pursue common objectives. Then the question becomes whether the leader is smart enough or disciplined enough to determine the right set of objectives and lead the organization in the right direction." John Birkler echoes the point: "I don't believe the leadership has to be charismatic. I think it just has to be competent. In many cases, you will find a charismatic leader can also be very shallow and not have much substance. That can get you by for a little bit, but not very long."

Lesson 6: High Performance Requires "Minimal Viability"

RAND researchers are not entirely convinced that organizations must be well managed to be high performing. Indeed, two-thirds of the Internet survey participants said that an organization could be poorly managed and still succeed, while another two-thirds said that an organization could be well managed and still fail. Putting the two sets of answers together, nearly half of the RAND researchers said that good management was neither necessary nor sufficient for organizational success.

However, I have never met a RAND researcher who believes that an organization can sustain high performance for long without at least some minimal organizational capacity. Any organization, no matter how moribund and inefficient, can generate growth or innovation for a year or two, if not longer. All it needs is extraordinary employees who are willing to persevere in spite of the barriers. The real challenge is to sustain that performance day after day without the burnout, turnover, and anxiety that come with poorly designed organizations.

Moreover, most RAND researchers would readily admit that organizations need some minimal capacity simply to mount a mission in the first place. RAND certainly makes that case for the military aircraft industry, for example, especially as the number of firms has dwindled from 16 in 1945 to just 3 major prime contractors today—Boeing, Lockheed-Martin, and Northrop Grumman. If the military merely wants to keep building the same airplanes, it need not worry about organization and management at all. After all, anyone who has the right parts and enough rivets can assemble an aircraft.

But if the military wants to produce innovative aircraft, it needs an industry with enough "minimally viable firms" to produce the break-throughs. According to a nine-person RAND research group, a minimally viable organization needs enough funding to maintain its design, development, and production capacity; enough skilled managers and workers to maintain a skilled workforce; facilities and equipment to convert the proto-types into production; and the expertise and structure to hold all of the above on course.[21] By RAND's own estimates, a minimally viable aircraft design organization today consists of 1000 to 2000 engineering and support personnel at a total cost of $200 million to $500 million per year.

As the team notes, the number of minimally viable firms is less impor-tant to innovation than the way in which the existing firms work and the future demand for innovation. Unlike in the 1940s, when aircraft firms operated in isolation, the aircraft industry today has adopted a number of practices that have changed the definition of just what constitutes a minimally viable organization. As the final report predicts,

> Industry structure will increasingly be defined through teaming
> arrangements and participation of all stakeholders throughout a
> product's life cycle. . . . Over time, even the characteristics of
> the prime contractors today may change radically. Future prime
> contractors will be more integrated across defense systems, and
> they may be smaller as a result of focusing on system-integra-
> tion activities while relying on partners from the supplier base
> for design innovation in key components and subsystems.

Whether there are enough minimally viable firms to produce inno-vation is an entirely different problem, however. As the team also contends, innovativeness is a product of national factors such as access to capital, the quality of the industry workforce, the ability of suppliers to generate new ideas, the level of research and development spending, national demand, and the right kind of competition. RAND clearly does not believe that compe-tition alone produces high performance. On the contrary, too much com-petition can diminish the resources needed for research and development, while too little can produce complacency.

Moreover, RAND research suggests that aircraft innovation often comes from firms with little or no history in the military industry: "Incumbents innovate in their old technologies in response to new entrants with the new technology. Eventually, and only in hindsight, the new technology prevails, driving out the old technology as it constantly improves, and at a faster rate than the old technology." Competition among a dwindling number of prime contractors does little to assure a steady supply of new ideas.

On the contrary, evolving business practice has changed RAND's definition of the minimally viable firm. According to a RAND research team led by John Birkler, prime contractors are increasingly relying on strategic alliances and teaming to assemble the skills required for major product development. Instead of building all this capacity in-house, prime contractors often concentrate on overall integration across a portfolio of reliable partners. In turn, they invest heavily in sharing information and developing virtual capacity to respond to new opportunities. As a result, the minimally viable organization has changed into a minimally viable design team composed of individuals and units drawn from several firms.

Such strategic alliances are increasingly common across government and business. The U.S. National Security Agency, which is responsible for collecting, decrypting, and analyzing electronic intelligence signals, has bet its future by outsourcing 1000 information technology jobs to the Eagle Alliance, a joint venture of Computer Sciences Corporation and Logicon, a division of Northrop Grumman. Under the Groundbreaker program, which weighs in at $2 billion over 10 years, the alliance is responsible for making sense of the agency's ridiculously complicated information technology, which included at least 68 independent e-mail systems in 2001.

Although it is too early to tell whether Groundbreaker will actually transform the agency, the contract reflects a clear embrace of partnerships as a source of viability. Because businesses increasingly prefer long-term relationships, or at least longer-term contracts, to repeated competitions for critical work, organizations must find ways to balance the pressure for full and open competition against the benefits of long-term partnerships that rely on strong incentives for performance, and the information sharing that goes with them.

Lesson 7: High Performance Requires at Least Minimal Competition

Competition dropped out of the winnowing process in the very first round, largely because it disciplined all organizations equally. Roughly half of the organizations that operated in a competitive environment were rated as exemplary or very good performers, compared to roughly half of the organizations that operated in a noncompetitive environment.

Yet, if competition does not assure success, its absence increases the likelihood of mediocrity. Roughly a sixth of the organizations that operated in a competitive environment were rated as mediocre or poor performers, compared to more than a third of the organizations that operated in a noncompetitive environment. Simply stated, organizations need at least some competition in order to stay awake.

As RAND's work on aircraft innovation suggests, there are times when competition is essential to the creation of new technologies such as the propeller monoplane, the supersonic jet, and the stealth fighter, and there are times when competition produces costly duplication and overlap. According to Mark Lorell's history of the aircraft industry, "the precise relationship between competition and increased innovation at the beginning of each new technology era is unclear. The competition to innovate during these periods was usually triggered by factors related to increased market demand, various technology developments, and military threat perceptions and system requirements."

Nevertheless, all of the aircraft breakthroughs of the past century have involved competition among at least seven experienced, credible prime contractors, which is four more than currently exist. As Lorell notes, the greatest stagnation in the industry occurred during the biplane era following World War I. "What explains this lack of innovation and design conservatism from the late teens to the early 1930s?" he asks. "We believe that, at least in part, it was likely caused by the relative lack of competition in military aircraft development, owing to the very small number of experienced, financially viable, and technologically credible firms competing for bomber and fighter contracts. This small number was in turn, caused primarily by the low demand from and the small size of the domestic market."

Yet, even as Lorell hints that Boeing, Lockheed-Martin, and Northrop Grumman may need company, other RAND researchers have come to believe that competition is not always desirable. This clearly the case in some areas of purchasing, where long-term, single-source vendor-purchaser partnerships are now preferred over yearly competitions. These private-private or public-private partnerships are based more on incentives and benchmarking than on traditional dog-eat-dog competition. As Frank Camm explains,

> Japanese auto firms that had previously assiduously cultivated at
> least two sources for all critical items ultimately came to realize

that they were paying a significant price by not going with the best source. They concluded, one after another, that if they could identify one source and build a partnership, with proper incentives, that the partnership could outperform dual sourcing over the longer term. That logic has generally been borne out. Imbedded in this logic is an idea used much more broadly— benchmarking has proven to be an effective substitute for competition in the context of partnerships.

(See Camm's briefing slide on the advantages of partnerships.)

Advantages of Partnerships

▶ Partners bring different comparative advantages.

▶ Partners use formal arrangements to align their comparative advantages.

▶ Partners are more likely to work together toward higher-level goals than firms using traditional approaches.

▶ Both partners invest in and share in the benefits of the partnership.

John Deere was one of the pioneers of this long view. Although Deere uses traditional competitions to purchase generic supplies, such as hardware, and longer-term competitions to purchase commodities, such as lubricants, it uses partnerships to acquire critical products, such as engines and transmissions. These "strategic supplier partnerships," as Deere calls them, can last up to 10 years and are designed to reduce the number of suppliers to the absolute minimum. It is only by working together over the longer haul that Deere and its suppliers can fine-tune expectations and incentives to produce the highest quality in the most important products.

Lesson 8: High Performance Thrives on Information

Five of the first- and second-round survivors and three of the third-round survivors were directly or indirectly related to information and communication. Three-quarters of the exemplary performers had what the RAND researchers labeled as adequate information systems, compared to just a third of the very poor performers; 88 percent of the exemplary performers had leaders who fostered open communication, compared with just 18 percent of the poor performers; and 94 percent of the exemplary performers measured the results of what they did, compared with 18 percent of the very poor performers.

This focus on how high-performing organizations saturate themselves with information pervades a great deal of RAND research, including Leland Joe's study of high-performing combat units and Beth McGlynn's work on health-care quality. As McGlynn recently wrote,

> Though many doctors use the most modern medical devices and treatments, most generally fail to take advantage of the latest technology to keep track of what they have done for their patients or to share that information with other doctors and with patients themselves. Doctors rely on handwritten medical records filed in folders just as they did 100 years ago, exchange information with other doctors via mail, phone or fax and communicate with patients in quick office visits or hurried phone calls.[22]

Neither Joe nor McGlynn believes that pure information is enough, however. "We need a real health-care system," McGlynn concludes. "We need to create teams of health professionals—doctors, nurses, health educators—who work together. Those teams must have the tools to help them quickly identify the best set of services for each of us. And they must be able to explain the choices we have in plain language so we can each decide what treatment is right for us."

Teams do not necessarily involve individuals and units, however. As RAND's research on shipbuilding shows, they can also involve very large assemblies of organizations. European shipbuilders have become highly competent at assembling large groups of suppliers who bring special expertise to each component of the product, be it a tanker or a cruise ship. While the shipbuilders specialize in constructing the hulls, subcontractors provide everything from the hotel functions, such as berths, food service, laundry, and waste management, to passenger cabins, gambling rooms, ship bridges, and modular anchor-handling machinery. Thus, a consortium of German firms, led by Germaischer Lloyd, is working to improve the life-cycle design of ships, including efforts to improve vibration prediction, loading effects, fatigue strength, the effects of fabrication methods on structural performance, and ongoing monitoring systems, while a consortium of Korean, Dutch, Finnish, and Norwegian firms has developed an engine-room diagnostic system to detect vibration and particle counts.

There is still room for competition among suppliers, but it is based more on cost-reducing innovation than on mere cost savings. Coartlauld Coatings has developed a new generation of paints formulated to dry more quickly and require fewer coats, for example, while Jotun has created fast-drying shop primers that support the just-in-time delivery of steel. Deerberg Systems (Germany), Norsk Hydro (Norway), and FOX Pollution Packers have all developed new systems for commercial shipboard waste management, each one tailored to a specific market.

RAND's interest is not in cruise ships, of course. It is in finding ways to reduce the cost and improve the performance of nuclear carriers. "We did not find any technological advances that would result, individually, in large cost savings if implemented by U.S. shipbuilders," RAND's research team concluded. "But foreign commercial shipbuilders are taking advantage of a wide range of existing production processes and technologies that have not been implemented in shipbuilding funded by the U.S. Navy." Without arguing that a hull is a hull is a hull, the RAND analysis suggests that innovation is essential to building robust hulls, even if they happen to contain a nuclear reactor.

At least among the organizations they know well, RAND researchers see information as an essential resource for performance. As Fukuyama and Shulsky concluded in assessing the virtual corporation, information flow is the most important consequence of organizational structure.

> Traditional theorizing about organizations tended to assume that sharing information within the boundaries of an enterprise was cost free and automatic, and that it would flow rapidly without obstruction along the lines of authority as indicated on the firm's organization chart. In fact, information is costly to acquire and transmit; the process takes time and effort, and it is not free from error and distortion.

RAND is working to enhance the flow of information through a variety of studies, including its effort to develop a first-of-its-kind system for tracking the quality of care given to the vulnerable elderly. Launched in 2000 in partnership with Pfizer, Inc., the Assessing Care of Vulnerable Elders (ACOVE) project has already produced a set of 22 evidence-based indicators to give older adults better information on the problems that they face.

These indicators can also be used as benchmarks against which to measure the actual quality of care. As RAND, Pfizer, and their research partners have learned, older adults often do not get the recommended care they need, especially when they are at risk of losing their independence. Barely half of the vulnerable elderly get the recommended health care they need in general, and less than a third get the recommended care for geriatric conditions such as malnutrition, pressure ulcers, dementia, and end-of-life situations. They also receive only half of the medications they need, in part because medical schools may not be providing the training required to diagnose and treat geriatric conditions, and in part because physicians may worry about overmedication and the costs of prescription drugs.[23]

The project involves more than research, however. It has also produced a number of short pamphlets for older adults that provide simple facts on a variety of conditions, including high blood pressure, osteoporosis, depression, diabetes, and dementia, all of which are based on evidence-based research into what older adults need.

The partnership itself reflects Pfizer's deep investment in research and development. In 2003 alone, Pfizer spent $7.6 billion on research, putting it ahead of DaimlerChrysler ($6.7 billion), Microsoft ($6.1 billion), Siemens ($6.1 billion), and IBM ($5.2 billion). It hardly makes sense to invest in new drugs if physicians do not know when or how to use them, which is one of the reasons that Pfizer asked RAND to assess the quality-of-care issue in the first place.[24]

Lesson 9: High Performance Thrives on Delegation

Delegating routine authority and embracing participatory management showed surprising strength throughout the winnowing process: As much as 95 percent of the high performers gave their staff authority to make routine decisions on their own, compared with 65 percent of the mediocre performers and just 26 percent of the poor performers; and 77 percent of the leaders of the high performers had a participatory style of management, compared with 40 percent of the mediocre performers and just 16 percent of the poor performers. The variation across all three sets of organizations was more than enough to earn these two characteristics a trip to the second round.

Although these findings can be explained in part by the earlier findings concerning what RAND researchers saw among high-performing organizations in general, RAND's research base also suggests the need to delegate and participate simultaneously. Businesses and the military alike rarely allow individuals and units absolute autonomy, particularly given the consequences of error. In 1757, RAND notes, Britain's Admiral John Byng was shot for deviating from the Royal Navy's *Fighting Instructions* after losing Port Mahon to the French; more than two hundred years later, Britain's Barings bank was brought down by the actions of a single trader in Singapore.

Delegation and participation also emerge as essential for treating clinical depression. Convinced that most patients with depression are not effectively treated in primary care settings such as doctors' offices, RAND's health program helped design and implement a five-year, five-state, 46-clinic, 27,000-patient trial of a program called *Partners in Care*.

The program was designed to address the enormous pressure on physicians to keep office visits short, which limits both the diagnosis and care of the one in five patients who show symptoms of depression. With depression well on track to become the second-leading cause of disability worldwide over the next decade, RAND decided to design a better way based on the basic principles of quality management. RAND's *collaborative care model* involved patient empowerment, case management by nurses, and teamwork between primary care providers and mental health specialists.

The goal was not to treat every patient with symptoms of depression. Rather, it was to ensure that the 6 percent who needed medication and/or psychotherapy received appropriate treatment, while helping the other 14 percent find less intensive help. "No one told the clinics, clinicians, or patients what to do," RAND reported. "They were encouraged to follow their own goals. Physicians and patients were informed about both medication and therapy, but they were free to make their own choice. In effect, the practices were trained to improve themselves."

The partnership produced stunning results compared with the traditional in-and-out office visit. Patients with symptoms of depression who visited a Partners in Care clinic were almost twice as likely to start treatment than those who visited a traditional clinic, which translated into better health and an increased likelihood of continued employment.

As we shall see, RAND researchers believe that champions are essential for successful change. But the focus is not on charismatic champions. It is on engagement, information sharing, and vision. "It has to start with the leader," says Robbins:

> He doesn't have to be charismatic, but he has to make it very clear that he's dissatisfied, that he wants to see the organization get better, and he has a reasonable attitude toward it. He's not just making everyone scared. He should be saying, "I want to encourage you to get better. I'm going to support you, but we WILL get better." And he needs to make sure he's there long enough to at least get it started.

Lesson 10: High Performance Starts and Ends with Mission

I have yet to find a RAND study that does not deal directly or indirectly with mission. Just as RAND and its researchers are not interested in uncertainty for uncertainty's sake, neither are they interested in organization for organization's sake. Either organization matters to the mission or it does not.

Thus, when asked specifically what the words *organizational effectiveness* meant to them, the 126 survey participants focused almost exclusively on mission. "It means carrying out its intended missions," one typical participant replied. "It includes an organization's capabilities to take action, its knowledge base to make that action effective, and its potential to learn and adjust to mold its efforts to a changing external context." Another defined the term as "the ability of an organization to do the right things to achieve its goals and contribute positively to the welfare of society in both the long-term and short-term." Still others defined it as "the ability to efficiently and effectively plan, implement, and complete tasks that advance the core goals of the organization," "the ability of a group to work together toward a common goal or vision—the key element is leadership that establishes a clear goal or vision," "an organization that is proficient in executing the present, while simultaneously positioning itself to be relevant in the future," "an organization that is successful at developing jobs, processes and related structure to support its stated vision and goals and to motivate its workforce toward obtaining this vision and goals," "having resources, plans, and results match expectations over a long period," and "meeting clients' needs, not their wants."

RAND is not interested in just any mission, however. Its work has long centered on the kind of "big hairy audacious goals" made famous in *Built to Last*, goals such as stopping the spread of HIV/AIDS, preventing nuclear war, reducing domestic violence against women, increasing educational achievement among poor children, and improving health care quality.[25] Nor are RAND researchers strangers to stretch goals, either—many are quite comfortable with the zero-tolerance standards that many organizations use for improving quality, workplace safety, and customer satisfaction.

At the same time, RAND and its researchers have learned to ask hard questions about the promises organizations make. Although they are quire willing to embrace audacious goals, most of the RAND researchers I met also believe in setting realistic expectations for progress. Hope as they might for audacious impacts, RAND researchers are mostly pragmatists who urge organizations not to promise more than can be delivered.

Part of the caution comes from RAND's collective experience comparing the rhetoric of audacious goals and the difficulty of lasting improvement. Indeed, RAND's education division even published a book titled *Rhetoric versus Reality* precisely to draw the distinction between the promise and performance of the promises embedded in the calls for school reform. As RAND's four-person team writes of tuition vouchers and charter schools, both reforms promise audacious returns, particularly for poorly performing students, but often yield less-than-stunning change.

The evidence, or lack thereof, suggests a much more cautious stance toward reform. Although there is some evidence that both reforms produce gains in parental satisfaction, there is very little proof that the reforms actually improve performance, which is, after all, the audacious goal. "The brevity of our list of knowns should send a note of caution to supporters and opponents of choice," the RAND team notes. "For most of the key questions, direct evaluations of vouchers and charter schools have not yet provided clear answers, and the list of unknowns remains substantially longer that the list of knowns."

These researchers are not making a case for the status quo, however. They clearly embrace the goal of better performance. But they also know that it is one thing to adopt a grand mission, and quite another to create the small wins that eventually add up to sustainable impact. Hence, the healthy dose of realism that most RAND researchers bring to the conversation about organizational mission.

Even with a realistic mission, RAND researchers might add that success depends at least in part on luck. "The U.S. has been very fortunate in having some adversaries who are not the sharpest knives in the drawer," says Stephen Hosmer.

> Milosevic made some terrible blunders during the crisis over Kosovo, particularly in believing that the massive ethnic cleansing of the Kosovo Albanian population would help his cause rather than hurt it. And his conceit was such that, at the end, he didn't listen to his advisors who warned him against calling an election. He believed he could win and had no sense of how far his political standing had eroded.

Even with such a weak adversary, however, the U.S. and NATO were unable to drive Milosevic to the negotiating table until the ethnic cleansing was almost complete.

As Hosmer continues,

> Saddam Hussein proved to be another less than bright bulb as far as strategy was concerned. He invaded Iran, but stopped short of occupying the Iranian oil fields, which would have given

him great leverage in that conflict. Then he invaded Kuwait before he had acquired a nuclear weapon to deter U.S. counteraction and again stopped short of occupying the oil facilities—those in Saudi Arabia—that would have given him enormous bargaining leverage. Finally, when threatened by an overwhelming military coalition led by the United States, he eschewed the opportunity to peacefully withdraw from Kuwait at little or no penalty.

In contrast, the "North Vietnamese leaders were very formidable opponents—much more realistic than our leadership about the nature of war and the strengths and vulnerabilities of the contending sides," Hosmer says. "They were very skilled at orchestrating military, political, diplomatic, and information operations to fight a total war." In that case, it was the U.S. leadership that made the mistakes.

> We didn't understand our enemy, particularly the North Viet-namese, and failed to develop the expertise needed to improve that understanding. At the strategic level, we mistakenly believed that South Vietnam could be successfully defended without permanently blocking the North Vietnamese infiltration routes through Laos. We also erroneously assumed that our public opinion would hold up over the length of the conflict, and that the Vietnamese communist forces wouldn't be able to sustain the attrition rates they were suffering. Thus, we underrated the enemy's capacity and overrated our own. Finally, and perhaps most important, we erred in starting the Vietnamization process too late and in failing to effectively posture and support our South Vietnamese allies to fight a protracted war on their own.

In short, even a high-performing organization cannot succeed with an impossible mission. It may have all the right components—a highly committed workforce, talented leaders, and more than enough resources to succeed—but it also needs a mission that is within reasonable reach.

CONCLUSION

The winnowing process discussed here is interesting for several reasons. First, it confirms some of the core findings of other research-based books such as *Built to Last* and *Good to Great* (neither of which I ever saw on a

RAND bookshelf).[26] Charismatic leaders turn out to be just as unimportant to the high-performing organizations identified by RAND as they were to the high-performing organizations that James Collins and his colleagues picked, for example, while participatory leadership turned out to be just as important.

RAND and its researchers are certainly not cut off from the rest of the world—they spend more than enough time in and out of organizations to have significant insights into what works and what does not. At the same time, RAND and its researchers spend relatively little, if any, time paging through the business best-sellers. They may know a great deal about who moved the ammunition, but they almost certainly know nothing about who moved the cheese. Thus, to the extent that organizations hunger for some kind of independent validation of the prevailing wisdom in such books, this winnowing process provides it.

Interesting though this information might be for confirming simple truths about what really matters to high performance, readers are right to ask just what kind of organization should care. Are the characteristics just as relevant to McDonald's as they are to the Air Force? Just as on point for IBM as for Intel? Just as important to chemical companies as to research firms?

Given the organizations that RAND knows best, the answer depends almost entirely on the level of external turbulence. Organizations that face a relatively calm, predictable future can cull from the pool of characteristics at leisure.

But as the next chapter will suggest, organizations that worry about sustaining high performance might want to pay closer attention. As already noted, the winnowing process produced more than just a random assortment of interesting characteristics. It also produced a common statistical portrait of organizations that perform particularly well in turbulent times— those that are alert to changing circumstances, agile in addressing vulnerabilities and exploiting opportunities, adaptive in creating new strategies and products, and aligned to achieve their mission. In short, the winnowing process produced an outline of what I call the robust organization. In a word, such organizations are *robust*.

NOTES

1   Katie Hafner and Matthew Lyon, *Where Wizards Stay Up Late: The Origins of the Internet*, New York:Simon & Schuster Touchstone, 1996, p. 55.

2   Hafner and Lyon, *Where Wizards Stay Up Late*, p. 57.

3 Hafner and Lyon, *Where Wizards Stay Up Late*, pp. 59–60.

4 Hafner and Lyon, *Where Wizards Stay Up Late*, p. 63.

5 Chuck Lucier, Rob Schuyt, and Eric Spiegel, "CEO Succession in 2002: Deliver or Depart," *strategy+business*, summer 2003, accessed at http://www.strategy-business.com, March 10, 2004.

6 Chuck Lucier, Rob Schuyt, and Junichi Handa, "CEO Succession 2003: The Perils of Good Governance," *strategy+ business*, summer 2004, accessed at www.strategy-business.com.

7 The study was conducted by Elisa Eiseman, Gabrielle Bloom, Jennifer Brower, Noreen Clancy, and Stuart Olmsted, and is cited in the bibliography.

8 The study was conducted by Debra Knopman, Susan Resetar, Parry Norling, Richard Rettig, and Irenee Brahmakulam, and is cited in the bibliography.

9 These quotes came in response to an e-mail I sent in March 2004 asking a handful of senior researchers for their insights concerning the findings described here.

10 I am grateful to RAND senior researcher Sandy Berry for fine-tuning the survey to ask respondents about a single organization, high-performing or not, instead of a group of high performers.

11 The first-round survivors were identified through simple Pearson correlations, which measure the degree of association between two variables, which in this case were the 34 separate characteristics and performance. A correlation can run from -1.0 to +1.0. For this analysis, a correlation of approximately +/-.175 is significant at the .05 level, which means that readers can be 95 percent confident that the association is other than random.

12 The second-round survivors were identified through nine separate ordinary least-squares regressions of the 29 surviving characteristics from the first round. Characteristics had to produce a significant predictive impact on performance within their respective category to remain in the pool.

13 The third-round survivors were identified through a single ordinary least-squares regression of the 13 surviving characteristics from the second round. Access to information was the number one predictor of performance, with a significance of .003, followed by having the funding to invest in new ideas at .005, having a clear mission at .005, delegating authority for routine decisions at .007, creating strong incentives for high performance at .008, fostering open communication at .015, and measuring results at .032.

14 This second look involved a factor analysis of the 13 second-round winners using principal component analysis with varimax rotation. The four factors covered 64 percent of the variation among the 13 characteristics, with each one accounting for between 18 percent and 14 percent of the sum of squared loadings.

15 These lessons are drawn in part from the RAND studies cited in the bibliography.

16 Jim Collins, "Built to Flip," *Fast Company*, March 2000, p. 131.

17 Terry M. Moe, "Toward a Theory of Public Bureaucracy," in Oliver E. Williamson, ed., *Organization Theory: From Chester Barnard to the President and Beyond*, New York:Oxford University Press, 1990, p. 127.

18 The study was conducted by Russell W. Glenn, Barbara R. Panitch, Dionne Barnes-Proby, Elizabeth F. Williams, John Christian, Matthew W. Lewis, Scott Gerwehr, and David Brannan, and is cited in the bibliography.

19 My Brookings colleagues Ivo Daalder and Michael O'Hanlon titled their history of the conflict *Winning Ugly*, Washington, D.C.:Brookings, 2000.

20 Leland Joe draws upon Guy Norris, "Boeing's Seventh Wonder," *IEEE Spectrum*, Institute for Electronics and Electrical Engineering, October 1995.

21 The team was composed of J. L. Birkler, Anthony G. Bower, Jeffrey A. Drezner, Gordon T. Lee, Mark A. Lorell, Giles K. Smith, F. S. Timson, William P. G. Trimble, and Obaid Younossi.

22 Elizabeth McGlynn, "Sharing of Health-Care Data Needs a Tuneup," *Los Angeles Times*, June 26, 2003, p. A18.

23 For a detailed introduction to the indicators, see Neil S. Wenger, Paul Shekelle, Frank Davidoff, and Cynthia Mulrow, eds., "Assessing Care of Vulnerable Elders: Methods of Developing Quality Indicators," *Annals of Internal Medicine*, Supplement, vol. 135, no. 8 (Part 2), October 16, 2001, pp. 647–652.

24 See Cecily Fluke and Lesley Kump, "Innovation," *Forbes*, July 5, 2004, p. 142, accessed at http://www.nexis.com, July 16, 2004.

25 James C. Collins and Jerry I. Porras, *Built to Last: Successful Habits of Visionary Companies*, New York:HarperBusiness, paperback edition, 1997.

26 See Jim Collins, *Good to Great: Why Some Companies Make the Leap . . . And Others Don't*, New York:HarperBusiness, 2001.

THE FOUR PILLARS OF
HIGH PERFORMANCE

RAND has long been considered a premier source of analysis of what organizations do, but has only recently become known as a source of insight on how organizations work. Even in its early work, however, RAND and its researchers worried about what they called "systems design," which they defined to include everything from equipment and fuel to strategies and organizations. Why bother creating the perfect strategy if the system cannot deliver?

RAND clearly understood that some systems were better at execution than others. "Analysis is easier for strong systems," Albert Wohlstetter wrote in 1958. "It is also easy for very bad ones." Strategies have a high probability of success in the former, and a very low probability of success in the latter. "The really bad ones don't hold us for very long because, for example, we needn't worry about the interdependence of a destroyed plane and a destroyed fuel system."[1]

RAND and its researchers have never believed that weak systems are doomed to perpetual failure, however. Organizations can make weak systems stronger, good systems stronger, and strong systems almost invulnerable. It is relatively easy to reduce the vulnerability of a runway by merely adding more taxiways, Wohlstetter noted. Multiplying the number of taxiways is not only relatively inexpensive when compared with other measures, it also improves the odds that at least some usable portion of runway will survive an enemy attack. "If we do this we have a taxi way-runway system which is considerably stronger. We can have a higher confidence in its survival."

Then as now, the key question is not whether there is one best system—Wohlstetter called the question "beside the point." Rather, the question is how to make a given system better. As RAND's recent study of innovation and change at the Marriott Corporation shows, there is a great difference between having *some* robustness and having *enough*. Although Marriott might have survived the market turmoil of the early 1990s, it took another path, no doubt reminded of its own mortality by the two heart attacks of its president, Bill Marriott, who had taken the reins of the company from his father.

It might have survived with its heavy debt load even if it had not changed, however. It had been opening hotels at a stunning rate in the 1980s, and was buying almost everything in sight, including fast food chains and amusement parks. Even with $1 billion in new construction a year, and a weakening real estate market, it had enough resiliency to tough it through.

But Marriott and its leadership saw the volatility ahead and decided to act by splitting the company in two in 1993. As RAND's research team chronicles the history, Host Marriott took control of the vast inventory of properties, while Marriott International entered the hotel franchise and food services industry.[2] By 2004 Marriott International operated or franchised 2700 properties in 68 countries and territories, 47 time-share resorts, 155 senior-living communities, 26 golf courses, 19 hotel reservation centers, and a food distribution system that served 7000 wholesale customers through 13 regional distribution centers. Marriott International is consistently rated as one of the nation's leading corporations, and was one of the 13 companies identified by James Collins and Jerry Porras as a visionary company in *Built to Last*.

Marriott's robustness does not reside in the division of responsibilities, however. Rather, it resides in a set of core practices that allow it to respond to continued instability without compromising its core values of customer service and quality. As Bill Marriott writes, "All of our intense attention to detail translates into consistent quality. Consistent quality leads to high customer satisfaction. Customer satisfaction translates into high occupancy, repeat business, and good room rates. Those in turn bring home good profits and attractive returns to property owners."[3]

Marriott International's continued high-performance also resides in the four pillars of robustness uncovered in the winnowing of characteristics— *alertness*, *agility*, *adaptability*, and *alignment*.

Marriott certainly became more alert in the early 1990s, whether through market analysis of travel patterns, the balanced scorecard, or simple green-light/red-light metrics that track customer satisfaction at individual hotels. Under its customer satisfaction metrics, for example, hotels that receive green lights achieve what RAND's team calls "celebrity status" within the corporation. "In the past, Marriott hotels had a comment card in every room, which was usually only filled out by guests who were either angry, elderly, or young," the RAND team writes. "Similarly, employees learned to skew the system, stuffing the comment box with positive comments to make the hotel appear better than it really was."

Today Marriott uses a much more rigorous guest satisfaction survey that provides reliable data on both current and potential customers—the ones who show up, as well as the ones who pick the hotel next door. In turn, the data help fine-tune a host of small-to-large decisions, from where to locate electrical outlets in a hotel room to how to greet quests at the front desk.

Marriott also became more agile during the 1990s. Although it is steady in its operating plan, its core portfolio of lodging brands such as Courtyard by Marriott, the Marriott Residence Inn, and Ritz-Carlton is highly sensitive to undulations in market demand. Because most of its hotels operate under franchise agreements, it can jettison properties as demand declines, and add new properties in growing markets. It can also acquire specialty properties such as its Le Merigot Resort in Santa Monica that enhance its visibility and prestige.[4]

Marriott also became more agile through a combination of information and Internet technologies that capture economies of scale and provide instant opportunities for adjustment. It created one of the first hotel frequent-flier programs that allows members to earn and redeem points by staying at any of the Marriott hotels, one of the first web-based reservation systems, and e-mail alerts to advertise promotions during the slowdowns that vary season-to-season across its network of properties.

This alertness and agility would have been useless if Marriott did not adapt to changing conditions, however. Although Marriott has developed standard operating procedures that assure continuity across its hotels, which assure alignment around its core values, as well as occasional ridicule across the industry as a whole, it also delegates authority to the local level where hotel managers can innovate to their heart's content provided the change does not undermine customer service or violate proven operating procedures. It also diffuses innovation through its internal web site and *Marriott World Magazine*, which is sent to employees at every hotel.

Marriott has also worked to ensure internal alignment around its mission through a mix of franchise and incentive fees based on a negotiated share of each hotel's gross revenues, as well as heavy investments in training and recruitment, frequent site visits by Bill Marriott himself, and the development of what it calls an *Associates First culture* that applies to all

128,000 employees. The combined effort has kept the company on *Fortune's* lists of America's 100 Most Admired Companies, and the 100 Best Companies to Work For year after year.

The Associates First effort reinforces Marriott's commitment to employee loyalty, and covers everyone from hotel managers to sous chefs. The initiative was not designed to brand Marriott as the place to invest, however. Rather it was designed to brand the company as a place to work. Recognizing future volatility in the labor market, Marriott has sought to attract and retain high quality employees, while building employee loyalty for the long haul. As part of the effort, it provides a variety of training opportunities, both voluntary and mandatory. Senior associates receive a 90-day orientation program and 10-minute daily training sessions as part of the 21 hospitality standards developed at headquarters. In addition, all associates are required to take at least 16 training hours per year, using Marriott's "mouse touch/human touch" to access CD-ROM-based information.

Innovation at Marriott

▶ Transformed model from hotel ownership to management

▶ Blended consistency with innovation

▶ Used performance measures to manage brand protection

▶ Segmented hotel market by customer preferences

▶ Created culture of "associates first" to retain employees

▶ Used information technologies to improve service and profits

---

As this chapter will argue, Marriott's enduring success came from increased robustness. No one could have predicted the collapse in hotel occupancy in late 2001 because no one predicted September 11, 2001, but Marriott was well positioned to survive. No one could have predicted the Saudi Arabian unrest either, but Marriott's hotels in Jeddah, Madinah, and Riyadh were still booking rooms when this book went to press. The measure of Marriott's success is not in keeping hotels open, but in staying alert to the changing world, moving quickly to address vulnerabilities and opportunities, adapting to reality through new strategies and products, and aligning the organization around a common vision.

DEFINING ROBUSTNESS

Although Webster's Dictionary defines robustness as "showing rigor, strength, or firmness," RAND and its researchers would also define it as the ability to withstand, even exploit, turbulence. In a world of many futures, high-performing organizations succeed against the unknowable by minimizing damage (hedging) and maximizing impact (shaping).

The term is hardly new to organizational life. Engineers use it to design buildings and bridges, statisticians use it to describe equations, coffeehouses use it to describe flavor, and planners use it to describe operating strategies. When used to describe bridges, equations, coffee, and operating plans, robustness means tolerance, ability to recover, rigorous, goodness-of-fit, and even flavor. But when used to describe organizations, robustness means the ability of an organization to protect itself against external turbulence, whether by hedging against the kind of vulnerabilities discussed early in this book or by exploiting opportunities as they arise.

Thus, a robust organization does more than just guard against surprise. It achieves extraordinary performance by adapting to changing circumstances. As Steven Bankes, Robert Lempert, and Steven Popper write in *Shaping the Next One Hundred Years*, "People learn. Over time, they will gain new information. Accordingly, adaptive decision strategies are the means most commonly used to achieve robustness because they are designed to evolve in response to new data. Faced with a multiplicity of plausible futures, a decision maker may settle on near-term actions but plan to adjust them in specific ways as new information renders some futures implausible and others more likely."

The concept of robustness comes directly from RAND's work on uncertainty-sensitivity planning. The centerpiece of that work involves the effort to "harden" organizations against both environmental turbulence and their own vulnerabilities. As James Dewar argues in his short primer titled *Assumption-Based Planning*, a predictable world allows predictable plans—the past becomes simple prologue to a familiar future.

However, during highly unstable times, the past is merely a gateway to a variety of possible futures. As Dewar explains, "Plans that assume the likelihood of one particular world run the risk of being seriously wrong." By hedging against vulnerabilities in their plans and operations, organizations can reduce their regret in following a particular course. By planning for an alternative future, they can assure a greater likelihood of success. "Making backup plans to move a picnic indoors in case of rain should be done regardless of whether you are looking forward to the picnic in the first place," Dewar argues. The possibility of rain will turn a good picnic into a bad one, and a bad picnic even worse.

Simply stated, robust organizations assume that surprises and downturns are inevitable, watch for signals that a given future is coming true, and take action to hedge against threats and vulnerabilities, while shaping the future to their advantage. As such, robust organizations are certainly resilient, as Gary Hamel and Liisa Välikangas define the term.[5] "The goal is a strategy that is forever morphing, forever conforming itself to emerging opportunities and incipient trends," they argue. "The goal is a company that is constantly making its future rather than defending its past. The goal is a company where revolutionary change happens in lightning-quick, evolutionary steps—with no calamitous surprises, no convulsive reorganizations, no colossal write-offs, and no indiscriminate, across-the-board layoffs. In a truly resilient organization, there is plenty of excitement, but there is no trauma."[6]

But resilient organizations are not necessarily robust. Take the notion that resilient organizations must reduce the time to go from "that can't be true" to "we must face the world as it is." Robust organizations certainly do just that, but they also continue asking themselves about "worlds as they may be" by remaining alert to subtle changes that reveal a coming change. As such they can be very boring places to be, especially if the future is stable.

Take the notion that companies can become victims of turbulence if their strategies are too narrow. Although Hamel and Välikangas are absolutely right, robust organizations such as Volvo address the challenge by adopting strategies that perform reasonably well against a range of possible futures. To the extent the actual future deviates greatly from the scenarios they have planned against, they adapt; to the extent the future remains within the envelop of possibilities, they may decide to stand firm.

Finally, take the notion that companies falter when they invest too much in "what is" and too little in "what could be." Robust organizations do that, too, but they also create internal structures and procedures that are themselves pliable. They do not need to move resources from one idea to another in part because resources such as people and systems are already able to shift to new missions and opportunities.

As noted earlier in this book, organizations must do more than just imagine the possibility of surprise. They must prepare for it. Organizations of all kinds have been challenging themselves with what-ifs for centuries, and have made both good guesses and bad. But as the world becomes more complex, what-ifs cannot suffice. Organizations must plan against a wide range of what-ifs simultaneously and structure their organizations to move quickly if necessary. They can be exciting or dull, traumatized or calm, but they must be an alert, agile, adaptive, and aligned organization behind it.

THE FOUR PILLARS OF ROBUSTNESS

Large, international organizations are not alone in adopting the four pillars of robustness. Al Qaeda has mastered them, too. As RAND's Brian Jenkins writes in *Countering al Qaeda*, "Al Qaeda is more than just an organization; it is also a process, and its principle resource is human capital."

Violence is not just a source of status, power, and satisfaction for al Qaeda; it is the primary product for holding the organization and its recruits together. "Violence is their *raison d'être*. The enterprise of terrorism provides status, power, and psychological satisfaction. It attracts new recruits. It demonstrates their devotion and gives them historical importance. Without terrorism, al Qaeda would collapse into just another exotic sect."

As other RAND studies show, al Qaeda has harnessed this hatred through a highly decentralized structure that produces the alertness, agility, adaptability, and alignment to succeed. According to RAND, terrorists will almost certainly continue to rely on information-age network designs, which means moving away from *great man leadership* centered on mythic figures such as Osama bin Laden to decentralized designs that are "internetted." The result will be more groups and greater coordination. "In short, terrorism is evolving in a direction we call *netwar*," RAND's John Arquilla and David Ronfeldt argue:

> Pictorially, an all-channel netwar actor resembles a geodesic "Bucky ball" (named for Buckminster Fuller); it does not resemble a pyramid. The design is flat. Ideally, there is no single, central leadership, command, or headquarters—no precise heart or head that can be targeted. The network as a whole (but not necessarily each node) has little to no hierarchy, and there may be multiple leaders. Decision-making and operations are decentralized, allowing for local initiative and autonomy. Thus the design may sometimes appeal acephalous (headless), and at other times polycephalous (Hydra-headed).

In some ways, terrorists are merely following best business practices pioneered by Marriott and others. "In the business world," Arquilla and

Ronfeldt maintain, "virtual or networked organizations are being heralded as effective alternatives to bureaucracies—as in the case of Eastman Chemical Company and the Shell-Sarnia Plant—because of their inherent flexibility, adaptiveness, and ability to capitalize on the talents of all members of the organization. What has long been emerging in the business world is now becoming apparent in the organization structures of netwar actors."

In contrast to a chain-link network that passes information and material along a designated line of contacts or star/hub/wheel network that sets basic standards for its franchisees, an all-channel network connects each semiautonomous unit to each other. Although the all-channel network is the most difficult to build and sustain, if only because each unit must have some contact with the others, it is also the most potent for the kind of pulsing that Arquilla and Ronfeldt describe in their research on swarming. Bluntly put, terrorist organizations have become some of the most successful organizations in the world largely by drawing strength from all four pillars of robustness described below.

Alertness

Alertness is the first pillar of robustness. Organizations have little reason to reallocate, retrain, renew, or realign if they do not see the change coming. As Dewar explains it, "alertness is just paying attention to what's out there because you are under state-of-the world uncertainty. You keep getting more and more data and finally you start to see."

Staying alert does not involve just collecting piles and piles of data, however. Dewar writes of two kinds of events, or signposts, that signal a change in conditions. One involves a change in the validity of a given assumption, meaning that the assumption is starting to fail, while the other involves a change in vulnerability, meaning that the assumption is increasingly at risk. As Dewar writes, "suppose a company's plans rely heavily on the assumption of a favorable regulatory or judicial ruling at some point in the future. There are two possible outcomes: the ruling is not favorable— in which case the assumption fails—or the ruling is favorable—in which case the assumption remains valid and the vulnerability surrounding that assumption disappears."

Alertness involves more than planning techniques, however. It also resides in a basic commitment to rigorous monitoring of how the organization is doing at any given point in time. According to John Birkler, who led the RAND study of how the Defense Department selected Lockheed-Martin to build the new Joint Strike Fighter, "If organizations don't have the data we need, they're probably pretty poorly run. We keep asking basic questions: What do things cost? How long does it take? My experience is that if they can't answer those questions quickly or don't have that work already done, they're just not functional." (See Jacob Klerman's briefing slide for the basics of good measurement.)

Essentials of Measurement

To manage performance, we must:

▶ Define performance explicitly

▶ Be able to measure something correlated with it—promptly, accurately, and inexpensively

▶ And, we do not want a measure of gross performance; we want net performance

---

Quinlivan made a similar point in telling a story about visiting the Saturn automobile plant in Spring Hill, Tennessee. The exchange is worth reading in the whole:

JAMES QUINLIVAN: My wife bought a Saturn. It's true—they treat owners differently. They will fix things. She lost her key once. My wife has to drive nearly three miles to get to work. She leaves herself notes once a month to get gasoline. In southern California, this is not what you call a particularly heavy auto user. They came over, pulled the number and got her a key quickly.

When we were on vacation—we were actually doing Civil War battlefields on the campaign down to Chickamauga—Spring Hill was right there, and we had to go do the Spring Hill plant tour.

PAUL LIGHT: Were you driving your Saturn?

JAMES QUINLIVAN: No, actually I had a rental. We had to go take the tour. You see their little postings and things. You're just watching people work. I've seen an assembly line before. In fact, one of the things hanging in our house is a Diego Rivera print that shows a Detroit assembly line in the 1930s. I've always found it sort of awe-inspiring. In fact, I went through Ford's River Rouge assembly line when I was a kid; I couldn't have been more than seven.

PAUL LIGHT: Where did you grow up?

JAMES QUINLIVAN: I grew up in Chicago, and I had an uncle that worked in Detroit. He sold things to Ford. I remember walking on that catwalk; as a small kid, it was awe-inspiring.

At Saturn, you could just watch these people and see their little postings on charts. You could say that looks like people are using those charts, that the system is actually in use. They're not doing it for me just because I'm on this tour; that group of people actually has some meaning that they derive from the charts.

PAUL LIGHT: Postings about what, like metrics?

JAMES QUINLIVAN: Yeah, you could see the little things on faults. Or there was one thing on which you could make out bars. It looked like some sort of production thing that was being done, but it was hand updated. It wasn't something that somebody had just posted there. It looked like somebody had integrated it as part of a process.

Any time someone can explain to me the equivalent of following a quality-control chart—they actually show something other than "I do this and that and then draw a line there" and can give sort of an idea about why they record this number for that and what they see in that linking to their own job—I am really impressed. It says that somebody bothered to explain the measures all the way down the line.

It is a classic RAND story, repeated in different forms by many of the researchers I encountered over the life of this project. It is also evident in RAND's case studies of how private firms assess environmental impacts, including Hewlett-Packard's approach, which was never designed to produce "full-blown life-cycle analyses of all environmental impacts" for every design decision. Rather, according to RAND's study team, Hewlett-Packard concentrated its focus on efforts with the largest payoffs. By working through the product value chain and life cycle, from R&D to disposal, and performing gross assessments of environmental impacts, Hewlett-Packard was able to build the foundation for what the RAND research teams describe as "broad, generic design-for-environment guidelines on packaging, consumables and supplies, manufacturing processes, and end-of-life strategies that decision makers could apply to all products."

Much as they like metrics, RAND researchers also share a uniform skepticism about potential measurement abuse. Reflecting on his own experience as a baseball and soccer coach, Dertouzos argues that winning and losing often have nothing to do with ability: "You know when you're a good coach. You know parents don't complain when you win. My son happens to blossom as a pitcher and no one can beat us and suddenly all the other parents love me." Dertouzos says the same about the Army recruiting command: "They can't do anything right in a booming economy, but can do nothing wrong when there's a 9/11. Suddenly everyone wants to join the military." (See Jacob Klerman's briefing slide of how to select good measures.)

Selecting Measures

▶ Choose outcomes carefully

  • What gets measured gets done

  • Beware of unintended side-effects; "be careful what you ask/pray for…"

  • Consider requiring minimum amounts of secondary measures

▶ High stakes measurement provides incentives for cheating (especially if the people doing the measurement are the ones getting paid)

  • You have to audit intensively

  • Punish fraud severely

Beth McGlynn echoed the sentiment in her discussion of health-care metrics. At one level, there are only two outcomes that truly matter: death and disability, mortality and morbidity. Death is pretty easy to measure, and disability has a relatively precise definition. But, as McGlynn cautions, "the more complex an individual patient gets, the less you have any sense of what the critical thing was that led to the outcome. I think that the value of the outcome piece is to keep asking ourselves in health care what we want at the end of the day. What is it that we're trying to produce? How does the doctor-patient encounter contribute to the thing that we're after, whether it's health, well-being, or whatever.... I think we're saying that what gets measured gets done. That's sort of the mantra in quality of health care."

McGlynn's work on health-care quality bears that concern. "I think the progress we've made in the last two or three decades on quality measurement is really getting the metrics right, and really being much clearer on how we measure things, and how we even pick the standards by which we measure things. But I think we've done really badly on communicating that information outside the small elite club that does the measurement."

Thus, much as they look for hard metrics as an indicator of a well-run organization, they generally prefer a mix of measures to sketch the fullest possible portrait of success. All things being equal, most RAND researchers would favor a blend of both quantitative and qualitative measures, the former allowing careful tracking over time, the latter allowing nuanced interpretations of hard-to-measure activity. As RAND's study of environmental management shows, "quantitative metrics by themselves can rarely capture everything important about a decision-making position. Proactive firms typically supplement their quantitative metrics with qualitative metrics on the overall operation of important processes."

This is certainly how Procter & Gamble conducts its environmental site audits at individual plants: "Personnel from one plant helped conduct audits at other plants to calculate metrics that each plant could use to measure progress against its own past performance; such cross-plant audits helped transfer lessons learned across sites. The audits subjectively rated each site, using a scale of 1 to 10, on specific factors related to government and public relations, people capacity, direct environmental impact, incident prevention, and continuous improvement." Although the audits were embedded with hard measures, they also gave intuition and judgment a say, which is essential to any effective measurement system.

Agility

Assume that an organization actually sets a signpost and discovers that a load-bearing assumption is somehow failing and has the warning time to act. Although the knowledge might be interesting as a harbinger of turbulence ahead, it is useless unless the organization can react.

The media arts provide a perfect example of the need for agility. According to RAND, the media arts are dramatically different from the traditional performing, visual, and literary arts. Not only do they lack the long history of other arts forms, they place a premium on innovation and experimentation and depend to a much greater extent on emerging technology. Produced by using or combining video, film, and computers, the media arts depend on agility for success, especially given the fickle audience for their products.

The problem is that the arts world is particularly unsteady today. Funding is unpredictable, audiences inconsistent, and tastes ever changing. "In combination, these developments are reshaping the organizational ecology of the arts world and blurring the traditional distinctions among sectors, disciplines, and media," RAND reports. "Instead of a sharp demarcation between a nonprofit sector's producing the high arts and a for-profit sector's producing mass entertainment, the arts world appears to be increasingly divided along the lines of small versus large organizations and those that cater to broad markets versus niche markets." Survival appears to rest on organizational agility—the ability to adapt quickly to funding opportunities and exploit audience share.

Some of RAND's most notable work on agility has focused on the Air Force, which is under enormous pressure to go anywhere, anytime to meet new threats. Gone are the days when the Air Force could count on predictable deployments and long periods of rest. It spent the 1990s mounting quick strikes against foreign targets, leading the bombing campaign over Kosovo, policing the no-fly zones over Iraq, and flying more than 500 humanitarian missions to Eastern and Central Europe alone. "The constant drumbeat of these contingencies during the 1990s has taken a toll on the Air Force," RAND writes, "and shows no indications of slackening."

Expecting more of the same far into an uncertain future, the Air Force decided to reorganize itself into an anywhere-anytime Expeditionary Aerospace Force composed of roughly 10 Air Expeditionary Forces, each with a mix of fighters, bombers, and tankers, two of which will always be on-call for crises and able to move into battle within 48 hours.

The only problem is that going anywhere in 48 hours takes a very different kind of organization. Aircraft can get off the ground in an instant, but their bases and housing cannot. Having been designed for a world with just two theaters—Western Europe and Northeast Asia—the Air Force is increasingly operating in areas where it has no main operating bases, and few, if any, temporary sites. In both a literal and figurative sense, the Air Force must have the organizational scaffolding to achieve its goal, which means more than just a large number of heavy cargo plans. "It takes forever to get one of these planes open because the stuff is so heavy coming in," said Robert Roll, a RAND specialist on the agile Air Force.

According to a series of RAND reports, that scaffolding requires a new way of organizing called *agile combat support*. At a minimum, such a system requires the Air Force to create a global infrastructure capable of moving a selected set of support resources such as heavy maintenance equipment, spare parts, shelter, and munitions into place quickly. Although new aircraft such as the Joint Strike Fighter may reduce the need for bulky support equipment, the Air Force will still need to build new bases and provide shelter. As a recent report argues, "the Air Force goal of deploying a nominal expeditionary package (a 36-ship mixed fighter squadron of air defense suppression, air superiority, and ground-attack aircraft) within 48 hours to an unprepared bare base cannot be met with today's support processes. That timeline can be met only with judicious prepositioning, and even then only under optimistic assumptions." This study does not question the need for agility, however. The changing Air Force mission demands nothing less. The only question is how to get there.

Drawing upon examples from the business world, one recent RAND report even recommends a virtual command structure modeled on the Rolling Stones' 1994-1995 *Voodoo Lounge* concert tour, which traveled to 26 countries, played a record-breaking 130 dates (including five secret club concerts), played before 6.6 million people, and made $320 million, which is still the record today. The tour was just as complex as many Air Force missions, although hardly as dangerous.

The tour employed 250 workers, required 56 trucks and 9 custom-fitted buses to move from city to city, two 747s and a Russian cargo plane to move from continent to continent, and consumed nearly 4 million watts of electricity per concert delivered by 6000 horsepower generators.[7] The 200 x 85 x 92-foot stage took four days to construct, required three different steel crews leapfrogging from site to site, 8 miles of power cable, the world's largest Jumbotron video screen, 45 tons of water ballast (roughly the size of an Olympic-sized swimming pool), 1500 lights, and a customized 1.5 million-watt sound system. The stage was so tall that it actually required aircraft warning lights under Federal Aviation Administration regulations. "This is like moving an army around the country," one of the production directors said at the time. "At times, it feels as though it would be easier to organize the D-Day Landings."[8]

The Air Force faces the same logistical pressures. According to RAND's report on the virtual air staff, the Air Force "is always 'on the road' and must employ the same miniaturized information connectivity and processing power to allow a staff to coordinate a plethora of issues that include planning (adapting to changing opportunities), logistics (juggling resources), personnel (employee relations), and intelligence (market research)." It also must accept new "bookings" on short notice, and operate from any quarters, no matter how tight or distant.

The Air Force has a long way to go before looking much like *Voodoo Lounge*, however. It has to shake off the organizational inflexibility associated with the Cold War, the problems in retaining pilots on extended tours of duty, and the natural wear-and-tear on its aircraft.

The Air Force is not the only RAND client looking for agility, however. The Army wants it, too, whether for reducing the vulnerability of lightly armored forces or reducing the cycle time in delivering spare parts.

Given its rapidly expanding inventory of missions, the Army has been looking for ways of moving light forces into battle quickly, while strengthening them against a range of both heavier and more widely dispersed adversaries. Although the Army is still quite capable of fighting major wars against massed enemies, the question is how well it can do in limited engagements such as the 1992 peace-keeping mission to Somalia, where the lightly armored 10th Mountain Division was asked to patrol a densely populated city with the equipment and training for rapid assault across open territory. The results were disastrous, as *Black Hawk Down* documents.[9]

Several recent RAND studies recommend an entirely different approach built around a *task organizing* or *tailoring* strategy in which units are mixed and matched for specific missions, and moved into place as fast as possible. "First, the Army needs to be able to assemble the right forces quickly, especially when drawing from a combination of units," one report urges. "Second, it must facilitate their rapid movement to the combat theater." Not only would this mean greater decentralization of traditionally centralized organizations, it would also require a new command structure that links the dispersed units together into a virtual force.

The Army must also get faster at supplying units in distant locales. If the Army wants to move "as far as it can get," as Velocity Management expert Marc Robbins notes, it must move spare parts as far as it can get, too. According to Robbins and his colleagues, the Army has already made great progress in doing so, largely by abandoning its old image of supply chain management:

> We had huge, elaborate modeling for warfare in which you deploy 10 divisions at extremely high operational tempo and mobilize the entire industrial base. That didn't seem to be terribly relevant anymore. The kinds of problems we saw our clients dealing with were more mundane. How do we fight this small war here? How do we deploy here? How do we give them the

supplies they need when they can't take it all with them? It all sounded more and more like what manufacturing firms have to deal with. We decided that the only way we could really help them was to actually look at what they did and help them try to fix it.

Working with others in the Army-funded Arroyo Center, Robbins and his colleagues eventually developed a Velocity Management system based entirely on the notion that supplies had to move quickly into battle. Before the Army began rebuilding its distribution system, it could take 50 days for material to simply get out of the United States, which produced constant hoarding and over-ordering.

Ten years later, the logistics process had been turned inside out. Just-in-time delivery came just in time for the war in Afghanistan. Since commercial carriers such as FedEx and Worldwide Express do not have regular routes to Karshi Khanabad, Uzbekistan, where U.S. troops were stationed, the Army had to invent an entirely new and agile system. According to RAND, end-to-end shipping times averaged just 16 days during the war, even though the tonnage of material increased dramatically.

Over time, the Army is raising the bar on agility. As the Velocity Management team's leader John Dumond explains, "A whole bunch of people in the Army were just used to 25- or 40-day order and ship times. Now they're used to seven-day order and ship times. We have a generation of new soldiers who weren't in the Army when you had those long delivery times, so they have come to expect seven days. That's kind of a nice thing. If it's not there in 10 days, they think it's bad."

Agility is also essential to effective teams. According to Leland Joe's study of high-performing combat units, teams must be able to respond to changing conditions, new threats, and the "fog" of battle. Joe's research focused in part on the 3rd Army in World War II "because it was prepared to make an attack into Germany, but were able to adapt and change their mission very quickly when the Germans attacked into the bulge," and the 1st in the 1991 Gulf War "because they performed a breaching operation of Iraqi defenses, then were later called to participate in the left hook envelopment of Iraqi forces," which meant that they "had the ability to do multiple missions effectively and react in a very short period of time, even though they had not planned to do them all."

Joe found three characteristics of high-performing units. First, commanders worked hard to cut through the fog of war, which Joe described as "getting less dense, but will always be a challenge." "We found that commanders had trained all their personnel to be able to report back information by going outside channels. In some sense, all the people knew that they had the ability to reach back and tell the commander directly what they felt was relevant information."

Second, every high-performing unit had "work-arounds" of some kind. "Every staff has strengths and weaknesses," says Joe. "I think the important thing was that high-performers were able to take advantage of the strengths and sort of avoid the weaknesses. It was very important in military organizations, because people do get killed or wounded."

Third, high-performing units were aligned around a common purpose: "The biggest, greatest characteristic was the common approach to the problem that the units took—the commanders had trained their units to react the same to various situations prior to the exercise. A lot of the focus was on how you move information around and share information to help foster that common perspective."

Adaptability

Adaptability is not a synonym for innovative. Rather, it is the ability to rapidly adjust strategies and tactics to meet changes in the environment. Sometimes, adaptability requires a technical breakthrough of some kind such as Intel's multi-core chip; other times, it involves incremental adjustments in response to market pressure. As such innovation is a form of adaptation, but not all adaptation is innovative.

At an operational level, whether on the factory floor, emergency room, or in the battlefield, adaptability refers to an organization's ability to react quickly to a diversity of scenarios, some that might seem predictable, others that involve great surprise. At a strategic level, adaptability refers to the organization's overall business model, and captures its ability to shift with state-of-the-world unrest. But whether operational or strategic, adaptability requires the organizational capacity to react.

Most organizations are already familiar with the concept of adaptability, especially if their executives drive a luxury car. Toyota's 2004 Lexus LS430 will tighten the seat belts, increase the driver's braking pressure, and even put the car in a defensive crouch closer to the ground if its radar senses an impending collision. Cadillac's XLR sports car is equipped with adaptive cruise control that will brake the car if its senses sudden movement in its path. BMW offers an optional active steering system that will override the driver under emergency conditions. The Mercedes S-Class will soon provide a system for closing the sunroof and returning seatbacks and table trays to the upright position just before an accident.[10]

Drivers are not about to let go of the steering wheel, however. They still want the sense of control. But with the Global Positioning System able to pinpoint both position and movement, the world is moving steadily toward the self-driving car. "Combine GPS with radar-aided cruise control," says the editor of *Car and Driver*, "add a lane-changing system and throw in a transponder, or cameras, and pretty soon you could have a car that drives itself in a middle of a bunch of conventional cars."

Organizations are still some distance from the self-driving plan, but are moving closer to assisted steering and the defensive crouch through the kinds of uncertainty-sensitive planning discussed in the previous chapter. They are also installing organizational radar to anticipate impending accidents and opportunities for acceleration.

Adaptability involves more than just preparing for surprise, however. It also involves efforts to stay ahead of the traffic through both continuous and disruptive maneuvering.

The mining industry provides a first example. According to a recent RAND report, the industry faces an unstable market, increased consolidation, an aging workforce, and heightened scrutiny of everything it does. Given this future, the industry has adopted a profoundly defensive crouch, avoiding risks, struggling to boost paper-thin profit margins, and cutting back severely on technology and research development. Metaphorically speaking, the industry has closed the sunroof, deployed the airbags, and hit the brakes as it worries about what might happen next.

The industry is not a monolith, however. The metals industry is less concerned about big trucks and blasting technology, and more focused on high-precision drilling technologies and the acquisition of high-yield mines. The coal industry is less concerned about productivity-enhancing technology and more concerned about regulations governing the use of high-sulfur fuels. The stone and aggregates industry is less concerned about finding new mines and more concerned about productivity increases.

Despite these differences, all segments of the industry are worried about declining investment in research and development. Because most firms do not have in-house R&D units, they have relied on incremental improvements to existing technology for most of their productivity gains. If there is breakthrough around the corner, it will have to come from outside the industry.

Not only does the industry need to think more aggressively about using new technologies such as the Global Positioning System to map and monitor its mines, it must prepare its workforce to deal with a very different future. Mine workers still carry lunch-pails to work, but they often eat atop huge machines with high-tech-like dashboards. According to RAND's research, workers are becoming more, not less, critical to high performance. As mining equipment gets bigger and more technologically sophisticated, individual operators are playing a greater role in determining mine output. They are also gaining unprecedented access to information and control over the equipment they are operating. Absent the multidisciplinary skills and freedom to fully utilize the new technology, the industry cannot generate the productivity gains needed to compete.

The U.S. military offers a second example. As the world's strongest military, the U.S. would seem to have an absolute advantage in virtually any battle setting. But past revolutions in military affairs suggest otherwise. If current power had anything to do with future power, the French cavalry would still rule the world. As the French discovered in 1346, knights on horseback were particularly vulnerable to English longbows, which in turn were particularly vulnerable to artillery, and so forth down through history.

On the surface, RAND's work on revolutions in military affairs confirms the worst fears of built-to-last, good-to-great companies. After all, the dominant power is almost never the source of the revolution. However, as RAND also shows, most revolutions are almost always adopted and fully exploited by someone other than the inventor. The machine gun was invented by the U.S. but exploited by the English and Germans; the armored tank was invented by the British but exploited by the Germans; and the first aircraft carrier was built by the British but exploited by the Americans and Japanese.

Moreover, most revolutions involve combinations of technologies rather than a single great breakthrough. Thus, the blitzkrieg was enabled by the tank, two-way radio, and the dive bomber; while the Intercontinental Ballistic Missile was a combination of long-range rockets, lightweight warheads, and accurate guidance systems. In addition, most revolutions take years, even decades, to achieve results. In other words, it is often creative reconstruction, not destruction, that produces the big impact.

Monsanto's entry into biotechnology provides a final example. Convinced that the number of chemical solutions to crop management was limited, Monsanto joined with Harvard University in 1972 to develop new chemicals for regulating plant growth and behavior. The Harvard collaboration was one of what would become many joint projects with universities and individual scientists, and reflected what RAND describes as Monsanto's paradigm shift toward research-based product development, which led to an internal research group.

Like the revolutions in military affairs described above, Monsanto did not achieve results overnight, nor was the effort always linear. Its scientists started their genetic engineering work on petunias and tobacco, for example, but eventually made their breakthrough on soybeans, which led to further breakthroughs in potatoes, tomatoes, and cotton, all of which were engineered to withstand herbicides and/or insects. The breakthroughs came almost 25 years after Monsanto's initial investment in biology, more than 40 years after J. D. Watson and F. H. C. Crick described deoxyribonucleic acid (DNA) and 139 years after Gregor Mendel began his experiments. According to Monsanto's Law, which is modeled on Intel's experience with integrated circuits, the amount of genetic information used in practical applications will double every year or two.

It is important to emphasize that all of this adaptability has been based on rigorous research and measurement. Although there have been mad scientists along the way, innovation is considered anything but accidental. To the contrary, it is the natural consequence of investment, research, and imagination. At least in these cases, adaptability depended on the kind of organization RAND researchers appear to like best—the innovative, entrepreneurial organization led by the honest, trusting, yet decisive leader.

If readers want a nearly perfect example of how that kind of research can work in other settings, they need read no further than RAND's work on preventing crime through early childhood investment. RAND's study was designed to compare four very different prevention strategies: (1) home visits during the first two years of childhood followed by four years of day care; (2) parental training for parents with young school-age children who have shown aggressive behavior; (3) cash programs and other incentives to encourage disadvantaged high school students to graduate; and (4) mentoring of high school students who have already exhibited delinquent behavior. Parental training was by far the least expensive of the four programs, averaging just $3000 per participant, while home visits were the most expensive at $29,400.

The RAND research team was not interested in cost, however, but rate of return. As the team found, parent training and graduation incentives were far more cost-effective in preventing crime than either home visits or delinquent supervision. Parental training cost $6351 per crime averted, while graduation incentives cost only $3881. By comparison, the home visits/daycare option cost $89,035 per crime averted and delinquent supervision $13,899. Both options become even more attractive when compared with California's three-strikes-and-you're-out law, which mandates life in prison for the third felony conviction at a cost of $16,000 per crime averted.

The research is particularly important for understanding how organizations allocate resources to any activity. Should they invest early or late? What are the short-term costs versus the long-term costs? Where can they get added value through small investments? Unfortunately, as RAND's research team argues, California's state government is so balkanized that there is no government agency with a primary interest in alternative interventions. As a result, it may take some kind of interagency, boundary-spanning organization to actually test the more cost-effective interventions on a broader scale. Lacking such an organization, law-enforcement agencies will continue to support imprisonment as the answer, while health and human service agencies will continue to focus on early-childhood programs.

Alignment

It is one thing to change the Air Force planning process or create whole-school reforms, and quite another to implement a relatively small-scale program to help children. But whether the change is massive or targeted, the organization as a whole must be aligned to mission.

For Beth McGlynn, alignment in health organizations is about being known as a patient. "It's the ability to move across doctors at any number of different levels and be known, meaning that your history is known, where you are in any sort of treatment path is known, that you're not having to re-explain yourself at each step of the way." As such, being aligned is about the communication system in an organization: "Is the organization designed in such a way that information gets transferred with you or actually just ahead of you so that you're not starting over at each step along the way?" asks McGlynn. "I think organizations can only do that if they have thought about it; that's the kind of thing that doesn't just happen. There has to be some malice aforethought to make sure those kinds of things happen."

Frank Camm sees the same kind of alignment at Wal-Mart, which has used information technology to change its business model. "Wal-Mart has basically gone to its suppliers and said, 'We're not even going to touch your stuff. We're just going to give you shelf space, and you're going to pay us for what we sell,'" says Camm, who has worked on everything from how companies react to energy and environmental controls to Air Force acquisitions. "Now that's a well aligned system. They have linked their information systems so that the guy selling knows what gets sold as soon as Wal-Mart does, and that guy is in there every day restocking the shelves."

Camm also believes that alignment involves cost controls and careful measurement, and remembers how high-performing companies used information on their toxic waste emissions:

What was fascinating to us when we went to talk to these companies is that they said their senior executives had no idea that they were emitting this much stuff into the environment. They were upset about the kind of liability they were exposing themselves to, but they were equally upset by the fact that their processes were so far out of control that this sort of emission could occur. Just from the straight total quality management point of view, they were saying, "This is unacceptable."

It's an alignment of mission to say that the senior management says, "Here's an opportunity for profit on our point of view by tightening up our processes." That's the alignment of mission, recognizing that what they traditionally looked at as a compliance cost they had no control over was something they could control in a way that increased their profits. In a competitive industry, if you can get even a very small change in your profit rate, you can drive your competitor out of business. They had a very strong incentive to react that way.

RAND's James Dertouzos sees high-performance in the alignment of markets and goals. His current research suggests wide variation in how military recruiters respond to relatively small changes in their recruiting goals. As he explains, "we're getting estimates that suggest people's effort can decline by as much as 20 percent just because their mission is unachievable. They essentially give up. I don't know whether it's a morale issue or whether it's responding to incentives in a very calculated way or what. When missions are not allocated appropriately either over time or from market to market, you get these incredible diminutions in observable effort. You can gain 10 to 20 percent gains in productivity in certain markets by just aligning markets and incentives."

Alignment is essential in broad public experiments such as Pittsburgh's Early Childhood Initiative. Launched under the auspices of the local United Way in 1996, the initiative was designed to help at-risk children with a portfolio of high-quality services, from health care to pre-school. At its peak, the program served only 680 of the 7600 children it had originally wanted to reach.

Although the program was a "noble bet," as RAND's study team calls it, the administrative structure governing the program was a nightmare. Only nominally under the United Way's control, the program was run by what RAND calls a "labyrinthine leadership structure" that led to unresolved power struggles between the program and United Way management and neighborhood frustration. "Venture capitalists making an investment of comparable scale might insist on a leadership team that includes a CEO with entrepreneurial experience as well as general management experience," the team reports.

Unfortunately, the initiative not only lacked an independent board, its chief executive did not have enough authority to make operational decisions for the initiative. Although everyone involved had the right motivation, the initiative desperately needed a CEO with what RAND describes as "experience in managing large endeavors and in starting them from scratch (as well as an administrative structure that permitted the exercise of strong leadership)."

Alignment is also a central contributor to the lean manufacturing process designed by Eiji Toyoda and Taiichi Ohno at the Toyota Motor Company after World War II.[11] Designed to eliminate wasted motion at each step in the manufacturing process, Toyota's system depends upon the combination of standardization and employee involvement reflected in the winnowing of characteristics discussed in Chapter Two. On the one hand, jobs are intricately scripted in a coordinated attack to reduce statistical variation. Parts move rigidly along the assembly line, employees always receive assistance from the same manager, and supplies are delivered with absolute precision "just in time."

On the other hand, employees and managers have complete authority to shut down the entire line if they spot a deviation. Toyota workers are scientists of a kind, using rigorous methods to improve their performance by creating the conditions for controlled inquiry, while developing deep knowledge of both how the process works and what the organization values. As RAND's Heather Barney and Sheila Nataraj Kirby note, "information gleaned from standardization and hypothesis-testing is not sent off to a team of industrial engineers who redesign jobs or pathways using theoretical models and then impose their design on workers. Rather, the workers use their own knowledge of their work to design and implement improvements for the plant, assisted by managers who act as teachers and resource guides."[12] As a result, problems are solved while they are still small and localized.

The co-authors suggest that the system is easily transferable to public schools where it could be vital for shifting the debate from inputs such as spending to outputs, while instilling a commitment to *jidoka*, which instructs every level of the organization not to pass problems along. "It suggests that educators put more energy into identifying and dealing with problems immediately and at their source." Having identified a problem, teachers would take action before a student or class moves onward and upward, diag-nosing problems through scientific assessment, and solving them through hypothesis testing and experimentation.

As Barney and Kirby readily admit, however, schools are hardly paragons of alignment. Teachers, parents, principals, superintendents, and political leaders often disagree sharply about the quality of the final prod-uct, and often punish schools for daring to experiment. The problem is not a lack of standardization, especially in the new testing requirements, but great risk in the kind of experimentation and problem-solving that might honor jidoka but close the "plant."

RAND TRANSFORMED

Few organizations know the basics of robustness better than RAND, and not just because it studies other organizations. RAND itself confronted an extraordinary period of instability with the end of the Cold War in 1989, in no small part because the 1980s had seen a sharp reduction in its policy research on social and economic problems.

The insecurity only got worse as the years rolled by and federal spend-ing caps took hold. With the Clinton administration looking for cuts just about anywhere in defense, while Congress looked for cuts just about every-where else, RAND was clearly facing more than statistical uncertainty. Hav-ing put 85 percent of its budget in the federal basket, RAND could either wait for the next surprise or change. As RAND's executive vice president, Michael Rich, remembers, there were two reasons to change.

The first was simple fatigue surrounding the post-Cold War transi-tion. "We had begun using those terms—'post-Cold War Transition'—in 1989, after the breakup of the Warsaw Pact, and in 1991, after the fall of the Soviet Union," he says. "By 1994, 1995, we said 'enough already,' and decided that we had to begin talking about the new era and the new period, not just the transition out of the old one. We'd better figure out what our situation was and what the future held for the institution."

The second reason involved the midterm elections of 1994, which produced the first Republican Congress in forty years. "It became clear that both political parties at the national level were committed to a bal-anced federal budget that would almost inevitably mean cuts in discre-tionary resources, including those for policy research and analysis," Rich says. "We were heavily diversified in the federal sector, but we were basi-cally a federally funded organization for the most part. Our feeling was that it just wasn't prudent to count on that as a recipe or a design for the future. It was time to reexamine our assumptions." To mix metaphors, RAND had put all of its eggs in a single basket, but could hear the water-fall just around the bend.

It was RAND's president, James Thomson, who began to use the waterfall imagery to portray the risks of standing firm. "There's a point where you can hear the danger, but you cannot see it," Rich says. "The challenge is to turn the boat before you get into the white-water that you can see. Once you see the danger, it's too late."

Like any organization facing a volatile future, RAND's challenge was to identify a new course and follow it. The problem was that RAND's revenues had risen dramatically from the early 1980s, when its budget was roughly $70 million in 2003 dollars, to $105 million by 1995. "We decided not to wait for full recognition by everyone because we realized by the time everybody in the institution would see the danger, it would be too late. We committed to the change ourselves, and then dedicated ourselves to bring along the rest of the institution."

Revenue was not RAND's only concern, however. In a very real sense, RAND had become becalmed. Its attrition rate had fallen to less than 5 percent per year, which meant the median tenure at RAND of the research staff was growing quickly. By 1994 half of the research staff had worked at RAND for nine years or more. "That, to me, was a danger sign for an organization like RAND that is so dependent on creativity, innovation, new ideas, and so on," Rich remembers. "Now, you can compensate for that with outsiders involved as visitors and reviewers and speakers and so on. We were doing a lot of that stuff, but we thought we ought to be concerned about this weak flow of analytical talent in and out."

Given its tradition, RAND did what it thought any good organization should do. It created a *scenario space* of possible futures.

One family involved a return to RAND's original core business in defense. "We would be smaller, profitable, and thus able to sustain our existence," Rich says, "but we would have had to divest a lot of the work that we had developed on social and economic policy." By circling its wagons around its defense research business, RAND would continue at roughly $80 million a year far into the future.

A second family involved diversification. "The idea here would have been to diversity into new areas that would be financially lucrative, which would generate funds for reinvestment and also enable us to expand our coverage of important policy problems." Diversification required new capacity, however, including an expansion of staff expertise well beyond the hard sciences that had given RAND its strength in the 1950s and 1960s, as well as the social sciences and humanities that had enabled RAND's diversification into social and economic policy research in the 1960s and 1970s.

A third family involved the eventual end of RAND. "We were serious about creating and studying dissolution options, motivated by one of our 'devil's advocates' who argued that RAND was a creation of the Cold War, and should reexamine whether it still needed to exist or whether there should be other organizations to take its place in and for the new era."

The scenarios formed the basis of a two-and-a-half-day board meeting in November 1995 that ended with a consensus to pursue the second set of options. "We felt that losing the work we would have had to divest would be harmful to the performance of our mission," Rich said of the first family of options. "The divested research was within the scope of our mission of helping improve policy and decision-making through research and analysis. It was high quality work and objective, and therefore met both of our core values. Shedding it would damage the reason that we existed."

RAND also saw the social and economic work as essential to its core business with the Defense Department, in part because it helped the organization recruit top-flight labor economists who knew nothing about the military, but who were attracted by RAND's research on social and economic issues. "Once they got here, they realized that some of the most complex and challenging analytical problems, and some of the best clients and most sophisticated databases, were actually in the defense work."

Equally important, RAND's own internal labor market allowed researchers to move across boundaries to work on any project that interested them, provided that the project was interested in them. Unlike most professional service firms, RAND does not have a system for assigning researchers to projects. Instead, researchers put together their commitments by marketing themselves to project leaders. As a result, RAND could not eliminate any one stream without risking harm to all the others.

Finally, RAND already had considerable expertise in diversifying. It had expanded its agenda in the 1960s with research on education, crime, health, energy, and the environment, and again in the 1970s with civil justice and research for other nations. "Diversifying further was plausible," Rich says. "We felt we would be able to cover more policy areas, broaden our client base, reinforce the financial health of the institution, and, in the process, increase the stream of earnings that we could reinvest in self-initiated research." By the end of the meeting, the board had hammered out a new business strategy designed to grow the organization, but not too fast. (Rich's briefing chart shows the basic thrust of the final decision.)

Rand's New Business Strategy for 1996 and Beyond

▶ Overarching objective: diversity and grow, so as to:

- Address a broader range of issues, obtain a wider client base

- Improve financial position through higher margin work

- Increase the flow of new recruits into RAND

▶ Three key strategy elements:

- Strengthen relations with national security clients, especially the department of defense

- Develop new non-national security clients in the private sector consistent with our mission and dedication to the public interest

- Maintain and build other nonmilitary work consistent with unit income goals

The plan was not self-executing, however. RAND clearly had to change its organizational structure to make the strategy work. It strengthened its alertness by improving front-office communications; installing new finance, planning, and analysis systems; and bulking up its external affairs and fundraising units.

It increased its agility by removing a layer of management that had been built in the 1950s around academic disciplines such as economics, mathematics, and so forth. "We felt that the pendulum needed to swing toward the business side so our research units go find new clients, go after new problems, adapt their products and services, and so on. Instead of separate departments, each with their own hiring approach, staff development, review and appraisal process, we decided that we wanted one organization, which came to be the Research Staff Management Department." Under this flatter structure, everyone on the RAND staff is organized into groups—economics and statistics, management sciences, and so forth—but is recruited, trained, appraised, and rewarded as part of a whole.

RAND increased its adaptability by eliminating another layer of management—the Domestic Research Division—and decentralizing responsibility to its various business units—Army, Air Force, national security, health, education, criminal justice, labor and population, public safety and justice, science and technology, enterprise analysis, and RAND Europe. While not quite boats on their own bottoms, metaphorically speaking, the units were given significant authority to develop their own revenue streams, and were rewarded for doing so with reinvestment resources.

RAND quickly realized that it also needed to strengthen its alignment. As business units became diversifying, so did their individual logos and letterhead. "It was like 'where's Waldo?'" Rich remembers about trying to find the word *RAND* on report covers. "It was in the upper right hand corner, upper left, small and large. There was really no consistency. The pendulum was swinging too far toward enterprise."

The chaos reflected RAND's own struggle to create a unified brand identity across its diverse marketplace. Mention RAND in the Department of Defense, and clients think about the Army, Air Force, and national security divisions. Mention it in health care, and clients think of RAND Health. Mention it in the private sector, and clients think of science and technology or labor and population.

RAND eventually responded by developing its first branding package, including a common format for all reports and letterheads. "Where a publication gets printed is not a core value of RAND. Frankly, I couldn't care less where it gets printed. But it has to be in publication series and use the right document number so every publication can be referenced. You have to meet our quality standards and other basic requirements, but you don't have to use our presses."

At the same time, RAND resisted the temptation to standardize everything. "We tried to be tough-minded about what really needs to be in common." RAND insisted that its business units use its facilities and financial architecture. It also insisted on a unified quality assurance process, and common security apparatus. But it did not insist that units buy RAND services such as travel, printing, and survey research, nor has RAND ever insisted on one kind of computer brand. In fact, Rich uses a Macintosh, while Jim Thomson uses a PC. "In a narrow accounting sense, it may be more expensive to operate with so many different computers and software packages," Rich explains. "In our line of work, however, the choice of computer is just as personal as the choice of journals to read. It's really intrinsic to the creative process here."

It is important that RAND refused to change its mission or its core values of quality and objectivity. "We were very explicit about staying constant. Was the 1995 client base the key to our success? Well, not really. The client base had changed over the decades, from just one client to dozens. Instead, we concluded that the keys to RAND's success were in its core values and mission."

By almost any measure, RAND's new strategy has worked. Revenues increased from $120 million in 1995 (in 2003 dollars) to just under $200 million in 2003. Similarly, the number of endowed research chairs jumped from two in 1995 to 11, total employment surged by 40 percent to 1417, and the median age of the RAND research staff dropped significantly without any reduction in the level of professional degrees. Equally important, the research staff became more diverse—whereas the hard sciences of engineering, math, computer sciences, and physical sciences accounted for 38 percent in 1995. It accounted for 26 percent by 2003; whereas arts and humanities, law and business, and policy analysis accounted for just 20 percent in 1995, it accounted for 31 percent by 2003.

This expansion was driven by a much wider funding base. In 1995 the federal government accounted for 81 percent of RAND revenues; by 2003, the percentage was down to 65 percent. In 1995, defense and national security accounted for 62 percent of RAND revenues; by 2003, the percentage was down to 50 percent. Along the way, RAND decided to sell its old building and parking lot just across the street from Santa Monica City Hall, and build a new headquarters a half block away. With property values sky high, the land sale pumped $53 million into RAND's endowment.

These changes clearly brought stress. As Rich acknowledged in 2004, the infusion of new people, young and not-so-young, created the potential for inconsistency. "That's strain number one: the challenge of adequate supervision, mentoring, and acculturation given our rapid growth and geographic dispersion." In addition to growing, RAND added new research sites, growing from three sites in two countries in 1995 to eight sites in five countries by 2003, including Qatar, Berlin, Cambridge, Leiden, Santa Monica, Washington, Pittsburgh, and New York City. "Then we've got 30 researchers in places where we don't have offices such as in Philadelphia and Chicago," Rich notes. "That has meant new challenges in making sure that every problem and every client should have the best talent from all of RAND, not just the best talent from the zip code in which the project leader is located."

This is not to argue that there is a trade-off between adaptability and alignment, but the two pillars can create tension against each other. RAND confronted the problems in its Science and Technology Institute, which had been funded by the White House Office of Science and Technology

Policy, and came up for renewal in the early 2000s. Although the Institute was generating $4 to $5 million in revenue per year, the new contract focused heavily on short-term assistance driven almost entirely by client requests with very limited authority to initiate projects and even heavier constraints on public dissemination of important findings and methods. Under RAND's informal "rules of the road," as the senior leadership calls them, the contract was simply too restrictive. So RAND said no and basically divested itself of the program.

When the government of oil-rich Qatar called, RAND saw a different kind of opportunity. Not only did the government ask RAND to use all of its expertise to help build a new school system, it invited RAND to help strengthen a variety of civic institutions and policy processes such as health care, information technology, and the environment through the creation of a joint RAND-Qatar Policy Institute in the nation's new "Education City." Launched in October 2003, the institute houses a small RAND staff that oversees an increasingly broad agenda of research, including education, environmental, and national security research, while accounting for 5 percent of total organizational revenues in 2004.

BENCHMARKS OF ROBUSTNESS

RAND's own transformation raises three fundamental questions about the basic concept of robustness: Can an organization be robust without strength in all four pillars? Are there different degrees of robustness? And just how would we know a robust organization if we saw one?

RAND's own transformation helps answer all three questions. There is no doubt, for example, that RAND was both alert and aligned in 1995 when it began exploring the futures ahead. There is also no question that it could have continued for years on its existing course, albeit with increasing vulnerability in an uncertain funding environment. But it did not have enough agility or adaptability to be robust against all plausible futures, most notably the futures that included a continued erosion in federal government support. Absent strength in all four pillars, it was much too vulnerable for comfort.

This is not to suggest that RAND was either inflexible or indifferent in 1995. Nor did RAND start its transformation from scratch. It had been through diversification before, and already had a broad client base. But it clearly was not as agile or adaptive as it needed to be if it wanted to control its own destiny. Even if one can argue that RAND had some robustness in 1995, most notably in its alertness to the changing environment and the alignment to move as a sum greater than its parts, it did not have enough agility and adaptability to assure success under a wide range of possible futures.

Toward both ends, it flattened its hierarchy, pushed more autonomy downward to its business units and the subunits therein, and strengthened incentives for diversification. It also increased its internal controls to protect alignment from the centrifugal forces it created with the new strategy, and strengthened external outreach in search of new markets and funding. Buffeted once by the end of the Cold War and again in the 1994 elections, RAND had no intention of waiting for another surprise. It chose instead to address its vulnerabilities, and shape the future to its advantage.

RAND's experience suggests that all four pillars of robustness are essential for high performance under external instability. Alertness signals the need to adjust; agility provides the speed to adjust; adaptability provides the new strategies and products to hedge against vulnerabilities and shape a hoped-for future; and alignment assures that the organization acts as a whole.

Organizations can clearly over-build one or more of the pillars, however. They can become so worried about the many futures they face that they cannot act in the present, become so consumed with the performance of "light" forces that they cannot bring anything heavy to a task, so focused on adapting that they forget to stand pat, and become so frightened of inconsistency that they drive out the creative spirit and experimentation needed for adaptability. They cannot be so tightly aligned that no one can breathe, but cannot be so lose that individual units might as well be flying the skull and crossbones.

Just because an organization *can* adapt does not mean it *should* adapt, for example. Rather, it should be able to adapt when necessary. Just because it can turn quickly in response to surprise does not mean it should always turn. Rather, it should only turn when its signposts show either increased vulnerability or a potent opportunity. Finally, just because it can see changes ahead does not mean it must act. If it has enough warning time, it might be better off standing pat to see just how a given future evolves.

Viewed as such, robustness is a form of organizational capital—it resides in the ability to act. As noted earlier, it hardly makes sense to adopt a robust plan if the organization does not have the alertness, agility, adaptability, *and* alignment to adjust the plan if and when events require a change. The issue here is not whether an organization is robust or not per se, but how much robustness it can muster against the futures it faces.

When asked where one might look for robust organizations, RAND researchers offer a mix of benchmarks. Several argue that robustness is nearly impossible in a start-up, for example. "If you look at a little start-up company, then they're likely to bet the whole company on a single future," says Dewar. "If you look at a multinational, then maybe they'll do robust decision-making across 90 percent of the company, while the other 10 percent takes flyers and hope that some of those will pay off. I just don't think of a little start-up company as being agile or very alert. They're just going to build whatever they want to build and hope it works. Robust decision-making says, 'Okay, I'm light on my feet. I'm going to do the following for now and pay attention. And when I see how the world's coming, I'm going to move to adapt.' A little start-up company's not doing that at all."

Other researchers say that robustness is only revealed in periods of turbulence, if only because time-tested strategies continue to work reasonably well in the calm. But as Lempert argues, robust organizations are revealed when the environment changes quickly and/or dramatically. "That's when the organization that cannot implement robust adaptive plans may fall behind. I am thinking of the observation that many private sector firms that are market leaders in some dominant technology fail to make the lead when a disruptive technology comes along. The organizations can't change rapidly enough to adapt to the new world."

Still others talked about an organization's ability to take a punch, response to a crisis, or overall alertness to market fluctuations—in other words, organizations find out how robust they are when the future changes suddenly. In the short-run, robust organizations may actually under perform against their competitors, if only because they keep at least some of their capital in reserve to hedge against surprise. They may also look less innovative than their peers, if only because they may be less willing to bet the company on a single breakthrough. In the long-term, however, robust organization should produce higher growth and more innovation, if only because they have protected themselves against vulnerability and can re-deploy resources quickly to exploit new opportunities. As such, robust organizations would tend to show up in books such as *Built to Last* and *Good to Great*, not in books about gales and tornadoes. Although robustness is no guarantor of survival, robust organizations tend to be in the cellar when the storms hit, ready to get back to work and adapt as necessary once the clouds clear. (See Nancy Moore's briefing slide on the scaffolding of innovation.)

The Scaffolding of Innovation

▶ Establish clear goals and metrics

▶ Structure to mission

▶ Empower and mobilize employees

▶ Use information technology to transform business

▶ Pay for innovation

▶ Build external relationships

This is not to suggest that robust organizations are somehow indistinguishable until moments of great stress, however. Think back to the winnowing process used in Chapter Two, and RAND's study of innovation at the Customs Service, Food and Drug Administration, Veterans Health Administration, DuPont, Marriott, and Procter & Gamble. As RAND's research team concluded, innovative organizations must have both the "hardware" of high performance structure and the "software" of employee commitment.

All six organizations started their transformations with a mission. Several merely restated their old mission in new language, while others adopted a new mission entirely. Whereas the Veterans Health Administration shifted its focus from a hospital-based system to integrate service networks built around its dense networks of 172 hospitals, 132 nursing homes, 73 home health care programs, 40 residential care programs, and 600 outpatient clinics, Marriott broke itself into two discrete corporations, one to manage its properties and the other to manage hotels.

All six organizations also introduced new measurement systems to enhance accountability and reinforce priorities. Whereas the Veterans Health Administration created performance contracts with the heads of each integrated service network, Marriott adopted a balanced scorecard to track financial and nonfinancial measures of organizational health. Whereas the Customs Service introduced a set of new measures to track the movement of cargo in and out of ports, DuPont tracked its performance against its innovation agenda and 10-year plan.

The six organizations did follow the same path on structure, however. Whereas the Customs Service and Veterans Health Administration consolidated, the Food and Drug Administration flattened; whereas Marriott dispersed, DuPont consolidated through its new Center for Creativity and Innovation. Regardless of their final structure, however, all six created internal and external networks to accelerate the movement of new ideas from start to finish. Whereas DuPont created over 400 formal and informal networks to transfer technology, Procter & Gamble created 20 communities of practice as part of its broad "connect and develop" initiative that tied new ideas to customer demand.

All six also invested heavily in information technology. Whereas the Customs Service invested in an entirely new tracking system that allowed shippers to monitor the movement of cargo in and out of ports, DuPont and Procter & Gamble invested in new e-mail and group discussion software to connect their research teams. At the same time, all six organizations provided extra resources for new ideas, whether through innovation investment funds or new congressional appropriations, and increased their interactions with clients and customers, whether through first-ever customer satisfactions surveys in the government agencies or more rigorous measurement at Marriott.

Viewed from a distance, all six organizations adopted the same kind of systems thinking that has long characterized RAND's other research. They came to view their organizations as merely part of a larger system composed of competitors, clients and customers, and events that shaped their futures. Although their primary aim was either process or product innovation, all six organizations clearly improved their robustness along the way. Indeed, one can easily argue that innovation was a by-product of other organizational changes that made all six organizations more robust. In turn, I believe the robustness created the potential for innovation.

At least at Customs, it also created the organizational capacity to quickly change directions after September 11, 2001. Having focused on becoming much more agile in tracking cargo on behalf of importers and exporters, Customs was the fastest of the homeland security agencies to change its focus to the war on terrorism.

CONCLUSION

One of the reasons many organizations bet the future on a single future is that they do not have the resources to do otherwise. Robustness is not free.

It requires investment in all corners of the organization, and potentially disruptive changes in how the organization operates. It is easy to tell an organization to measure results, for example, but more difficult to develop the right measures and track them accurately. It is also easy to tell an organization to delegate authority for routine decisions, but much more difficult to train employees to use that authority wisely. It may be easiest of all to tell organizations to regularly survey their clients and customers, but much more difficult to make sure they ask the right questions, invest in the best ideas, and use the results to calibrate strong incentives.

There are times when betting the organization on a single future is the only way to survive, however. As James Collins and Jerry Porras write, Boeing bet the company on the 707, leaving McDonnell-Douglas in its wake (at least until it bought McDonnell-Douglas in 1997). IBM made a similar big bet in the 1960s when it put its engineering muscle behind the 360 computer, which Collins and Porras describe as the "largest commercial ever undertaken."[13] But adopting these big hairy audacious goals would have been nearly impossible if Boeing and IBM did not have the capital and organizational capacity to survive. As the next chapter will discuss, robust organizations survive and prosper in part by placing the best bet across a range of futures. But this does not mean they never gamble. By strengthening each pillar of robustness, they ensure that they can give a punch as well as take one.

Robustness also requires more than a broad embrace of alertness, agility, adaptability, and alignment. Organizations must also make those pillars present through a set of operating practices that actually produce the desired outcomes. It is one thing to celebrate alertness, for example, and quite another to accept the notion that there is no single future out there against which to plan. It is one thing to celebrate agility, and quite another to invest in contingencies that may never come to pass.

As the next chapter will show, robustness also involves a much more detailed set of organizational practices that occasionally challenge the prevailing wisdom about best practices. As much as one can encourage organizations to connect the dots, for example, RAND's research encourages organizations to collect the right dots first. As much as organizations are right to "think lean" about how they work, RAND's research also suggests at least some redundancy for unanticipated surprise. And as much as an organization can celebrate the widespread embrace of balanced scorecards against which to track current performance, RAND's research supports parallel efforts to unbalance the scorecard, whether to protect against cheating or guard against complacency.

NOTES

1   Albert Wohlstetter, "Systems Analysis Versus Systems Design," P-1530, October 29, 1958, accessed at www.rand.org/publications/classics/wohlstetter/ P1530/P1530.html.

2   The project was conducted by Debra Knopman, Susan Resetar, Parry Norling, Richard Rettig, and Irene Brahmakulam in 2002, and is cited in the bibliography at the end of this book.

3   The study team cites J.W. Marriott and Kathi Ann Brown, *The Spirit to Serve: Marriott's Way*, New York:HarperCollins, 1997, in their case study of Marriott, which is contained in the larger report, *Innovation and Change Management in public and Private Organizations: Case Studies and Options for EPA.*

4   Truth be told, I stay at the Le Merigot whenever I can—small hotel, beautiful rooms, great staff. The only problem is that the previous owners did not buy the lot between the hotel and the beach—most Le Merigot rooms now look into an apartment building.

5   Gary Hamel and Liisa Välikangas, "The Quest for Resilience," *Harvard Business Review*, September 2003, pp. 52-63.

6   Hamel and Välikangas, "The Quest for Resilience," p. 53.

7   These statistics are from Its Only Rock and Roll, the Rolling Stones European Fan club, and can be found at www.iorr.org.

8   The quote is from the Rolling Stones press kit, accessed at http://www.stones.com/retro/press/stage.txt on June 16, 2004.

9   Mark Bowden, *Black Hawk Down: A Story About Modern Warfare*, New York:Atlantic Monthly Press, 1999.

10   These examples and the quote from the editor of Car and Driver come from Danny Hakim, "Robo-Cars Make Cruise Control So Last Century," The *New York Times*, April 4, 2004, p. A1.

11   See James P. Womack, Daniel T. Jones, and Daniel Roos, *The Machine that Changed the World: The Story of Lean Production*, New York:Harper Perennial, 1990.

12   The discussion is part of a larger volume on accountability edited by Brian Stecher and Kirby, cited in the bibliography.

13   James C. Collins, and Jerry I. Porras, *Built to Last: Successful Habits of Visionary Companies*, New York:HarperBusiness, paperback edition, 1997, p. 101.

HOW ROBUST ORGANIZATIONS OPERATE

RAND and its researchers have been asking how to build and strengthen the four pillars of robustness since the 1940s. They have invented new techniques for imagining alternative futures, monitoring performance, making choices, streamlining bureaucracies, managing and buying equipment, igniting innovation, and enhancing command and control. Although they often say that the letters in RAND stand for research and no development, they have also imagined or invented a variety of tools for organizational success, from world-circling spaceships to computer-modeling techniques for simulating the future.

At least some of these techniques were designed to help RAND improve its own performance. In the early 1950s, for example, RAND engineers decided to build their own version of a new computing machine designed by Princeton professor and RAND consultant John von Neumann. With IBM still years away from pursuing the 360, and just four other "Princeton-class" computers under construction elsewhere in the country, the computer team staked out a few hundred square feet in the basement of RAND's 4th and Broadway headquarters and began building the machine one vacuum tube at a time. Named in honor of its designer, the JOHN-NIAC started crunching numbers in 1953. (Nine years later in 1962, IBM president Thomas Watson, Jr., invited the head of RAND's numerical analysis department to a dinner celebrating his company's decision to switch from punch-card equipment to computers. "We were pushed into it," Watson reportedly said, "and these guests were the people who pushed us."[1])

The JOHNNIAC gave RAND instant mathematical agility, but also required entirely new programming, data management, memory allocation, and storage space, as well as innovative mathematical algorithms designed to reduce computing time. In short, agility was not enough to assure high performance. RAND engineers had to develop the alertness to use the new technology, the adaptability to extend its reach, and the alignment to manage its inputs and outputs.

A half-century later, RAND continues to work toward greater robustness, whether for itself or its clients. Although industries and organizations differ in important ways, all enterprises share common vulnerabilities and opportunities that respond to greater alertness, agility, adaptability, and alignment. The challenge, therefore, is to convert the broad outlines of robustness described in this book into more specific advice, all of it based on a deeper, more interpretative reading of the RAND knowledge base. Accordingly, this chapter is built around four "mini-chapters" on how robust organizations operate:

1. *Robust organizations think in futures (plural) tense.* They prepare for uncertainty by creating landscapes of possible futures; accept the inevitability of surprise; challenge their assumptions about the futures they face; reduce regret by adopting robust, adaptive plans, avoiding unintended consequences, and reducing vulnerability; and focus on the direct, indirect, and cascading effects of what they do. As such they are highly alert.

2. *Robust organizations organize for lightning.* They recruit their workforces for maximum flexibility; train for agility by drawing the right lessons from the past, reducing the cost of learning, and cultivating corporateness; set just-beyond-possible goals; provide authority to act; and think lean about every aspect of work. As such they are highly agile.

3. *Robust organizations challenge the prevailing wisdom.* They create both the freedom to learn and the freedom to imagine; aggregate expertise by creating teams and networks; unbalance their scorecards by measuring in futures tense, using multiple measures to avoid complacency and cheating, being careful about what they measure, and inviting intuition; and strengthen command and control to assure that investments are well spent. As such they are highly adaptive.

4. *Robust organizations lead to mission.* They grow and groom their own leaders; lead in futures tense; communicate through images and stories; anticipate their adversaries through careful study and assessment; and ignore irrelevant issues that impede command. As such they are tightly aligned.

Running Robust

1. Think in futures tense (alertness)

2. Organize for lightning (agility)

3. Challenge the prevailing wisdom (adaptability)

4. Lead to mission (alignment)

THINK IN FUTURES TENSE (ALERTNESS)

Robust organizations do not take any future as a given. To the contrary, they believe that many futures are possible. "Forecasting is inevitably a hazardous business," writes Charles Wolf. "To paraphrase Yogi Berra, 'It's dangerous to make predictions, especially about the future.' "[2]

Because RAND researchers reject the notion that any one future is knowable, they have specialized in developing methodologies for creating inventories of possibilities. Although some futures may be more likely than others, RAND researchers recommend that organizations take control of their destiny by thinking in futures tense, thereby abandoning the old *predict-then-act* model of action in favor of an *explore-then-adapt* approach that produces strategies that do well across a landscape of possibilities.

Thinking in Futures Tense

1. Explore the landscape of futures

2. Expect surprise

3. Challenge assumptions

4. Reduce regret

Explore the Landscape of Futures

Most organizations already accept the notion they face many futures, the only problem being that they only look at one or two futures at a time, often in isolation. The planning department may have one scenario of the future, the marketing department may have another, and the financial department may have still another. Instead of reasoning across a range of plausible futures, they often rush to define *the* most likely future.

The challenge is not to build consensus around a single future, however. It is to make sure that the organization understands that range of futures that might affect its performance. For organizations and industries in stable environments, doing so might involve little more than an occasional conversation built around signposts, or harbingers, of possible change. Under conditions of light turbulence, organizations make fewer assumptions about the future and face fewer vulnerabilities as a result. But as turbulence rises, so does the number of assumptions about the future, and the vulnerabilities to surprise.

Alternative futures become more valuable the further organizations look into the future. As RAND's John Gordon and Brian Nichiporuk write, trend projections are useful roughly 10 years into the future. For organizations that must make long-lasting decisions about product lines, recruitment strategies, training programs, and modernization plans, alternative futures provide an opportunity to examine common needs across a range of futures. The U.S. Army equipment needs in the dark future they label "chaos-anarchy" are very different from the equipment in the more hopeful future they call "democratic peace." In the first alternative future, the Army will need more light infantry with light armored vehicles and airborne support, as well as deep investments in protection against chemical, biological, nuclear, and toxic weapons. In the second, the Army will need a much smaller force, advanced nonlethal weapons, and more training for policing and peacekeeping activities. (See my modifications to Gordon and Nichiporuk's slide on the value of alternative futures for planning.)

The Value of Alternative Futures

▶ Trend projects are only useful for 10 years or so; beyond that they have much less utility

▶ Using a spectrum of futures enables one to see a range of possible modernization requirements for the organization

▶ Alternative futures make it easier to pursue a hedging strategy

  • What common needs might we see across a range of futures?

  • How appropriate is an organization's strategy and structure for various possible futures?

For organizations and industries in unstable environments, robustness starts with a sense of just how many plausible futures they face. Are there six compelling scenarios, as in the Army study just discussed? Three dozen, as in the Volvo SUV decision? Three hundred, as in global warming? Or three thousand, as in population planning?

The key term here is *possible futures*. Organizations are not required to imagine every alternative world out there. But they can develop very broad landscapes containing a wide range of possible, if not probable, futures. Just because there is no rain in the forecast, to use the picnic analogy of James Dewar, the director of RAND's Center for Longer-Range Global Policy and the Future Human Condition, does not mean that rain is impossible. It is one of many possible futures that might require a bit of action such as a contingency plan for moving the picnic table inside.

In an ideal world, organizations would adopt the plan that performed best across the landscape and let events take their course. However, the world is anything but ideal, and the future anything but fixed. Almost by definition, a robust plan will produce less than optimal results—it may perform reasonably well against all possible futures, but will almost always under-perform against any single future. More importantly, organizations may become so fixated on reducing volatility that they reject risky strategies that could produce great gains.[3]

The answer is not to abandon the search for robustness, however, but to adapt as events unfold. Organizations cannot adapt if they cannot spot the events, however, which is why RAND recommends creating signposts, or checkpoints, well into the future. As already noted, signposts reveal an important change in the validity or vulnerability of a key assumption about the future. As Dewar writes, signposts are closely related to three other concepts in traditional planning—aim points, which involve goals, targets, and/or objectives such as DuPont's 10-year innovation plan; strategic control, which compares strategic goals to progress made; and military indications and warning (I&W), which uses indicators such as social and political unrest to determine potential threats.

Whatever they are called, signposts constitute an early-warning system that helps organizations respond to impending change. RAND does not pretend to be expert in interpreting signs, which has spawned a separate research discipline called *semiotics*. Nor does RAND have an answer for every information bias. But RAND does believe organizations should establish signposts of *important* change, which Dewar defines as anything significant enough either to require a new plan or raise an alert, and be acutely aware of the problems in actually declaring a problem.

Organizations need to recognize the concept of defensive avoidance, for example, which leads individuals to reject unfavorable information as a shield from stress. They must also prepare for the kind of cultural and organizational avoidance that led U.S. automobile makers and Xerox to misinterpret the strength of the Japanese production system in the 1980s, and guard against bad or missing data, as well as plain old deception. As Dewar suggests, no one has come up with a better approach to identifying signposts than simply looking for ways in which a given plan can fail.

Expect Surprise

RAND researchers are just as fascinated by surprise as anyone, in part because surprises are so common. As Paul Davis argues, surprises are not occasional annoyances in an otherwise predictable word but, rather, a common occurrence in every field. Few predicted the Cuban missile crisis, the fall of the Shah of Iran, the disintegration of the Soviet Union, or the terrorist attacks on September 11, 2001.

"Why do so many predictions fail and surprises occur?" Davis asks. "The reasons include the constant competition of measures and countermeasures, the tendency to keep weaknesses out of mind only to have them attacked by the adversary, prosaic failures of design or execution, and a failure to appreciate the frictions of war...."[4]

RAND has long believed that the way to deal with uncertainty is to think of the world as a complex system in which small events can have major consequences. Who knows where a repair convoy might turn? Who knows which bunker holds the target and how many civilians might be nearby? As Davis cautions, "uncertainty is not only ubiquitous and large, but also impossible to get rid of by merely working hard to do so."

Noting that strategic planning can be either torture or insightful, expensive or lean, Davis and his colleagues at RAND recommend a planning sequence in which organizations start with a *no-surprises future* built on a simple extension of the present, then use branches and shocks to create alternative futures, develop hedges and contingency plans against those alternatives, and deploy capabilities that can be used against as many of these threats as possible.

The point is never to develop a single scenario against which to hedge. Rather, it is to develop a set of scenarios that allow one to test current action against alternative possibilities through techniques such as assumption-based planning. As Steven Bankes, Robert Lempert, and Steven Popper write, "No matter how inclusive the information gathering, how effective the analytic tools and techniques, how profound our insights, and how careful the resulting preparations, the future is certain to follow paths and offer events we did not imagine. Surprise takes many forms, all of which tend to disrupt plans and planning systems."

Surprise also involves challenges to the status quo, a point well illustrated in RAND's research on revolutions in military affairs, which involve sweeping changes in how wars are fought and won. Almost all of history's revolutions involved some sort of conceptual breakthrough that simply could not have been anticipated in advance—for example, Germany's use of the blitzkrieg, or lightning war, to overwhelm French defenses at the start of World War II, or England's use of the longbow to defeat French armored cavalry at Crecy in 1346.

Asked why some nations are more innovative than others, RAND's Jeffrey Isaacson, Christopher Layne, and John Arquilla answer that external threats, ambition, and the lack of resources all create incentives to innovate at the national level, while "product champions," career paths open to reformers, and recent failure all facilitate innovation at the organizational level. Drawing upon three detailed case studies, the RAND team concludes that *asymmetrical*, or one-sided, innovation is more likely to occur in weaker nations that face insurmountable threats than in stronger nations that are unchallenged. Unable to copy the military strategies of their more powerful opponents, these militaries have the greatest incentive to invent alternatives that allow them to win against high odds.[5]

From a robustness perspective, the team's most interesting example involves Paraguay's victory over Bolivia in the Chaco War, which lasted from 1932 to 1935. Paraguay had no business winning the war—Bolivia had a much stronger army and much greater incentives to occupy the lowlands between the Andes Mountains on the west. Moreover, Paraguay had almost no money to fight a war. In contrast with Bolivia, which had its oil revenues and all the modern technology available, as well as German military advisors, Paraguay had no tanks, only a few airplanes, and less than half as many soldiers. What Paraguay did have was 10 advanced mortars, and a novel strategy for fighting the war. The story of Paraguay's victory is every bit as compelling as any told about "Big Blue," Toyota, or General Electric.

The Paraguayans maneuvered their forces separately, employing decentralized, small (company-sized) units supported by their trench mortars, which had a highly disconcerting effect on the Bolivians. Though maneuvering separately, the Paraguayan detachments could also combine against portions of the Bolivian

Army. In this manner, the swarming tactics of the Paraguayans soon disrupted the Bolivian offensive, not least because the former avoided a classical decisive battle in favor of disrupting key nodes of the extended Bolivian logistics chain. The Bolivians fought with great valor, yet, despite their superior overall numbers, they fought most of the battles at a numerical disadvantage—they were being defeated in detail. The Bolivians had decided to imitate the most advanced armies of their day, but found themselves being defeated by a smaller, less-equipped force that had found a way to innovate.

As Isaacson and his coauthors conclude, the Bolivians were unable to defeat Paraguay's main force "mostly because there wasn't one!" Bolivia lost the war and all the territory it had occupied through years of encroachment, "not because it performed so poorly, but because the Paraguayans innovated and performed much better relative to their foes."

Although there is obviously a place for creativity in such revolutions, the study also suggests that most large-scale revolutions involve a number of innovations in technology, strategy, and organization in an often disorderly process that cannot be easily anticipated and can fail at several turns. "The necessary technology may exist, but the contemplated devices prove impractical," RAND's Richard Hundley writes. "It may not be possible to turn the new devices into viable systems. No operational concept may exist to employ an otherwise viable system concept." Even if all these conditions are met, the industry may be unable to accept the reality of change. Serendipitous invention may be the spark for the revolution, but it by no means a guarantee of ultimate success. Alertness to changing circumstances is essential, too.

Challenge Assumptions

Assumptions shape every aspect of performance—they help define problems, causes, and solutions, as well as images of the future. Social Security actuaries use three different sets of assumptions to describe the future: worst-case, best-guess, and best-case. During the bitter debates surrounding the 1983 Social Security funding crisis, the actuaries actually used five estimates: worst-worst-case, worst-case, best-guess, best-case, and a best-best-case based on the Reagan administration's own budget forecasts, which the budget director described as a "rosy scenario."[6]

RAND rarely accepts assumptions about the present as a given. According to RAND's John Birkler, "a lot of research shops will be committed to the position that the client wants. The Navy might say, 'Well, we need 12 carriers.' I'm not sure whether we need 12 or not. But when we were asked to do an analysis we can say, 'What are the implications of not having 12, or having more than 12?' So I'm not committed to a point of view that says we need this certain force structure. I think more in terms of, does that do the job and best accomplish your objectives relative to other systems or other approaches."

The number of carriers depends, therefore, on the Navy's mission. As Birkler and his colleague John Schank write in *The Atlantic Monthly*, there may be good reasons to build at least three more carriers:

> During the recent Iraq war only eight of the 12 U.S. carriers were deployable; five played important roles in the conflict, leaving only three available for action elsewhere. Simply keeping even those eight carriers deployable required that maintenance and crew-rotation plans be deferred—something that can't be done indefinitely. If a nuclear standoff with North Korea had escalated to war, or if Israel, Japan, or Taiwan had required U.S. military assistance, or even if the United States had simply needed to project power into the Indian Ocean or the Philippine Sea, taking adequate action would have been difficult.[7]

As noted early in this book, RAND has even invented a simple technique for questioning present-tense assumptions. *Assumption-based planning* is about as simple and inexpensive as planning can get. First, organizations identify the load-bearing assumptions underpinning their plan. Second, they identify the vulnerabilities embedded in those assumptions. Third, they define signposts that reveal the potential breakdown of an assumption. Fourth, they take shaping actions that address the impending breakdown. Finally, they select hedging actions that will reduce the impact of failed assumptions if and when they occur.

Assumption-based planning is best done when decision makers can compare their vision of the future against alternative *worlds*. "In our usage," stated Dewar and his colleagues in their easily readable introduction to the method, "a *world* is a hypothetical future situation in which a vulnerable assumption has been violated for one (or more) of the plausible reasons identified in Step 2. Such a world is not complete in the sense that it describes how every aspect of today's world has evolved. It is intended only to add to the plausibility of evolving from today's world into one in which the vulnerable assumption has changed."

Assumption-based planning is much easier than more formal strategic planning. All it requires is a commitment to questioning the assumptions that underpin a current plan. As such, it is not a planning technique, but a way to test a plan after it has been made. As Lempert explains, "Assumption-based planning is a very nice framework for finding vulnerabilities. It's very cheap, and it's simple.... You've got a plan and you look for vulnerabilities."

Just because it is simple does not make it costless, however. It can be just as disruptive as more elegant strategic planning, especially when it raises serious doubts about the basic assumptions on which an organization based its hopes. Moreover, assumption-based planning works better when plans are more detailed than loose, largely because the underlying assumptions are more easily described. It also works better when plans cover longer periods of time, largely because shaping and hedging actions take time to work their will. Finally, it works better when plans are being reviewed at the highest levels of the organization where resource decisions are made.

The allure of assumption-based planning is obvious. It can be used by organizations at virtually any stage of their life cycle. For the young non-profit, assumption-based planning can create a needed reality check about its very purpose for being; for the older manufacturing firm, assumption-based planning can force hard choices about a rapidly changing world. If a plan has no violated assumptions, organizations can move forward with a relatively small number of signposts that reveal important changes in the world—e.g., funding cutbacks by a state government, radical innovation in a market. If a plan has violated assumptions, organizations can decide whether they can shape and hedge themselves out of the problem. If so, they can take appropriate action; if not, they must change the plan.

Having helped design the methodology, Dewar now has his hands full as the director of the Frederick S. Pardee Center for Longer Range Global Policy and the Future Human Condition. According to its mission statement, the Pardee Center was established "to improve our ability to think about the longer-range future—from thirty-five to two-hundred years ahead—and to develop new methods of analyzing the potential long-range, global effects of today's policy options in order to design sound policies that are sensitive to those effects."[8]

Reduce Regret

RAND does not have a crystal ball for imagining the future. Rather, it has invented a wide range of techniques, some formal, some informal, but all rigorous, to create a "scenario space" that includes a number of possible futures against which organizations can hedge.

Some of those futures involve what RAND researchers characterize as deep uncertainty. "Basically, deep uncertainty is when decision makers don't know or can't agree on the model that relates actions to consequences, don't agree on the probabilities, and don't agree on the values that should be used to judge the desirability of various outcomes," Lempert explained to me. If decision makers face a lot of factors that affect outcomes, but can characterize all the probabilities, they can use some variation of standard decision analysis. If they're running an electric grid or building an airplane, they can use that pretty easily."

In other words, standard models work particularly well if the world behaves a certain predictable way. But what if the world does not behave predictably? "We're interested in situations where decision makers really don't know the model," says Lempert. "They can do A, B, or C, but having pulled the lever, they're not quite sure what the response is going to be. They might know something about the possible responses, but there's the Paul Light theorem, the Robert Lempert theorem, and others competing for attention."

Steven Popper describes this as the *three-apes problem*:

A fruit-laden tree grows on a prehistoric savanna. A bipedal ape-human comes to the edge of the brush and ponders the risk of crossing the grasslands to gather a meal. Is a lion lurking in the high cover? She notices the swish of a tail: "Swishing tail→ Active lion→Danger." She withdraws. Later, a second ape long familiar with this patch comes by. No swishing tail, yet she knows that every so often a troop mate has been lost in gathering fruit here. How often? She considers the risks, balances her need, and determines whether to cross. Now a third ape approaches this stretch of savanna for the first time. She can draw upon neither concrete information nor familiarity with this patch as a basis for logical deduction. She is, however, quite hungry and her survival hangs in the balance. She searches for familiar patterns and weighs them against her experience. She takes a few steps forward and then looks for changes in the patterns. How far can she proceed and still scramble back to safety? Where might a lion hide in this brush? Is that movement over there solely due to the wind? She ventures forth step-by-step, updating information, planning for contingencies, perhaps tossing a rock or two to probe for any lurking predators. In this manner she proceeds into a potentially terrifying unknown.[9]

As Popper says, human beings often find themselves in a similar situation. "This is still the way people reason under uncertainty—for we must certainly call this reason. It is not the deductive, fact-based process we rightly consider one of the glories of human civilization. Rather, it is based on a precivilized, near-innate system of inductive analysis that has stood, and continues to stand, our species in good stead. It is not a system inclined to produce unbiased estimators."

Unfortunately, it is a system that performs poorly, if only because there is so much information about so many alternative futures that no one human being or organization can handle it all. Tempting though it might be to bet the company on gut instinct, many RAND researchers argue that organizations should aim instead to reduce regret across a range of plausible futures, which is exactly what Volvo did in introducing the XC90. Reducing regret involves a commitment to robustness, a focus on unintended consequences, and efforts to reduce vulnerabilities through deliberate action, not hopes and prayers.

Reducing Regret

▶ Start robust, then adapt

▶ Avoid the unintended

▶ Reduce vulnerability

Start Robust, Then Adapt RAND's work on preparing for alternative futures is clearly about helping the third ape. "I think what we're trying to do is really systemize and better support the types of thinking that people intuitively do," Lempert says. "We want to help them do it much better."

Under these conditions, RAND recommends "robust, rather than optimal, strategies that perform 'well enough' by meeting or exceeding selected criteria across a broad range of plausible futures and alternative ways of ranking the desirability of alternative scenarios." Decision makers should work together to construct a plan, then try to break it and send it to the computer, which tries to break it again, then bring it back to decision makers who try to hedge it. The result is a robust, adaptive plan.

Unlike assumption-based planning, which is relatively simple to implement, robust adaptive decision making demands extensive interaction between humans and computers in search of a plan that fails most gracefully. Basically, robust adaptive decision making allows decision makers to look for unknown vulnerabilities with the help of a computer. The focus is on robustness, not achieving the greatest immediate gain, recognizing that the most profitable plan in an expected future may not be the safest across all plausible futures. A plan can be called robust if it has considered a variety of alternative futures, threats, and possibilities, and come out with the best results.

Lempert describes the methodology as follows: "When you think you have the right strategy, you use the computer to try and break it. When you're stuck or when the computer suggests a robust strategy, then you challenge people to try to break it. When you can't find a plan that you think works, the computer can help you. When the computer's stuck, then you try to add other things that can fix it."

As Lempert notes, robust adaptive decision making is most appropriate when the future is complex. "We can elicit experts from Exxon-Mobil in one room and the experts from Greenpeace in another" to come up with probabilities relating to future climate change, for example, Lempert says, and "lo and behold, the distributions are very different. If I put all the experts together, I get a food fight, not better distribution. Exxon-Mobil and Greenpeace have very different assumptions about how the climate will evolve. Science can resolve many of these differences, but we may have to wait to find out who is right. We don't want to do that."

Dealing with complexity does not always require robust, adaptive planning, however. "You don't consult a planner in raising your kids," says Lempert. "It's a complex system, but one with which we have a huge amount of experience that you expect has some bearing on your individual kid. Parents gather up folk wisdom to get their intuition going and explore multiple scenarios in their head. People oftentimes make pretty good decisions in situations of deep uncertainty because they have some intuition about how the system works."

As Lempert contends, people are pretty good at other things, too:

> If you have a room full of people and everybody picks something different, then what do you do? People are pretty good at saying, "Gee, how about if we approach the problem this way and do this? We could reach a compromise. This will get us what we want."
>
> They're also good at games or challenges. If I come up and say that no one can think of any plausible future that can break this scenario, people are really good at coming up with counter

examples. There's the wonderful deep literature on the strengths and weaknesses of human decision making that says cab drivers can basically tell you all the things that people do wrong. They can see patterns where they don't exist. They convince themselves that things are true that they want to be true, which are demonstrably not true; you can spend a little more time showing they're not true in those group things. It's all that sort of stuff.[10]

As noted earlier in this book, robust adaptive decision making is designed to marry computer capacity with intuition to support the thinking that people intuitively do. The computer loop is designed to test plan after plan to see which ones produce the greatest regret. The human loop is designed to break the computer model. "You go back, people come up with hypotheses, and you wire those in as best you can into your models, and test those." The result is what Lempert calls the irreducible trade-offs:

> For example, here's strategy A, and here's strategy B. We've made them both as well hedged as we can make them. The world might break this way, in which case B is better. Here are some scenarios that are really hard to hedge against, two really different sets of scenarios or futures. If you want to hedge against both of them, you don't do very well in either. You can guess this way and hedge as best as you can against those, but you've got to choose A or B.
>
> Ultimately what the analysis is doing is trying to come up with clever strategies that hedge as best as they can to try and reduce those tradeoffs from 40 or 50 different things you have to worry about to just a couple. Then you characterize them for the decision makers, and the decision makers have to guess which way to go. That's what they're paid for, right?

If decision makers will not make the decisions, however, no amount of future focus will help. Doing so is not about charisma or intelligence. It is about the willingness to choose. Thus once a robust adaptive plan is made, the organization must be willing to change directions if circumstances change.

Avoid the Unintended RAND researchers have plenty of experience studying unintended consequences, starting with the bomber study. Although some unintended effects are impossible to predict, many are the products of sloppy analysis and simple errors in judgment.

Consider RAND's ongoing studies of California's effort to cut class sizes by offering school districts roughly $800 for every student enrolled in a class of 20 or fewer students. By 1999 the program covered 1.8 million kindergarten to third-grade students at a cost of more than $1.5 billion a year.

The question for RAND was not whether the program succeeded in an absolute sense—class sizes did go down. Rather, RAND asked how the schools achieved the results. Did students do better in smaller classes, and what did the schools do to push the numbers down?

The answer revealed a small gain in student performance but significant declines in teacher quality. According to RAND's ongoing evaluations, which it conducted in partnership with three other research organizations, teacher quality went down with class size. "The proportion of teachers with full credentials decreased in all grades, as did the proportion of teachers with the minimum level of college education (only a bachelor's degree) and the proportion of experienced teachers (those with more than three years of experience)."

Although there were several potential explanations for the decline, including a growing school-age population, RAND found that the problem of underqualified teachers was greatest exactly where the class-size reductions occurred, in elementary schools. RAND also found that teachers in smaller classes spent more time on individual and small-group instruction, and reported more satisfaction with their ability to meet student needs. However, teachers in both big and small classes covered just about the same amount of material over the year. Although the benefits of smaller class size appeared to last into fourth grade, it did not close the gap between low-income, minority, or English-learner students.

Given that the program was only a few years old at the time of its second evaluation, RAND has been appropriately cautious about the actual impacts. Some would take the small positive effect as proof-positive that the program had worked, while others would wonder whether the benefits were worth the cost. At least in 1999, RAND's researchers could not make a judgment on whether smaller classes were part of high-performing schools or not.

Those who want an even more cautionary tale about unintended consequences need only talk with RAND's senior researcher, Stephen Hosmer. As Hosmer says, his research on operations against enemy leaders covers a range of questions: "How might you make the best use of air power in such operations? What are the lessons for the decision maker based on the experience to date? Except where substantial U.S. military forces have participated in the overthrow of a regime, U.S. attempts to oust enemy leaders have proved very difficult. Operations to remove enemy leaders by direct attack or through U.S. support to coups and rebellions have mainly failed. And then there can be catastrophic unintended consequences." Consider Hosmer's analysis of the 1993 attack on the headquarters of Somali rebel leader Mohammed Farrah Aidid as an example: The idea was to cripple the command structure of Aidid's Somali National Alliance's organization, and if possible, to eliminate Aidid himself. Unfortunately, the attack killed a number of elders and religious leaders from Aidid's subclan.

> This had three bad effects. First, it greatly strengthened Aidid's political backing in Somalia at a time when we were trying to reduce it. Second, it made it almost impossible to reach a negotiated solution of the conflict we had with the National Alliance. And third, it motivated Somalis to kill Americans. They were so motivated that more than 1000 Somali men, women, and children were killed and wounded in suicide-type attacks against the U.S. Rangers following the crash of a Blackhawk helicopter in October 1993.
>
> The U.S. losses from the shootout precipitated our eventual withdrawal from Somalia. That retreat, along with the earlier U.S. withdrawal from Lebanon, apparently encouraged Osama Bin Laden to believe that the way you get Americans out of the area is to kill them.
>
> That was a disastrous counterproductive operation. The lesson for decision makers is that they must very carefully assess the downside of leadership attacks. And doing so requires accurate intelligence and informed advice from area specialists who understand the culture and what effects a leadership attack is likely to have.

As Hosmer demonstrates, the U.S. has rarely succeeded in such operations. Direct attacks against enemy leaders such as Aidid and Saddam Hussein have created enormous unintended consequences, while coups and rebellions appear to work only against weakly protected governments.

The fact is that most enemy leaders take at least some care to protect themselves, making such operations difficult at best. "Over the past 50 years," writes Hosmer, "the United States has had no success in removing enemy heads of state by direct attack and only very limited success in promoting the overthrow of hostile regimes by coup or rebellion. The only consistently successful way the United States has been able to remove hostile governments during the post–World War II era has been by invasion and occupation—and such takedowns have been attempted only against weakly armed opponents."

It is important to note that Hosmer's analysis is intensely rigorous, but not quantitative. He takes great care in describing each case, but has no cost-effectiveness model at the end of the book. His analysis of the 1986 air strike against Libyan leader Muammar Qaddafi is dispassionate, but chilling nonetheless. Although the laser-guided missiles came within 50 feet of Qaddafi's residence, and left him psychologically shaken, the attack reportedly killed Qaddafi's 15-month-old daughter, seriously injured two of his sons, and may have injured his wife. But because Qaddafi was probably in an underground bunker at the time, he escaped uninjured.

Despite the hope that the raid would deter Qaddafi from terrorism, it may have played a role in Libya's decision to orchestrate the bombing of Pan Am Flight 103. As Hosmer notes, the Lockerbie tragedy killed more U.S. citizens than the Berlin disco bombing that prompted the air strike in the first place. Even more important perhaps, the raid may have led Qaddafi and other heads of state toward the more indirect and dangerous forms of non-state-sponsored terrorism that al Qaeda represents.

Reduce Vulnerability Organizations that think in futures tense must identify their vulnerability to threats and surprise. Doing so involves a simple process for highlighting the load-bearing assumptions that support a given plan, and the vulnerabilities that might break them.

As Dewar maintains, assumptions can be vulnerable in many ways. During the Cold War, for example, the Army's plan for preventing a Soviet invasion of Western Europe relied on putting thousands of U.S. troops in the way. There were many ways that the plan could have been wrong. As he says, "The threat could have disappeared (as has happened), Europe could have been overrun, the Europeans could have asked the Army to leave, public opinion in the United States could have forced the president to call for troop withdrawal, and the United States could have disbanded its army. At any given planning horizon, these specific changes were more or less plausible. As a rule of thumb, *any* plausible change in the world that would cause an assumption to fail within the planning time horizon is sufficient to identify that assumption as vulnerable."

Once basic assumptions have been identified, organizations must create signposts of possible breakdown. Dewar believes that "the best approach in an uncertain planning environment is do what needs doing *now* and to watch out for changes that will resolve the uncertainties in the future." As noted earlier signposts are merely events or thresholds that clearly indicate the changing vulnerability of an assumption—either the assumption is holding firm, which requires no action, or it is starting to break.

Take book publishing as an example, Dewar says, where literacy rates could rise or fall, television viewing could increase or decrease, bookstores could stay open later or close earlier, and pulp prices could fall or rise. Signposts do not have to be negative to act—publishers might sign more books if literacy rates are increasing, for example, or increase their sales force if more bookstores are opening.

But whether positive or negative, signposts carry implied action. Simply asked, what will the organization do to control or shape a situation so that an important assumption does not fail? A shaping action is simply another form of adaptation—an organization spots an impending breakdown and responds.

Dewar contends that the decision to act depends on a mix of alertness (warning time) and the agility (the ability to act). If an organization has enough warning time and can move quickly, it does not need to act at all until the failure becomes more certain. If it has enough warning time but cannot act quickly, it must take shaping action as soon as it sees an impending breakdown. In turn, if an organization has little or no warning time and can move quickly, it can wait until the future becomes clearer before it must act. If it has little or no warning time and cannot act quickly, it must take shaping action as soon as possible. Alertness provides the warning time, while agility (and the adaptability and alignment to go with it) provides the ability to move quickly. (See Dewar's warning tree.)

If shaping actions are impossible because warning time is limited or the future is turbulent, robust organizations can take hedging actions to prepare themselves for the potential failure of a critical assumption. Whereas shaping actions take place in response to some future event, hedging occurs in the present and involves an effort to prepare the organization for the failure of a load-bearing assumption. Doing so might involve further Delphi research or a more structured approach such as RAND's Vulnerability Assessment & Mitigation Methodology (VAM), which it invented to deal with a host of threats to information systems, not the least of which are human weaknesses such as gullibility or rigidity.

But whatever the technique, be it intuitive or highly structured, robust organizations worry about the vulnerabilities that reside just beyond tomorrow, and take action when needed to shape and hedge. As a result, such organizations are *fault tolerant*: Their current plans are well-hedged against volatility, and their signposts are well positioned to reveal possible breakdowns that cannot be foreseen.

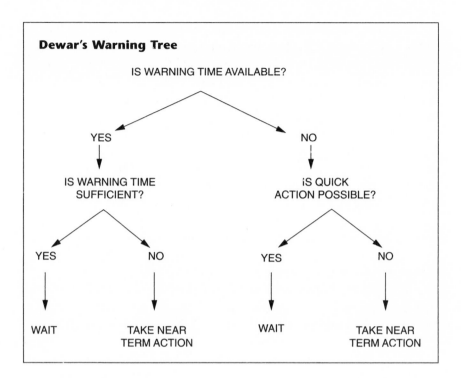

Dewar's Warning Tree

IS WARNING TIME AVAILABLE?

YES — IS WARNING TIME SUFFICIENT?
- YES → WAIT
- NO → TAKE NEAR TERM ACTION

NO — IS QUICK ACTION POSSIBLE?
- YES → WAIT
- NO → TAKE NEAR TERM ACTION

Focus on Effects

It is one thing to caution organizations to avoid unintended consequences and quite another to give them the tools to "focus fire" on an intended effect. Moreover some negative effects may be simply unavoidable.

The effort to help organizations create intended effects has produced some of RAND's most promising recent research, including much of its work on creating more accurate ensembles of possible futures. It has even prompted Paul Davis to imagine what he calls "a grand challenge for the analytical community" in thinking about effects-based operations as a core operating principle of a high-performing military. Despite its heavy focus on military success, the method is relevant for almost any organization interested in creating impacts, be it in the arts, education, or health, be it in government, business, or the nonprofit sector.

According to Davis, an effects-based operation starts with a basic commitment to *"mission-system capability,* which refers to the no-excuses ability to accomplish missions under a wide range of operational circumstances and to characterize the range of circumstances for which the capabilities are sufficient to provide different degrees of confidence." In other words, what do organizations need to succeed in a variety of settings?

Anchored in advanced mathematics and modeling, RAND's effort to advance the research on effects-based operations is often esoteric. It is also clearly rooted in what Davis labels "the revolt of the war fighters," including the young Air Force officers who were appalled by "the frequently mindless and ineffective use of air power in Vietnam....When their turn to lead came, they were determined to do better."

It is also driven by the "revolt against standard models and analysis." As Davis readily admits, "most modeling and analysis still encourages a mechanistic view of warfare that emphasizes firepower and attrition while ignoring other critical aspects of strategy, such as maneuver of forces and fires, command and control, and aspects that relate to each side's effort to attack its opponent's strategy, will, cohesion, and cognition—as in a drive for decision superiority." Substitute the words *sales, manufacturing*, and *services* for the word *warfare*, and you have a nice summary of the current frustration with academic research on organizational life.

The notion that organizations should develop plans based on what he calls the "direct, indirect, and cascading effects" of each option makes perfect sense. The challenge is to make sure that all the effects are fully understood. Although Davis might well take offense at the idea of an informal version of effects-based operations, especially given his deep commitment to modeling, the ethos of the method is applicable across almost every aspect of organizational life. Wars are not the only events that take place in complex systems that are mysterious and hard to predict.

RAND and its researchers have used very informal versions of effects-based evaluation to study a variety of programs. In 2001, for example, RAND released an informal effects-based evaluation of the California Wellness Foundation's $60-million Violence Prevention Initiative (VPI). Launched in 1993, the 10-year initiative seeks its impact through an interaction of community action, policy change, leadership development, and research, each of which is built around specific programs. Under the policy program, for example, the Pacific Center for Violence Prevention has been working to reduce access to firearms through legislation, while other grantees have held been working to educate the entertainment industry on the link between violence on the screen and violence in real life.

The question for the RAND researchers was not whether the collection of initiatives made sense, but whether they actually produced a measurable effect. As they report, the data on the actual decline in youth violence provides little evidence on the initiative's effects: "Violence did begin to decline at a faster rate almost everywhere VPI existed, and it is plausible to believe that these programs had something to do with that drop. But because violence dropped almost everywhere else as well, it is impossible to distinguish the drop 'caused by' VPI-funded programs and other factors that may have played an important role.... While the failure to find a statistical detectable proof that these programs 'caused' the drop in violence is a disappointment, what actually happened is a reason for celebration."

The most important contribution of the evaluation was not in the specific data, however. It was in the rounded analysis of the combined effects of the overall initiative. As the California Wellness Foundation notes in the preface to RAND's final report, "given the relatively modest size of our grants, a whole range of other simultaneous interventions, and a booming state economy, it would take real hubris to assert that the VPI should get the credit."

Effects-based planning might have helped increase impacts in two ways. First, it would have helped the California Wellness Foundation anticipate an alternative future that might have changed its grant-making priorities. Second, effects-based planning might have helped the foundation create even greater cascading effects across its collection of programs. As the foundation notes, the ultimate success of the initiative depends on creating a social movement of the kind one sees in RAND's case studies of networked organizations. Exploiting such opportunities requires an agility rarely found in philanthropies, but one well worth imagining through effects-based planning.

ORGANIZE FOR LIGHTNING (AGILITY)

Agility comes from many sources, not the least of which is technology. The Army designed the Stryker combat vehicle to move troops into combat faster, while the Air Force has reorganized itself into an aerospace expeditionary force designed to get anywhere within 48 hours. Together, the two are working toward deploying airborne forces quickly and safely, creating what one RAND report calls *lightning over water*.

According to the analysis, agility involves more than just a change in strategy and new technology. It also requires an agile workforce. Robust organizations worry constantly about preparing their workforces for the future, not the past. They focus on putting the right people in the right jobs with the right incentives and achievable goals. In doing so, they expand their talent base, not by adding staff, but by increasing productivity.

RAND has plenty to say about building a robust workforce, much of it drawn from studying military recruitment on behalf of the armed services, particularly the Army and Air Force. Regardless of the sponsor, however, RAND clearly believes that people matter to performance.

My favorite RAND study on the question is titled *The Effect of Personnel Quality on the Performance of Patriot Air Defense Operators.* Published in 1994 with a pale green cover, it is just about the most unattractive RAND report in my files. But it also happens to be one of the most important. Simply put, the study found that smarter soldiers hit more hostile aircraft, thereby wasting fewer missiles. Moreover, smarter soldiers need less training and experience to do their jobs well. A one-level change in the standard measure of quality equals or surpasses a full year of experience.

This is not to suggest that training is irrelevant. As the study concludes, soldiers learn key skills on the job, most importantly whether and when to engage aircraft. Even more importantly, they tend to learn more when they are trained as part of a unit than as individuals.

I am not the only one who likes the study. "I'll tell you what I like about it," says RAND's Beth Asch. "First of all, it's really difficult to measure performance in so many ways. When you can measure performance, who cares because the job isn't all that important? Here's a case where performance was multidimensional but with a lot of thought and effort the researchers were able to measure performance by watching individuals in simulations and monitor their actions. It was also a really important study especially since it came out just after the Gulf War. Most important, the policy implications were really dramatic about the effects of aptitude on productivity."

People are only part of the equation, however. Robust organizations organize for lightning deliberately. They do not just recruit anyone for the job, for example, nor do they delegate authority randomly. Rather, they recruit for a range of futures, train for changing circumstances, set incentives carefully, and streamline their systems to be as lean as possible.

Organizing for Lightning

1. Recruit in futures tense
2. Train for agility
3. Set just-beyond-possible goals
4. Provide authority to act
5. Think lean

Recruit in Futures Tense

RAND has spent an enormous amount of energy over the years learning how to recruit employees, much of it for the military. Once the U.S. abandoned the draft for a voluntary force, the military had no choice but to learn how to attract and retain high-quality talent. After all, the military relies on a closed, single-entry-point system—there is only one way in, at the bottom.

As the military would almost certainly admit, the learning curve had to accelerate with the changing labor market. During the 1970s and 1980s, the military met its annual targets by concentrating on high school graduates who had no intention of going on to college. By the 1990s, however, college had become the destination of choice for two thirds of high school graduates. Either the military had to get much better at recruiting college-bound students or target a dwindling share of the labor market.

The military has made some progress with experiments, such as the Army's *College First* program, which repays up to $65,000 in college loans and pays money stipends during the first two years of college, and the Navy's *CASH* and *tech-prep* programs, which provide similar benefits for students who intend to pursue key occupations such as hospital corpsmen and nuclear-related fields.

However, RAND states that the military still has some distance to go, especially given the coming talent war over skilled employees. Although the College First program shows significant promise, the military must do more than promise its recruits new skills for a highly-competitive labor market through its *Army of One* advertisements, or locate recruiting posts in shopping malls, which RAND calls "going to the mines to look for diamonds."

The military must also become much more aggressive at defining its recruiting goals. Consider James Hosek's analysis of the twenty-first century soldier as an example.[11] "The future may or may not threaten a major war, but it requires the ability to fight and win one," Hosek writes. The emphasis must be on both versatility and leadership at all levels of the armed services, which requires a robust workforce planning process that will create a robust, adaptive workforce.

The first step in building such a process is to imagine the future. According to Hosek, there are at least six different visions of what soldiers might be asked to do in the future. Some will be *cyber soldiers* who enter enemy territory in advance of conflict as spotters for precision weaponry. Others will be *information warriors* who provide the first line of defense against netwar. Still others will be specialists in humanitarian aid and policing, or experts in running highly automated equipment.

Hosek's descriptions of the cyber soldier could be easily amended for any private firm, albeit absent the war-fighting language: "The cyber soldier belongs to a small unit whose mission is to penetrate enemy territory, engage in surveillance and reconnaissance, with the assistance of advanced sensors, and call in remote-fire precision guided weapons." Armed with advanced sensor technology, secure information networks, and computer software capable of tracking large numbers of targets, the cyber soldier will be entrusted with life-and-death decisions that once belonged to senior officers, and will need both the training and integrity to use this authority wisely.

Like the other soldiers of the future, cyber soldiers must come from the top of the labor market, not the bottom. The question, therefore, is what the military can do to compete against private and nonprofit organizations to win its fare share of the talent. The answer involves a mix of increased pay, guaranteed access to training, and experimentation with new recruiting packages, all of which demand increased flexibility in organizations that were built on conformity.

It is not enough just to recruit talent at the bottom of the organization. The military must also become better at holding onto middle- and senior-level talent. It must also become better at holding onto experience, especially among personnel who face the turmoil associated with boiling peace.

The military is hardly the only industry that needs to deploy in futures tense. According to RAND's 1996 study, local bus and rail agencies face two very different problems as their employees confront increasingly sophisticated transit systems, one involving a shortage of technical skills among current and future maintenance workers, and the other involving the transition from traditional to high-performance organizations.

Even if the first problem could be solved through more aggressive recruitment and higher pay, the second problem will only yield to the creation of learning organizations. Drawing upon lessons from leading private firms, RAND research shows that transit organizations must understand the need for change: "Where there is an external catalyst, such as the threat of contracting out work or cuts in funding, then the case for change may be clear. In the absence of an external threat, however, able leadership can still bring about radical change. The key is to start the process by sharing the rationale for reform and the vision for the future with employees."

As RAND's transit research shows, recruitment is only the first step in preparing the workforce to succeed. Organizations must also set clear expectations for workforce engagement, a point well made in RAND's work on lean manufacturing where the engagement of all participants in the value chain is essential for success. This means more than just motivational speeches and tales about fish or whales. Workers must receive training on new methods of production, for example, and must learn how to conduct the kind of root-cause problem analysis that James Quinlivan saw on his Saturn tour.

This does not mean that everyone becomes an admiral or general, however. Rather, it means a new relationship in deploying an organization's human capital. As the RAND research team reports, "Even the newest mechanics and operators have some insight into the machines, the processes, and the practices based on their day-to-day experience.... As holders of critical expertise, manufacturing operators should be given the authority to make decisions relevant to their work, without having to get approval from a manager for routine decisions." As the RAND team also notes, they should also expect their ideas and suggestions to be taken seriously, which ultimately requires a commitment to trust and mutual assistance on both sides of the traditional labor-management dialogue.

Train for Agility

Recruiting in futures tense is only the first step in creating an agile workforce. Once recruited, employees must be trained for a changing world.

However, many organizations still rely on educational and training models designed to meet the needs of the past. As RAND notes, the current system was built on the notion that most employees would arrive at their first job with most of the knowledge needed for a 40-year career.

The notion fails on two counts today. First, many employees arrive at their first jobs without the agility needed to succeed, and, second, many employees cannot get the training they need to gain agility once they start work. Even if the educational system provided the basic knowledge needed for global competitiveness, which it does not, most organizations do not provide the training to stay current as the world changes.

Most international organizations know what they are looking for, however. They want professionals with a repertoire of skills built around attitudes and traits, not professional and technical knowledge. The demand is clear in RAND's study of 75 international organizations such as Accenture, AIG, Bank America Corporation, BP Amoco, Cisco, General Mills, Hewlett-Packard, Merck, Microsoft, Pfizer, Procter & Gamble, Schlumberger, Sun Microsystems, TRW, and Unocal.

Asked to rank 19 attributes of a successful professional, the business respondents ranked general cognitive skills such as problem solving and analytical ability first; followed by interpersonal and relationship skills, tolerance for ambiguity and adaptability; personal traits such as character, self-reliance, and dependability; innovation and ability to take risks; competitiveness and drive; and ability to work well in different cultures. Written and spoken English language skills came in last on the list, just ahead of knowledge of international affairs, and managerial training and experience. (See Tora Bikson's briefing slide on the changing workforce.)

The Changing Workforce

▶ Across sectors, a majority of respondents report a desire for new competencies alongside the traditional:

- Advanced, specialized domain knowledge

- Continuous learning

- Teamwork and negotiation skills

- International experience and understanding

▶ Traditional competencies are still highly valued (e.g., general cognitive and interpersonal skills; personal strengths such as character, self-reliance; ambiguity tolerance, adaptability; strategy and policy thinking)

▶ An integrative repertoire of high-level competencies is in greatest need and shortest supply

- Substantive depth (related to the organization's primary business processes)

- Managerial ability (with an emphasis on motivating and guiding teamwork)

- Strategic understanding (seeing implications of the global environment and local context for primary business processes that cross borders)

- International experience and crosscultural sensitivity

If the demand for agile thinking is clear, the supply of agile employees is not. According to a recent Rand assessment, most organizations expect major skills deficits as the baby boomers begin to retire. Given the long lead times involved in changing the educational system, RAND's study team worries most about the middle- and upper-level of organizations, where training opportunities are generally meager and poorly designed, and career development is often self-initiated, ad hoc, and unrelated to the organization's strategic plans.

Organizations can either wait for the U.S. educational system to get better, or become much more aggressive at building agility once employees are hired. For organizations that decide act now by training in futures tense. RAND research suggests three general strategies toward this end: draw the right lessons from the past, reduce the cost of learning, and cultivate *corporateness* across the workforce.

Training for Agility

▶ Draw the right lessons

▶ Reduce the cost of learning

▶ Cultivate corporateness

Draw the Right Lessons   Paradoxically, the place to start training in futures tense is to stop training in past tense. Unfortunately, training programs are notoriously hard to change, in part because of organizational resistance. As the old joke goes, changing curricula is like moving the bones in a graveyard—you don't know who owns the bones until you start digging.

The voluminous literature on how the U.S. won the 1991 Gulf War is a case in point. In the rush to judgment that followed the 100-hour battle, many analysts drew the wrong lessons about success. Some argued that the Air Force had made the difference, celebrating the F-117 stealth fighter for its role in the campaign; others pointed to the logistics effort, noting that the U.S. moved more material by air to the Gulf in five weeks than it had moved in all 56 weeks of the 1948-1949 Berlin airlift; and still others emphasized the impact of electronic warfare, which crippled the Iraqi communication system. But as RAND's William Lambeth argued in 1993, there is a key distinction between the *little* lessons learned about how the war was fought and the *big* lessons that might shape future preparation.

Worried that the main lessons learned from the war might be limited to the need for better bomb fuses, Lambeth argued that the U.S. was "phenomenally lucky" in the days leading up to war. "For one thing, we had five and a half months to plan, build up forces, and train in theater to make this story come true," he writes. "This was definitely *not* a come-as-you-are war. We used every minute of time we had available to good effect. We could probably have used even more."

In addition, the U.S. benefited greatly from Saddam Hussein's decision not to invade Saudi Arabia, which could have created an entirely different outcome. "Whatever the Saudi reaction might have been, there is no way a few squadrons of American F-15s and F-16s could have prevented a determined Iraqi advance on the ground." As a result, the U.S. had the luxury of starting the war at a time of its own choosing.

Finally, the U.S. had Saddam Hussein as its adversary, a point discussed below. As Lambeth writes, Hussein misjudged how the U.S. would respond to the Kuwait invasion, and just about everything that followed: "About whether the United States would respond beyond words; about American staying power and domestic support once committed; about the cohesion of the allied coalition; about his former Soviet friends; about the effects of modern air power; about his defensive fortifications in and around Kuwait; and about the 'mother of all battles' and his prospect of sucking the United States into a bleeding war of attrition that would run up high American casualties before it ended."

Without discounting the role of diplomacy, preparation, 15 years of realistic flight training for fighter aircrews, a chain of command that worked, and the piles and piles of material shipped to the Gulf, Lambeth predicted that there would be a strong push from "some quarters," likely contractors and high-technology aficionados, to make technology the hero of the war. Although technology did make a difference, the U.S. succeeded in large measure because it had the right people in the right place at the right time with the right plan, not because of technology, smart bombs, or stealth. "We would have fought the war less brilliantly without them, and we would have paid a far higher price for our success. But with the leadership, the training, the quality of personnel, and the morale that we also commanded, it would have been for naught."

It is a lesson well worth remembering in designing any training curriculum. Helping employees master the revolutions in materials and manufacturing, information, and global commerce involves more than the latest gadget. It also involves the thinking skills discussed above and a deliberate effort to cull for lessons learned. RAND's own search for knowledge led to this book, for example, and underpins its general commitment to rigorous analysis.

This commitment also underpins a number of recent RAND recommendations for organizational improvement, including RAND's strategy for making the Los Angeles Police Department more professional. "Maintaining professional expertise is a continual process," RAND's research team concludes. "A profession will stagnate, lapse in its expertise, or otherwise fail in its service to society if it does not constantly update the knowledge of its members." Unfortunately, most police forces leave the learning to chance—officers learn on the job or in the wake of major controversies, such as the Los Angeles riots.

As RAND's researchers report, the LAPD is hardly the only organization that learns by accident. Having long suffered from similar problems during both war and peace, the Army created a discrete learning platform called the Center for Army Lessons Learned (CALL) in 1985. As RAND describes the center, "CALL collects lessons, observations, insights, and suggestions from the Army's major combat training centers.... The organization also allows any soldier, anywhere, anytime, to provide his or her observations on how the army might better prepare for conflict."

Organizations do not necessarily need a special unit to generate formal reports. What they do need is some device for collecting knowledge, sorting it, and disseminating it. There are thousands of lessons learned out there. The challenge is to pick the right ones for the situation at hand.

As for the Army's Center, its lessons learned became a little too public for the military's taste in October 2003, when a report on intelligence problems in Iraq surfaced in *The Washington Post*.[12] According to the report, U.S. intelligence was weak at best and useless at worst. The unmanned aerial vehicles (UAVs), which had had been the tool of choice for collecting information during the early phase of the war, were so slow that they were rarely close enough to an attack to be of value, while Army operators were often so poorly trained that they could not analyze the information collected. As a result, the "daily mortar and rocket attacks on bases and convoys became virtually undetectable to the UAVs."

Reduce the Cost of Learning New training programs are useless without the opportunity to learn. Unfortunately, many organizations continue to rely upon training methods that are anything but agile.

The problem is not so much a lack of investment, however, but a lack of access and strategy. According to the study of international organizations cited earlier in this chapter, most career development activities are self-initiated, ad hoc, and poorly linked to overall strategy. Moreover, as RAND concluded, the most widely used approaches (e.g., courses) are those least likely to yield the desired learning (e.g., integration of substantive and managerial skills).

These organizations face two challenges in helping employees learn. First, they must make it easier to say *yes* to learning, whether through direct assistance or new training technologies. Second, they must make sure the training programs are worth taking.

United Parcel Service (UPS) has made significant progress on the first challenge through its Earn and Learn program, which serves as both a recruitment and training tool. Launched in 1999, the program has paid out more than $47 million in tuition assistance in helping 30,000 employees attend college, boosting both productivity and loyalty. Available in 51 locations by 2004, the program provides $3000 per year in tuition for its part-time frontline employees and $4000 per year for part-time managers up to a lifetime maximum of $15,000 and $20,000 respectively.

In addition, part-time night-shift workers at the UPS Louisville hub receive free tuition at Metropolitan College, a virtual university created in partnership with the University of Louisville, Jefferson Community College, and Kentucky Technical College. The program has made the difference in recruiting employees to a difficult, but essential shift, while boosting productivity along the way.

Other organizations such as Marriott have made learning easier by exploiting Internet and computer technology to create the *Mouse Touch/Human Touch* system used across its hotels, while requiring all employees to promote common understandings of the organization's mission, values, and business objectives. Still other organizations are investing heavily in the development of CD-ROM packages, distance learning models, and *microworld simulators* that enable employees to practice decisions and maneuvers just as pilots do with aircraft simulators.

Such simulators have shown particular value in the Army logistics process, which relies on reservists to handle the top jobs in most deployments. As RAND's studies show, reserve training is especially difficult given personnel turnover, the geographic dispersion of units, and the need to refresh the knowledge base with new lessons learned. Not only is training infrequent, it often focuses on decisions that occur after deployment occurs. In addition, most training occurs over a few days, and cannot, therefore, simulate the intensity of real-world events.

Although the term *microworld* has been around for the better part of 30 years and was featured in Peter Senge's *The Fifth Discipline Fieldbook* as one of many tools for encouraging learning, there has been little research on how such simulators might actually work in developing needed skills.[13] Hence, RAND's efforts to both build and test an actual microworld simulation of supply distribution on the Japanese island of Hokaido. Designed to show the evolution of a distribution network over a 24-day period, the simulation consisted of 92 discrete points in time, each one requiring a real-world decision such as how to move jet fuel from a petroleum tank farm located at Bihiro to divisional forces at Shiranuka.

RAND's experiment with the Hokaido microworld suggests that reservists not only learned important skills about distribution from the three-hour simulation, but also gained new skills in finding trends in data, identifying the impacts of those trends, and making proactive decisions in response. Although expensive to develop and program, microworlds are inexpensive to deploy and use, especially for employees with limited training time.

As suggested above, microworlds are useless unless the knowledge they convey is relevant. It hardly makes sense to train reservists how to transport fuel in trucks when fuel is usually transported by ships, for example. Thus, agility also resides in helping employees develop the right skills. As RAND's study of the 75 international organizations suggests, it is not enough just to spend money on training. The training must lead to higher performance.

Hence, RAND's recommendation that organizations embrace the concept of portfolio careers that would allow employees to develop greater leadership skills through job rotations, stretch assignments, and movement across their organizations. Designed to emphasize competencies needed for future success, such careers would allow individuals to break free of the generic, one-size-fits-all nature of most training programs. Toward that end, human resource units must become strategic partners with senior leadership in shaping career-development programs, while working more closely with line managers in taking more risk with employee assignments.

Cultivate Corporateness Even as they adapt to the changing labor market by increasing employee agility, organizations must instill a sense of corporateness among their employees. This is certainly the goal at Marriott, where the Associates First program is designed to reinforce common goals, and at UPS where the Earn and Learn program is designed to promote employee loyalty.

It is also the focus of the environmental management programs that have evolved with increased government regulation and customer demand. In 1993, for example, AT&T joined with Intel to benchmark pollution prevention efforts at five firms considered among the best in the world in *going green* as part of ordinary business: Dow, DuPont, H.B. Fuller, 3M, and Xerox. According to Frank Camm, who authored one of RAND's studies on proactive environmental management, a successful pollution prevention program depends on high-level commitment and constant communication about the need for action. It also depends on careful measurement, formal goals and procedures, and employee motivation tied to compensation and performance appraisal.[14]

Given the organizational inertia against change, Camm believes that "the leadership must be clear from the start about the mission, goals, policies, and procedures associated with the new program. The pollution-prevention program must then communicate this information throughout the organization and secure the buy-in of the line managers of the relevant business units and plants." Much as early success depends on senior leadership, full adoption requires a broader motivational effort to remind, retrain, and reward employees for specific progress, all of which takes time.

At Procter & Gamble and Walt Disney World Resorts, for example, successful pollution control started with specific environmental goals stated in simple terms, followed by decentralization to promote innovation and agility, and continuous learning to promote adoption. According to RAND, Procter & Gamble's Mehoopany plant in northeast Pennsylvania uses a range of formal and informal devices to teach employees about environmental management, including teams, newsletters, e-mail, training classes, and an internal home page, while Walt Disney World Resorts uses cross-functional teams to spread the word about the need for improvement, as well as a monthly column on *Environmentality* in its monthly newspaper, *Eyes and Ears*.

Both organizations also use cross-functional task forces to address specific environmental problems. Cross-functional teams at Mehoopany developed the basic approaches that led to reductions in nitrogen oxides and chlorine, reduced its solid waste flow, and developed an aggressive environmental improvement plan. The Solid Waste Utilization Task Force also made sure that waste revenues and costs are tracked back to the appropriate business unit, which further reinforces the corporation's general environmental strategy.

Both organizations then proceeded to train their employee through a range of tools. At Mehoopany, for example, all new employees attend a 90-minute orientation built around the company's environmental goals, including the notion that nature is a Procter & Gamble customer. These goals are further reinforced by incentives for environmental stewardship, both through cash and noncash rewards linked to clear measures of performance.

According to Camm, Mehoopany is especially effective at using business cost methods to motivate environmental performance. All environmental costs are placed in well-defined pools; simple rules and supporting practices allocate each pool to a product; and the financial system provides accurate information on just how pollution prevention, or the lack thereof, is affecting costs. The plant tracks all waste streams, for example, and either charges business units for waste disposal or credits them for revenues generated through recycling. "To allocate the cost of all material passing through," RAND writes of solid waste disposal, "Mehoopany simply weighs each container coming from a product module to the transport point and allocates the cost proportionally. While this method is not absolutely precise, it is close enough to allocate costs."

The fact that all employees own Procter & Gamble stock is also part of the training program. Employees are shown exactly how environmental management affects company earnings, and can see the impact of their effort on the bottom line.

Set Just-Beyond-Possible Goals

RAND and its researchers have an ongoing and lively debate about where and how to set organizational goals. At one level, they all believe that organizations should set stretch goals that seek maximum impacts, whether in delivering the right treatments to patients, the right weapons to soldiers, or the right strategy for leaving no child behind. At another level, RAND researchers are mostly realists who recognize that there are limits on what organizations can actually achieve in a realistic amount of time.

It is one thing to set minimum standards in reading and mathematics by 2014, for example, and quite another to set yearly targets for actually implementing the goal. As RAND's Brian Stecher, Laura Hamilton, and Gabriella Gonzalez write, the "adequate yearly target" goals embedded in the law can only motivate educators if they are perceived as reasonable given available resources, and if they operate fairly for all schools. To the extent schools and teachers see the goals as impossible, the RAND researchers believe they "are likely to either abandon their efforts to meet them or resort to shortcuts, such as excessive coaching, to ensure success." At the same time, to the extent schools and teachers see the goals as too modest, they will feel little reason to change. The balance appears to be in setting goals that are neither impossible nor easily achievable, a stretch zone that I call "just beyond possible."

The Army is currently confronting the same balancing challenge in motivating recruiters. As RAND's James Dertouzos has discovered, the first step in setting goals is to understand that enlistment outcomes are affected by recruiter behavior, the difficulty of the mission, and market factors that are out of the recruiter's control.

A local recruiting market is determined by a bunch of economic and demographic characteristics. These characteristics, often called *supply-side factors*, represent the market quality. On the one hand, recruiters are given missions, or recruiting goals. If these goals do not match up well with the market quality, recruiters may not have incentives to exploit a market's potential. If the goal is too difficult, recruiters become discouraged and reduce effort. On the other hand, if the goal is too easy, recruiters don't have to work so hard to achieve success ("Made Mission, gone fishin"). In either case we actually end up observing an outcome that's significantly less than what the market would normally bear.

As Dertouzos concludes, the key is to set a just-beyond-possible goal:

Frankly, what could be more important in terms of managing people? Set a reasonable goal and reward them for either making it or failing to make it. Make it equitable, reasonable, and consistent with the organization's mission and you can set it at an individual level so people have incentives that are well in line with the organization.... Hiring the right people is important and motivating in other ways but trying to come up with individual incentives that are well aligned with your organization's incentives, rewarding people for doing the kinds of behaviors that achieve those organization's incentives, that's about as essential to management as you'll ever want to be.

Dertouzos reports that there is evidence that far-beyond-possible missions may have undermined recruiter morale, incentives, and effort in the late 1990s and early 2000s. Recruiters did better in expanding the market when missions were realistic, the irony being that the Army might have actually done better had it set it targets lower.

Once the goals are set, organizations must create the incentives for action. As RAND has learned through its ongoing work on proactive environmental management at firms such as Hewlett-Packard, DuPont, Ford Motor, IBM, Olin, Procter & Gamble, Volvo, and Walt Disney World Resort, incentives drive virtually every step in the process, including initial interest in environmental management.

At the corporate level, there are obvious reasons to invest in proactive environmental management, but being a pretty organization is not one of them. According to another of RAND's environmental studies, Intel invests in environmental technology to avoid the long and expensive process of securing air permits; Xerox's asset-recycle management initiative is designed to reduce waste; and DuPont is convinced that so-called *yield improvement technologies* can increase its environmental reputation, which can only increase sales.

At the business-unit and individual level, corporate incentives must be translated into metrics that measure and reward actual performance. "Metrics can motivate behavior only if linked to incentives," RAND's research shows. "Every firm seeking to improve its environmental management gives special attention to incentives; they tend to choose incentives that are compatible with their prevailing corporate cultures."

The incentives need not be financial, however. According to the team, "the most common form of incentive appears to be a direct, nonmonetary award to individuals who have tangibly improved environmental management. Firms emphasize the importance of giving such awards often, even for small improvements, to spread the importance of environmental management throughout the organization."

At Walt Disney World Resort, for example, the incentives have involved a mix of non-cash awards, including Jiminy Cricket pins for members of *Environmentality circles*, silver pins for a demonstrated commitment to the environment, and gold pins for a specific environmental accomplishment. All of the pins are awarded at an annual Earth Day ceremony at Epcot Center, and acknowledged in *Eyes and Ears*.

This commitment to environmental management extends well beyond Walt Disney World Resort, however. The Disney Company produces an annual *Enviroport* summarizing corporate achievements in recycling, waste reduction, and resource and wildlife conservation. The report itself is printed on 100 percent recycled paper certified by the Forest Stewardship Council, and printed in a facility that produces almost zero volatile organic compound emissions.

The company also encourages individual business units such as the Contemporary Hotel at Walt Disney World to create their own environmental action programs, which in turn involve everything from individual Jiminy Cricket certificates to a departmental awards program built around 9-inch statues of Sorcerer Mickey (energy savings), Ludwig von Drake (safety and security), and Jiminy Cricket (environmental management).

Incentives obviously send important signals about what gets valued and done. Yet, incentives for environmental management cannot be so powerful that they distract individuals and business units from other important goals, while negative incentives cannot be so draconian that they discourage risk taking. Thus, the RAND study notes the need to manage failures. "Trial and error offer great potential in any learning organization and are especially important in efforts to refine changes in an ongoing production process. Systematic learning depends on a system that supports flexibility and tolerates the right kinds of mistakes." Too many rubber chickens converts a culture that rewards trial *and* error into one that creates trial *for* error.

The study also suggests that some activities are so complex that they either cannot be carefully measured or involve competing goals. In such cases, organizations may choose a set of relatively weak or low-powered incentives over a single strong or high-powered incentive. As such, what gets measured *and* rewarded gets done. If some tasks cannot be measured, organizations are better off choosing low-powered incentives for the tasks that can be measured. A Jiminy Cricket pin is hardly a reward if Walt Disney goes out of business.

Moreover, even when activities can be carefully measured, the question is whether the incentives should be targeted at individuals or units. James Hosek might well answer "it depends."

> In the military, you have a unit that's going to be on call at some time to deploy and perform its function—that could be a battlefield function, combat function, etc. The individuals in the unit need to work together to get the job done. Well at some point individuals who deploy are going to be with their unit, called upon to do what the unit was trained to do. They were trained as a unit, they were taught to rely upon each other, and they literally may find that their life or death depends on whether their friends in the unit do what they're doing. In circumstances like that, where the unit is expected to pull together, it's really difficult to single out any individual as having higher productivity than another. This is a case of a contingency in which the unit must perform as a unit.
>
> On the other hand, let's shift back to peace time, which is a good 95 percent of the time a person is in the military, or if you're thinking of a large organization, most of the time it's not in an ultimate crisis mode where survival is at stake. People who work harder should be recognized—people who are putting in more effort, supplying more ideas; people who are available on the weekends,; people who are willing to cooperate, share information, work reliably, and exchange information in a trustworthy

way. Those are really good employees and you want to recognize them and single them out.

One way of trying to mesh these two things is by treating people equally when they're in a given status such as a certain unit or a certain rank or pay grade. There is also the possibility of advancement, an advancement that need not be the same for everybody but that could be tailored as you gradually go up. But whatever you do, you can't improve if you can't measure what you're doing. You can exhort people or use rhetoric but basically you won't know whether you've made progress unless you have specific yardsticks to judge against. They can be one person versus another. They can be one organization versus another.

Ultimately, the question is not so much whether incentives matter—the winnowing process ranked strong incentives as the third strongest predictor of performance. Rather, the question is just which incentives to use. As RAND's Susan Everingham cautions, "a lot of my colleagues will just say incentives, incentives, incentives. That's the economist's way of looking at the world. But I think it's more complicated than that. True, if you have the wrong incentives, you're going to get the wrong behavior. Maybe theoretically, there is some set of incentives that will get everybody to do what you want them to do, but I would be willing to argue that that set has never been found. And incentives alone are not enough. But they sure can cause a lot of damage if done in the wrong way."

Provide Authority to Act

Given RAND's work with soldiers, teachers, doctors, and a host of other frontline employees, it is hardly a surprise that its researchers might believe in delegation. Delegation is certainly part of achieving the agility that James Quinlivan saw on the Saturn factory floor, the recruiting success that James Dertouzos is studying, the cohesiveness that Leland Joe sees as essential for high-performing combat units, the commitment to quality that Elizabeth McGlynn hopes for in health care, and the successful interventions that Susan Everingham believes will reduce drug use.

As James Hosek argues, delegation is part of an overall culture of promise: "People need to believe in what the organization is trying to accomplish. They need to believe that they will be recognized for the effort they make. Their efforts will not be obliterated through sabotage or through misinformation. That they will be protected from the arbitrary turnover of personnel below or above them so that their record will not be lost if somebody leaves. That they will be given fair opportunities for actually doing the job they were hired to do so that there will be a flow of opportunities to them that's on par with their peers."

Delegation, and the employee engagement that goes with it, may also help explain the success of California's charter schools in matching public schools on student achievement. By all accounts, California's charter schools should be trailing their public peers. As a recent RAND shows, charter schools often succeed in spite of the obstacles. For example, California's charter schools spend less money per pupil, get less state education aid, and have less experienced principals and teachers.

Part of the disparity is that charter schools often lack the expertise to exploit funding opportunities. It can take months to fill out the forms for state aid, and years to master the rules. Moreover, many charter school operators may not even know that state aid is available, particularly for special needs such as nutrition assistance.

Part of the disparity is that individual charter schools must spend money on rent, utilities, maintenance, and storage that public schools automatically receive through property taxes or bonds. Landlords who know that charter schools operate under short-term authority often inflate rents, and start-up costs must be absorbed through lower salaries and fewer supplies.

Part of the disparity comes from the charter workforce, or lack thereof. Charter-school principals were less likely than their public-school peers to have a teaching or administrative credential, and more likely to take their jobs without prior administrative experience. Nearly three-quarters of public-school principals served as an assistant principal and/or principal of another school before taking their current post, compared with only 40 percent of their charter-school peers.

Given these funding and experience deficits, the question is how California's charter schools could generate rough parity with their better financed, more experienced public peers on student achievement. Yet, that is precisely what they do. As RAND's study team reports, "despite these operational differences, our analysis generally shows similar student outcomes. Most noteworthy, charter schools are achieving comparable test scores despite a lower reported level of revenue."

The answer appears to reside in *how* charter schools operate, not *what* they spend per pupil. Although charters and public schools put roughly the same number of teachers in the classroom, charter schools appear to give their principals and teachers much more of a say in what they do. Charter-school principals reported a significantly greater sense of control over teacher salaries and benefits than did the principals of matched conventional public schools, as well as a greater sense of control over the hiring, discipline, and dismissal of staff.

Further case studies by RAND "presented a picture in which principals often used their freedom to create a democratic atmosphere in which important decisions were shared with the teachers....Teachers in all of the schools visited said that they felt that they played an important role in decision making, and some teachers in schools that had been converted from conventional public schools felt that they were treated with more respect after conversation." In addition, charter-school teachers reported more mentoring, shadowing, peer-to-peer learning, and coaching.

Delegation goes well beyond giving principals and teachers greater authority over their work. RAND found greater parental involvement in their sample of charter schools than in the matched public schools. Charter schools were significantly more likely, for example, to create learning contracts between parents and schools. Although conventional public schools were more likely than charter schools to hold back-to-school nights, open houses, and ongoing contact through special events, the charter schools reported more parent participation in every kind of contact they provided, including volunteering, parent-teacher conferences, and workshops. RAND also found a much higher level of required participation, which suggests "a strong commitment on the part of the school to engaging parents in their children's education...."

Think Lean

Name an organization and it has likely done something over the past few years to "lean" out some process, be it purchasing, transportation, case management, product development, or customer relations. Lean thinking does not just involve efforts to reduce waste and inefficiency, however. It also involves a kind of organizational "triage" designed to sort products and processes into different categories that can be managed with the appropriate discretion and incentives.

John Deere did it in the mid-1990s by strengthening its relationships with suppliers based on the characteristics of the products it buys. Low-risk, low-value products such as nuts and bolts are defined as *generics*, and are purchased through standardized, automated systems using simple selection criteria to govern relatively short-term contracts, while low-risk, high-value products such as tractor tires are defined as *commodities*, and are purchased through longer-term contracts among a smaller base of suppliers.

In turn, high-risk, low-value products such as axles are defined as *unique*, and purchased through longer-term contracts with a small number of partners with whom it shares both information and expertise, while high-risk, high-value products such as transmissions and engines are defined as *critical*, and involve a tighter relationship. Because they significantly affect profitability, the company invests in its relationships. "It severely limits the number of providers for each product, sometimes moving to sole sources," RAND's study notes. "It purchases extensive data exchange and devolves considerable responsibility to these sources."

These strategic alliances assure a long-term relationship that depends on shared incentives, not competition for success. They also reflect a triage among providers into four classes: non-preferred, approved, key, and partner. "Until a supplier can demonstrate otherwise, Deere manages it as non-preferred," RAND's team writes. "Deere's long-term goal is to mature its providers over time....If things go well, trust accumulates between buyer and seller and they can enter into a deeper relationship that generates more value for both of them."

Setting priorities is only part of lean logistics, however. Many companies have reduced the number of suppliers dramatically. According to RAND, Allied Signal cut its supplier base from 10,000 in 1992 to fewer than 2000 in 1997; Boeing cut its 31,000 suppliers to less than 20,000 by 2004; 85 percent of IBM's purchases are now concentrated among 50 supplies; Intel has adopted a "n+1" benchmark in determining the maximum number of suppliers (n) needed in each commodity area; Merck cut its supplier base from 40,000 to 10,000 during the 1990s; and Whirlpool cut its supplier base by 50 percent in the late 1990s and early 2000s.

RAND has used these and other lessons from private firms to design and promote lean logistics and purchasing in all of the armed services. It has also explored the potential savings from lean manufacturing in the aircraft industry, where nearly all manufacturers had embraced the concept, if not the practice of lean thinking by the late 1990s. After summarizing the potential gains from lean thinking in engineering, tooling, manufacturing, quality control, manufacturing, administration, and even human resource management, RAND asks why so few firms have actually succeeded in wall-to-wall reform. "One answer lies in the difficulty of enacting any large-scale organizational change, especially one where the benefits to the companies are mixed with costs (as is the case in defense manufacturing, where more efficient production in cost-plus or cost-based contracts means lower profits for the manufacturer," RAND answers. Moreover, it can take years to build a truly lean factory. "And this transition does not just happen but requires a significant commitment and level of effort by the organization, its suppliers, and even its customers."

Thinking lean does not just apply to logistics and manufacturing, however. It also applies to basic strategy. As RAND's research on lightning over water suggests, organizations must also make whole units lean by giving them the training and equipment to deploy faster. If light forces are to be the instrument of choice in fighting limited engagement' across the world, the Army must decide how to give them greater survivability and firepower. Toward this end, RAND maintains that the Army has three choices.

- It can take current light forces such as the 82nd Airborne, and give them better and heavier equipment, including its own precision weapons that can be brought to bear against heavier adversaries.
- It can make current light forces smaller and more dispersed. Instead of using large numbers of light forces to contain an adversary in traditional head-to-head combat, the Army could create very small, highly dispersed, virtually independent teams that would move independently of each other, but come together in occasional swarms.
- It could make current light forces more maneuverable, and therefore more survivable. The maneuverability would require new, somewhat heavier equipment, as well as the ability to target heavier forces with coordinated air support.

RAND's research shows that the Army cannot continue with its "come as you are" force, especially if adversaries decide to stand and fight. Using simulations of light forces arrayed against the kind of heavier forces they faced in the 1991 Gulf war, RAND found that the current generation of light forces simply does not fare well against a powerful, armored opponent that decides to fight. Following the first choice outlined above would improve overall effectiveness in today's world, but not the increased need for anywhere, anytime responsiveness. Following the second choice increases responsiveness, particularly by reducing cargo weight, but reduces firepower and the ability to sustain a battle with heavier opponents. Following the third choice actually decreases responsiveness, but increases firepower and the ability to take on heavier opponents.

Whatever the Army decides, it must become more agile. Although the overall magnitude of threat faced around the world may have declined since the Cold War, the number and diversity of threats will most certainly increase. As RAND argues, "the threat has 'globalized,' meaning that the

U.S. Army may need to deal with a much broader range of opponents, in many diverse locations, and through many kinds of missions, perhaps more so than at any other point in its history." As a result, the American must rely on light forces that can be airlifted quickly, and a streamlined supply process that go to the farthest point on the globe with equal agility. Doing so requires the ultimate application of lean thinking.

Thinking lean even applies to research and development, a point well made in RAND's research on Xerox, which has been working for more than a decade to align its technology investments more closely with customer demand. Given the unpredictable markets it faced in the early 1990s, Xerox adopted a much flatter organizational structure, gave its product divisions greater responsibility for all steps in the product delivery process, and created a strategy council to formulate a strategic vision of customer needs and emerging markets. In the early 2000s, Xerox also called on General Electric Capital to fix its billing process, which had come unhinged in an administrative consolidation.

GE Capital also helped Xerox implement "Lean Six Sigma," which blends total quality management with Toyota's lean-manufacturing philosophy. Together the two approaches have helped Xerox reduce the number of research cycles needed to bring a product to market, shaving time and money from the design process, while reducing waste and environmental costs. Xerox not only used the system to develop its new DocuTech print-on-demand copiers, it has created its own fledgling consulting business to teach other companies how to move from being consciously incompetent to unconsciously competent.[15]

CHALLENGE THE PREVAILING WISDOM (ADAPTABILITY)

Adaptability involves a basic decision to challenge the prevailing wisdom, be it inside an organization or outside. Often times the challenge is anything but welcome, especially if it raises questions about existing strategies and procedures during relatively calm moments. Hard as they try to create the sense of urgency deemed so important to a change effort, organizations are notoriously fond of the status quo—the Army loves its tanks, Marriott must have loved its real estate, and Volvo certainly loved its cars.

Adaptation may never quite reach the zero-trauma goal that Hamel and Välikangas desire, but it can be made easier, or at least more natural. As I have argued, any organization can innovate once by hiring that mythical charismatic leader or driving fear down through the ranks. The trick is to innovate twice, thrice, and more by making innovation a natural event.

The same lesson holds true for adaptation, where organizations can either alter their future or be altered by it. The secret, if it can be labeled as such, is to create the organizational capacity to adapt by rewarding learning and imagination, aggregating expertise, unbalancing the scorecard of traditional financial and nonfinancial measures, and embracing the concept of command as a form of delegation and participation. As noted earlier, organizations do not have to adapt under all circumstances—there will be times when they decide that their course is safe even given new realities. But they must be able to adapt when necessary, whether by adopting entirely new strategies and products, or by altering course ever so slightly to keep pace with the futures they face.

Challenging the Prevailing Wisdom

1.   Create the freedom to learn

2.   Create the freedom to imagine

3.   Aggregate expertise

4.   Unbalance the scorecard

5.   Embrace the command concept

Create the Freedom to Learn

Robust organizations never stop learning. They see no purpose in saturating their units and employees with information unless that information is credible, rigorous, and based on deeper understandings of how the world works in past, present, and future tenses. As the old saying goes, garbage in, garbage out. From RAND's perspective, organizations must create knowledge. Reducing the cost of learning is no doubt part of the process, but far from enough to assure the requisite learning.

RAND may be the best teacher on this characteristic. Although there is no doubt that it creates knowledge, it operates at such high velocity, moving from project to project, that it must work hard to aggregate knowledge.

Part of the challenge lies in the tyranny of project research, which rarely leaves time for reflection. RAND researchers are so busy in the present that they have no chance to think back to the past. Part of the challenge comes from the internal labor market that allows senior researchers to move from project to project in search of the most interesting work. In a sense, autonomy becomes the enemy of organizational learning. "A lot of the value in RAND's work is never really captured," says Dominic Brewer, "because you have this group of senior people that's kind of in it for the fun of moving around and helping here and there."

RAND is aware of the challenge, which is why it has created it own learning platforms, most notably its own graduate school. Created in 1970 as one of eight public-policy programs funded by the Ford Foundation, RAND's Pardee Graduate School provides a two-way platform for adaptation. On the one hand, the students earn part of their tuition as research assistants on RAND projects. As they move from project to project, they carry knowledge across the research divisions. On the other hand, the school uses RAND researchers as its faculty, thereby creating opportunities for interdisciplinary learning. Because they are not tenured in any sense of the term, faculty members teach mostly out of a genuine love for learning, which infects the Santa Monica office with a kind of intellectual fervor that reinforces rigor and honesty.

One of the curriculum's most important courses is actually built around case studies of exemplary RAND research. Taught by the school's current and founding deans, Robert Klitgaard and Charles Wolf, the course asks a series of tough questions about what constitutes good research.

Focusing on 10 recent studies, Klitgaard and Wolf argue that successful analysis has a variety of characteristics. It can change the rhetoric about an issue by debunking an urban legend, or add needed complexity to an oversimplified debate. It can reduce a complex model to a usable equation, or provide a common factual basis for debate. It can change the actual question, or explore the translation of research into practice. Bluntly put, what you don't know actually can hurt you. As Klitgaard writes, "Recognizing what is not known and admitting uncertainties is perhaps more important than the researcher's instinctive quest for emphasizing what new bit of truth a piece of research has uncovered."[16]

Create the Freedom to Imagine

Many organizations leave the imagination to their planning units. Strategic planners are hardly the only people who think in futures tense, however.

Indeed, some might argue that they are wed to a highly inflexible, linear model of the future that leads inexorably to one future, and one future only.

This is why many RAND researchers believe in saturating organizations with information. Most of its researchers long ago abandoned the notion that imagination is the special gift of senior leaders in favor of a much more pliable model that allows creativity to flow from all levels of the organization at all stages of the innovation process. Innovation turns out to be much less predictable than strategic planners once believed, a conclusion noted by RAND researchers in studies of everything from environmental technology and information systems to mining, surgical procedures, the media arts, and weapons systems.

This is certainly what Leland Joe found in his study of high-performing combat units. As he suggests, "there is no cookbook for creating a high performance unit." However, there are shared characteristics of success. Not only must leadership be involved in obtaining and analyzing information, the unit "must be trained as a team and perform as a team." This means recognizing and sharing relevant information, cross-training team members so they understand the needs of the entire unit, and creating an open environment in which units have great freedom in determining what they need to know. Given the fog and friction of war, combat units must be able to adapt quickly.

This is also what RAND has learned from its recent study of the housing industry. Its study team suggests that the relatively low rate of innovation in the industry involves a variety of factors—"boom and bust cycles lead to low investment in employees and training to prepare them for innovation," "the fragmented nature of the industry slows information sharing and innovation acceptance," and the industry's "highly competitive nature may deter industry participants from adopting innovations because they want to minimize risks." In addition, home building takes place in the open and with multiple subcontractors, meaning that innovators may be unable to benefit from their innovations long enough to recoup their investments.

The question is how to spark innovation in what has become a risk-averse industry. Although the team does not discount the benefits of new patent protections and more federal funding on smart materials, its research suggests that the industry would benefit most from a deluge of information and incentives. Because innovation may or may not be affected by research funding, for example, the housing industry may need stronger incentives for innovation and greater access to information.

Take land developers as a first example. "The principal business of land developers is to buy undeveloped land, to prepare it for resale, and then to sell it," the team reports. Because money has value, speed is of the essence, which affects the innovation process in a number of ways. Developers not only need time to learn about an innovation, they also need time to convince government regulators, investors, and community stakeholders that the idea holds merit. Unless the knowledge base contains the needed information, the innovation will not take hold.

Take home buyers as a second example. Buyers look for many things in a home, the team writes, "but innovation is typically less important than are location, aesthetics, value, the chance for appreciation, and the quality of the neighborhood and surrounding schools." Home buyers may like the energy efficiency, durability, and low maintenance cost that innovation might bring, but will not pay the premium unless they can see a proven value added. Again, unless the knowledge base contains that proof, the innovation will be hard to sell.

The point is that saturating the housing industry with information at all stages and all levels of the housing process might lead to very different options for enhancing innovation, while targeting traditional activities such as research and development key incentives.

Imagination does not occur in a vacuum, however. It involves an appropriate mix of incentives, market pressure or demand, and a bit of luck. Although innovation almost always involves serendipity, revolutions involve a process that can be both observed and anticipated. Indeed, according to Richard Hundley's study, most revolutions in military affairs such as the blitzkrieg require a cascade of innovation to succeed. (See my modification of Hundley's briefing chart on a multiple-innovation model of revolutions in military affairs.)

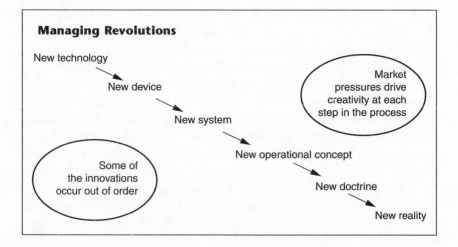

Managing Revolutions

New technology

New device

New system

Some of the innovations occur out of order

New operational concept

Market pressures drive creativity at each step in the process

New doctrine

New reality

The study also suggests that revolutions in military affairs are often adopted and fully exploited by a nation other than the one that invented the new technology. The original inventors were either unable to convert new technology into an actual device (nuclear aircraft engines were too heavy to use), a new device into a viable system (electromagnetic guns were too hot to fire), a new system into operational practice (machine guns were useless until trench warfare), a new practice into new doctrine (tanks were originally viewed as another form of transportation, not the leading edge of an infantry attack), or a new doctrine into a new reality (the British and French were too arrogant to believe that tanks were fast enough to end run the Maginot line). The market belongs to the organizations that can put all the linkages together, imagining how one innovation leads to another, and so on down the chain.

Successful movement through the chain involves a series of triggers. As Hundley recommends:

- You must have a fertile set of enabling technologies.
- You must have unmet military challenges.
- You must focus on a definite "thing," meaning a device together with a concept for deployment.
- You must ultimately challenge someone's core competency.
- You must have a receptive organizational climate that (1) fosters a continually refined vision of how war may change, and (2) encourages vigorous debate regarding the future of the organization.
- You must have support from the top, including senior officers with traditional credentials willing to sponsor new ways of doing things, as well as new pathways for junior officers who are willing to practice and experiment.
- You must have mechanisms for experimentation to discover, learn, test, and demonstrate.
- And you must have some way of responding positively to the results of successful experiments.

Established organizations face two great challenges in the list. First, they must be willing to reward inventors and rule breakers. As Hundley notes, history is replete with examples of inferior military powers that used a revolution in military affairs to overpower a superior adversary. Alas, history provides few examples of the superior military power that upsets it own core competency—the only exception known to Hundley was the U.S.

Navy's decision to embrace aircraft carriers, even though doing so rendered its battleships highly vulnerable and virtually useless.

Second, organizations must be ready to embrace revolutions started elsewhere, which requires a readiness to learn and adapt. "It takes a brave organization to make a part of itself obsolete," Hundley writes. "Historically, this has been rare in the military world." It has been equally rare in the business and nonprofit worlds as well.

Aggregate Expertise

Unlike most think-tank scholars, who usually work alone, RAND researchers almost always work in teams, often drawing colleagues who do analogous research in other divisions, while encouraging the kind of multidisciplinary, or cross-functional, work represented by its housing and petroleum studies. (See Moore's slide on cross-functional teams.)

Managing Cross-Functional Teams

▶ Tailor membership to the assigned activity

  • The right people with the right skills, experience, and training

▶ Guide efforts with performance measures and goals

▶ Provide needed organizational investments

  • Time, budget

▶ Grant authority to control internal activities and make substantive decisions

  • Increase with experience and success

▶ Appoint a formal team leader

▶ Link members' performance evaluations and compensation to team performance

---

These are more than just teams in a traditional sense. They are knowledge sinks where ideas and expertise mix together. As RAND's Bernard Rostker remembers the gays in the military study discussed later in this chapter, "We were able, given the breadth of the RAND research staff, to put together a team from many disciplines.... Some of our staff had backgrounds in military manpower, but many had never worked with the military before that project. This diverse group was comfortable working together. We were also comfortable working without 'hard data' and drawing conclusions based upon the observations we made from the formal literature and visits to analogous institutions.... We approached it in a very commonsense way, fully understanding the limitation of time and information."[17]

RAND has also used cross-functional teams to great effect, which is how Susan Gates moved from military manpower to education. "I had been doing work off and on in the education unit since I've been at RAND," she says, explaining her engagement in RAND's new study of school principals. "One of my first projects was on higher education as an industry. I knew the head of the education program, Dominic Brewer, who asked me for input when they were submitting the proposal. They were actually seeking insights from the military side about what they could learn about careers and career paths from the military perspective. I wrote a little segment, and as it turned out, that segment was what ended up getting funded as the whole project."

Although RAND researchers are free to work alone, the internal labor market reinforces multidisciplinary research, while allowing senior analysts to cover future gaps. "You have to work well independently, but also work as part of a team," says Bruce Hoffman of the RAND style. "You have to have the ability to work for a sustained period of time on one topic, but also to be nimble and flexible enough to be pulled off onto some short-term, high visibility project. You have to be willing to take on more than one thing at one time or more than three things at one time. And that's the satisfaction we all derive from working here, and the fact that you don't punch a time clock."

RAND does not believe teams are the only way to produce knowledge, however. Its own research on team-based health care provides ample caution. RAND reports that quality improvement (QI) in nursing-home care is more likely in organizations with an underlying culture of innovation. "Our results indicate that QI cannot just be implemented in any nursing home," the eight-member team concluded in its 2002 article. "Rather, the nursing home must be suitably predisposed to QI by having a culture that rewards innovation and teamwork."

Other RAND studies have confirmed the pattern in a range of organizational settings, most notably perhaps in the treatment of psychological depression. Initially, RAND's study team believed that a highly centralized approach to quality improvement would be less successful than a local approach. "We assumed that a purely centralized top-down intervention would be unsuccessful," the researchers argue, largely because local clinicians would be less likely to accept advice from on high. In turn, the researchers expected the local teams to be more successful, largely by "gaining buy-in from local practices and hence in designing enduring programs."

Contrary to their initial hunches, however, the local plans succeeded only "when the local environment was highly supportive and team leaders had high levels of expertise and commitment." Health-care organizations should use only local teams "when a team leader with interest or expertise in depression and time to participate is available, and when support from local practice leadership and/or support from mental health specialists is high."

Moreover, picking the right team depends on the task. The Army's Velocity Management project actually involved two types of teams: Army-wide process improvement teams that included technical experts on all aspects of the logistics process, and site-improvement teams that included local technical experts and consumers. The Army-wide teams were responsible for designing the general reform, while the site-improvement teams were responsible for tailoring the actual implementation.

Finally, as RAND's environment studies show, cross-functional teams cannot be so labor-intensive that they overwhelm the participants, and, in doing so, reduce corporate performance. Nor can they be allowed to drift without outside review. "Teams work best when governed by consensus, and, with experience, team members tend to develop skills that support consensus decision making. But to the extent that teams require leaders or that leaders need to intervene to manage a failure to reach consensus, the leaders come from a broad management background, not a functional specialty, such as environment."

Unbalance the Scorecard

Robust organizations are fearless about measurement. They create signposts that reveal the increased vulnerability of core assumptions about plans and operations, and monitor the effects of their actions. Creating a balanced scorecard composed of financial and nonfinancial measures is only the first step in creating the metrics needed to track results. Once created, however, organizations must be ready to unbalance the scorecard in search of new metrics that both unsettle complacency and encourage adjustment.

RAND's analysis of environmental management makes the case clearly. As RAND's research team argues, "successful firms manage what can be measured. The cliché can be overstated, but proactive firms rely on metrics as the foundation for managing improvement. Accounting is often called the language of business. Metrics extend this notion more broadly to reflect the importance of nonmonetary, as well as monetary, measures of performance."

Metrics can play many roles in promoting adaptation, not the least of which is tracking intended effects. At least for motivating behavior, however, the metrics need to be carefully designed to induce the right behavior, be compatible with the constraints at hand, be easy to collect and verify, and can be mutually understood and shared.

The Olin Corporation provides a case in point. As RAND's case study shows, Olin already had a quality culture when it began its environmental management program in the 1980s. It was no surprise, therefore, that Olin would use value-added as the basic measure of environmental remediation, whether in the form of cost avoidance, cost savings, or cost recovery. Once launched, Olin also regularly tracked cost management, changes in spending projections, relationship management, public perceptions of the remediation program, significant remediation accomplishments, extraordinary adverse effects, and individual site performance. The effort to measure relationship management involved short, formal surveys of key regulators and senior Olin leaders, while remediation accomplishments were tracked through traditional value-added indicators. Olin sought to manage remediation more like a profit center rather than a cost center.

Beyond urging organizations to find a range of simple, usable metrics, my interpretation of the RAND knowledge base suggests five principles for creating high-performance measurement: measure in futures tense, collect the right dots, avoid over-reliance on any one measure of performance, keep the measures relatively simple, and make room for intuition.

Unbalancing the Scoreboard

▶ Measure in futures tense

▶ Collect the right dots, then connect them

▶ Don't put all your measures in one basket

▶ Keep it simple

▶ Invite intuition

Measure in Futures Tense   Alongside a general commitment to thinking in futures tense, RAND would almost certainly recommend measuring in futures tense. The two are not quite the same, however. The former often involves highly sophisticated methods for creating a portfolio of formalized scenarios, while the latter involves rigorous methods to set present-tense metrics into a future context.

Consider RAND's recent work on the future of the performing arts. Given the lack of data on the state of the arts both past and present, RAND decided not to invest in formalized scenarios of the future. Indeed RAND faced a monumental task just measuring the current state of the arts. On the commercial side of the equation, the recording and media arts release very little data on the costs of their operations, no doubt in part because of royalty concerns with artists. On the nonprofit side, the data are more plentiful, but of lower quality.

But whether unavailable or spotty, the result is the same: "Because the data are fragmentary and incomplete," RAND's research team reports, "the literature on the art world suffers from several weaknesses: academic studies tend to be narrowly focused on areas where the data are plentiful; commentary for broader audiences tends to take on larger issues but usually provides only anecdotal evidence for support; and the field in general lacks a systematic framework for analyzing the data that do exist." Simply put, the plural of anecdote is not data.

Instead of creating new data, the team decided to synthesize every scintilla of available evidence to build first a trend line from the present to the past, and a second trend line from the present into a possible future. In a line that is analogous to a Surgeon General's warning, they caution this possible future is far from certain. Absent some miracle, however, it anchors a mixed-case scenario that holds both promise and peril. Specifically, RAND predicts that the number of organizations supplying live performances of theater, music, opera, and dance will simultaneously contract at the professional level and expand at the community level, which in turn could produce a narrowing of access in small and mid-sized cities, and a concentration of access in large metropolitan areas that are able to support high-budget nonprofit organizations with top-echelon performers and productions. At the same time, RAND also predicts that more Americans will have greater access to smaller, low-budget productions of great cultural and artistic diversity performed largely by amateur artists (and professionals willing to perform for little or no pay) in their own communities.

The question is whether this is the future that will be or just a future that might be. According to RAND's research, no one knows. Arts organizations cannot assume that time will stand still—either they measure things that matter such as audience depth, breadth, or commitment in futures tense, or they may well fall between the cracks of an increasingly fragmented industry.

Collect the Right Dots Although it is fashionable to argue that organizations are drowning in information, RAND's history of information failures suggests that there are two kinds of problems in collecting the right dots. First, organizations often collect the wrong information in the first place, and, second, even when they collect the right information, they often fail to circulate it.

Take the case of the Beltway sniper who terrorized the Washington, D.C. area in October 2002. There was clearly no lack of attention to information at the time—there were dozens of agencies involved in the investigation, as well as unrelenting media coverage. Moreover, eyewitnesses had reported that they had seen a blue Chevrolet Caprice at the scene of an early killing in the District of Columbia, which fit an even earlier report regarding a shooting at a Washington suburb. "In this case, weak signals were overwhelmed by noise: the spurious clue of 'the white man in the white van,' " the RAND researchers write. "Of course, the distinction between noise and too many dots may be obvious only in retrospect; there are millions of potential dots—some are part of one picture, some part of another, and most part of nothing. It is not easy keeping multiple conflicting patterns in place in the face of a strong desire to jump to conclusions."

Or take the case of September 11, where FBI agents in both Minneapolis and Phoenix alerted their supervisors to the flight training of potential hijackers. Had the two agents compared notes, they almost certainly would have discovered the pattern. Although the information was passed up to the FBI hierarchy, it was not shared laterally at any level. Similarly, earlier warnings of the 1998 terrorist attacks in East Africa were compartmentalized with the vast U.S. intelligence bureaucracy and never linked.

As RAND's Martin Libicki and Shari Pleeger write, there are many barriers to collecting the right dots, including a lack of awareness of the need for information, a lack of attention to the information collected, a misuse of standard templates such as balanced scorecards, medical charts, investigation checklists, and so forth, and territorial instincts among different units. In the Beltway sniper case, for example, police developed the investigation using a standard template based on the most recent information. They wrongly assumed that the killers were fleeing the scene of each shooting when they often stayed behind (even eating French fries), confident that they would not be seen.

Collecting the right dots is only the first step in assuring accurate information, however. Libicki and Pleeger also believe that organizations must bring scattered pieces of information into some proximity to each other. "Detecting that a fact merits note and forwarding is, for its part, often composed of two factors," RAND warns: "the awareness that something is a significant anomaly and the explanation of the anomaly as signifying something...."

Don't Put All Your Measures in One Basket Despite their collective focus on metrics as a marker of high performance, many RAND researchers urge caution in collecting and using metrics. No one metric or set of metrics can be allowed to eclipse a broader understanding of how an organization performs.

Thus, even as he maintains that measurement is essential for understanding the nature of a problem, Leland Joe also argues that there is such a thing as too much information. "There are stories of soldiers having so much information that they spend all their time looking at the screen, and trip and fall down."

Susan Everingham makes a similar point, simultaneously endorsing metrics, then urging caution:

> I think managers need metrics. I can see that. You can't get away from them. What people don't like about them is the fact that they oversimplify and they don't capture all of the nuances that need to be taken into account. But the key is finding the grades, the score, whatever your metrics are, that capture the most important information about your organization, and that will tell you whether you are heading in the right direction or not.
>
> From an analyst's perspective, the more data the better, and the more money to look at that data, the better, because you often don't know what you're going to find once you start digging into the data. So as far as you, the analyst, are concerned, you gather every piece of data you can and look at it every different way that you can. And if you could, you would take 5 to 10 years to do it. And you would probably find some fascinating things.
>
> But managers can't afford to do that. They have to respond in real-time, and they usually can't afford to collect all that data. They need to pick out the pieces of data that they think are really going to help them manage their organizations. From an analyst's perspective, data and measuring are good; from a manager's

perspective, it's the right data that's good. The wrong data is actually bad. If you collect the wrong data, you're going to be sending the implicit message to everybody that *that* is what you really care about, and then that's what people are going to start focusing on.

As Everingham suggests, measurement is essential for understanding whether an organization is, in fact, on mission and performing well. At the same time, it can focus too much on short-term variations, which drive out long-term thinking, or be so complex that it cannot be used by anyone without a Ph.D. "Did you see the story the other day?" Quinlivan asks. "Some inspector in Utah supposedly went out to a restaurant and told them one in four eggs had salmonella, so they should only have three-egg omelets." Ba-boom.

Health care provides a case in point. RAND researchers have been working for over a decade on designing an accessible, user-friendly set of measurements that doctors, patients, insurers, and policymakers could use to hold the health-care system accountable. But the data to do so is weak at best, misleading at worst. As RAND's team reports, the lack of unique identifiers for patients, providers, and facilities; the inability to compare data elements across systems; and missing information create a host of undesirable, even unintended consequences for the health-care system.

According to one recent RAND study, much of the available information does not apply to people with chronic disease: "If health plans that provide good preventive services are less successful in providing care for chronic conditions, and if the available information on quality focuses primarily on preventive health services, individuals who shift into health plans that provide poor chronic disease care may experience significant and perhaps irreversible declines in their health and functions."

RAND also reports that most health-care purchasers focus more on cost than quality, in part because the effort to develop quality measures is so difficult. "Without such information, excellent health plans that provide care at a somewhat higher cost may be driven out of the market or may choose to compromise the quality of care delivered to meet the cost requirements."

Although RAND and its researchers recognize there are no perfect measures of anything, they do believe some measures are better than others. As Shan Cretin notes, "Researchers are so focused on their thing that they don't understand that their thing is only one of many things the organization has to do well in order to succeed. Putting in a system to measure

2000 indicators may be the best thing to do in terms of getting a really unbiased look at quality of care, but health-care management might be satisfied to measure 50 or 100 things and put some resources into something else."

The challenge is to make sure that the search for the best does not become the enemy of the good. "It's hard to step back and recognize that you've shown something to be true, but people might get 90 percent of the value by doing something quite a bit less. If it's really that great, then a little bit of it is probably pretty good, too."

Keep It Simple   Once collected, metrics must tell users what they need to know in ways they can handle. This might mean a balanced scorecard of some kind, a dashboard of key indicators that all employees can access every day, or a report card. As the Velocity Management team reports, "Metrics must be developed that reflect what the customers of the process need and value. The metrics should be robust against gaming; that is, only desired behaviors should produce improvements in the metrics.... The choice of metrics is critical because what gets measured and reported is what gets attended to."

Whatever the format, *how* information is presented can be as important as *what* gets measured. RAND's research on health-care report cards makes the point. Much as consumers say they would use report cards on local providers and hospitals, most do not use the information they have. Sometimes, the information is not available when the patient needs it; other times, it comes too late to influence a decision; and still other times, the information is too dense to consume.

As Cretin says, researchers must pay special attention to consumer resistance to a given set of metrics: "It may not seem like a good reason to you and may not be totally on target, but it's real. For example, there are a lot of guidelines that say you need to have patients take this drug and do this if they have diabetes. The professionals are resisting this. Why are they resisting it? The patients don't come with just diabetes. They have diabetes plus other things."

Her analysis of evidence-based medicine is easy to apply in a host of non-health-care settings:

> The patients live in different circumstances that make it very hard for them to do the thing you are recommending, and the clinician may be trying to engage in a relationship with this patient over the long haul to get this patient moving in a better direction and willing to let them not do certain things now in order to build that relationship. That might be a reasonable thing to do.

It's not that the evidence is bad, but this might not be the most important thing to do for this patient. This patient may have other conditions, may also have asthma, for example, and helping them work through how to control their asthma may be more important at the moment than working on the diabetes or vice versa.

When you say it fast, evidence-based medicine makes a lot of sense. When you actually look at the evidence, there's probably really compelling evidence for four or five things to do for people with diabetes. There's a lot of not so compelling evidence and a whole bunch of other stuff.

When you look at the guidelines people come up with, they have literally hundreds of recommendations in them. They carefully annotate them and give references, but when you read the references, they're not all equally compelling. A lot of the randomized trials are done on rather clean populations; and that's how you do a trial. I get a good result by limiting myself to people with Type II diabetes, no evidence of cancer, heart disease, kidney involvement, etc., and I do the trial and I say this works.

Now you go out into practice and here comes this patient who's had breast cancer two years ago, has diabetes now, has some heart disease, and they don't fit in the trial model. It's not a slam-dunk. I'm not saying that ultimately you won't pull doctors over toward some of the evidence-based stuff, but you also may find them saying get real. A lot of what you're asking for there isn't that clearly evidence-based.

Invite Intuition   Not all measurements stem from objective sources, however. RAND has enormous respect for intuition and judgment as sources of future insight—respect that dates back to RAND's pioneering work on the Delphi method for creating scenarios of the futures. In 1959 two RAND researchers wrote a little-noticed paper arguing for the systematic use of expert opinion and pseudo-experimentation to build scenarios of the future in hard-to-predict or inexact sciences.

Named for the home of Greece's greatest oracle, the Delphi technique actually involves a highly rigorous system of anonymous interaction with a panel of outside experts who are asked to imagine alternative future. It is anything but "occult" or "oracular," as one RAND researcher complained in 1969. As Dewar explains, it is "used in strategic planning to project the future technical, market, and other developments, uncover fundamental differences of opinion, and identify nonconventional ideas and concepts. Participants first make initial projections of future events. After their initial projections are correlated and shared with the group, participants are then asked to explain (anonymously) their differences in a series of follow-up rounds."

The questions can be a bit unusual, to say the least. Consider how Dewar recently posed a question about energy policy in the year 2020:

> A time traveler from 20 years in the future will visit you early in the new millennium. The time traveler knows everything about the situation surrounding energy needs in the year 2020. What do you want to know about the future?

Yet, there is no doubt that the answers lead toward more precise images of the future. After three rounds of back-and-forth, Dewar's expert panel of 27 academics, government officials, and industry leaders agreed that the most important questions about the future clustered around global warming, hybrid/zero-emission automobile markets, natural gas, increased nuclear power use, oil prices, and the viability of fuel cells.

The method may seem unusual, but repeated experiments have shown that the Delphi technique does a much better job at projecting certain futures than high-powered, data-fueled mathematical models. If not informed by the Greek gods, experts appear to bring a mix of both judgment and data to bear on the questions they are asked.

Embrace the Command Concept

Command and control is essential to the other three pillars of robustness—it reinforces alertness, permits maximum delegation, and creates alignment. Successful command and control involves more than just issuing orders or a clear chain of accountability, however. It also involves the ability to adapt quickly to changing circumstances, delegate authority, and filter vast quantities of information.

Writing of the Air Force experience over Kosovo, RAND researchers argue that commanders and their staffs need systems that collect *decision-quality information*, meaning information that is complete and understandable enough to allow rapid learning. They also need control and communications systems that allow them to change targets while aircraft are en route, and instant information back on the actual execution of their orders.

But command and control also involves a broader image of just how a battle will play out. According to RAND's Carl Builder, a command concept should be so "prescient, sound, and fully conveyed to subordinates that it would allow the commander to leave the battlefield before the battle commences, with no adverse effect upon the outcome."

Defining the term *command concept* to mean a vision of a prospective engagement that informs decisions, Builder writes that an ideal command concept, or business plan, embraces the following elements:

- Time scales that reveal adequate preparation and readiness, not just of the concept but of the units tasked with carrying out that concept.
- Awareness of the key features of the outside world—situational awareness—that will allow the concept to succeed.
- A structuring of forces consistent with the tasks to be accomplished.
- Intelligence about what the adversary is expected to do, including the signposts that will announce the need for adaptation.
- A contingency plan in the event of failure of the concept and the resulting operation.

Drawing upon studies of six great battles, Builder also suggests that most command concepts, or business strategies, often suffer from an unwillingness to adapt in the face of clear signals of failure. Great commanders are mostly concerned with constantly addressing a simple stream of questions regarding their plans: "Are things going as we planned?" "If not, what is broken and needs fixing?" "Why and where are things going wrong?" "And is the plan wrong, or does it simply need adjustment?"

These were clearly the questions that U.S. Navy Admiral Chester Nimitz and U.S. Army General Douglas MacArthur asked as they prepared for the Battle of Midway and the invasion at Inchon, for example. Both had nearly ideal images of what they wanted to accomplish, and were well supported by their information and command systems. Indeed, the Battle of Midway may be a near-perfect example of the pure command concept. The plan never varied, yet subordinates had more than enough authority to adapt as necessary. "Nimitz could have gone on extended vacation when his carriers left Pearl Harbor;" Builder concludes; "his concept was sufficient to carry the burden of battle and ensure the victory."

In contrast, Field Marshal Bernard Montgomery failed to ask the questions as he prepared to take the Rhine bridge at Arnhem in September 1944. Instead, he tried to fit the operation to the available forces rather than make hard choices about which service would be best at the task, and ignored information that the operation was failing. Despite extensive rehearsals and briefings, Montgomery's plan failed because the ground commander had no system by which he could learn that the plan was failed. British radios at Arnhem worked so poorly that the commander could not even communicate with his own forces, and was almost captured.

As Builder writes, the Allies gambled that surprise would overcome the limits of the plan, not the least of which was insufficient capacity to airlift enough forces into combat. "The true situation at Arnhem—the key to success of the operation—could only be verified by a physical link up," they write. "The result of this conceptual error was the destruction of the British 1st Airborne Division as a fighting force." Of the 10,000 paratroopers dropped across the Rhine, less than 2200 made it back.

Finally, General H. Norman Schwarzkopf succeeded in the Gulf War because he had a strong command concept, and adapted quickly to events when his information and command system alerted him to changing circumstances. As Schwarzkopf later wrote, he knew that his plans needed to change when he heard that the Iraqis had destroyed the desalinization plant in Kuwait City:

> Since Kuwait City had no other source of drinking water, this could only mean that the Iraqis were about to leave. And if they intended to pull out of Kuwait City, I reasoned they intended to pull out of Kuwait.
>
> At that point, I knew that I had to act. Timing is everything in battle, and unless we adjusted the plan, we stood to lose the momentum of the initial gains. I'd fought this campaign a thousand times in my mind, visualizing all the ways it might unfold, and from the fragmentary reports coming into the war room, I could discern that the Iraqis were reeling. If we moved fast, we could force them to fight at a huge disadvantage.[18]

As Builder continues, Schwarzkopf's decision to accelerate the battle plan was the only variation he made in the original battle plan. He did not innovate, nor did he invent. He merely adapted the plan to a simple signpost that sprang up almost by accident in the stream of information flowing from the battlefield.

As the case studies suggest, command is far more than simply issuing orders. In fact it may not involve issuing orders at all. To the contrary, it starts with the simple willingness to question the prevailing wisdom, even if it comes from oneself.

LEAD TO MISSION (ALIGNMENT)

Virtually every success story in this book involved strong, often self-effacing leadership at the top. Although these leaders almost always delegated significant authority downward and embraced participation, they also took responsibility for aligning the organization around a clear vision of the hoped-for future.

At the same time, virtually every example of frustration in this book has some lesson for the leaders of robust organizations, whether in the willingness to question assumptions, the effort to create agility, or the need to embrace the leadership potential at all levels of the hierarchy and beyond. RAND's focus is not just on issuing the right orders, but on who gives the orders, what the orders say, how the orders are informed, and how adversaries behave.

Before turning to RAND's specific recommendations on alignment, it is important to remember their lack of enthusiasm for mythical charismatic leaders who toss off decisions straight from the gut. They clearly believe in courageous action, but want the courage to be well informed; they also believe in execution, but want action to be built around robustness and adaptability; and they want organizations to take leaps of faith, but want the leaps to be measurable and the consequences understood. Asked what he meant when he said that organizations need courageous leaders, Robert Roll answers that "I don't mean blind guts. I mean thoughtful courage, the willingness to listen to people who have other ideas. You can ruin a lot of lives and cause a lot of pain and suffering. You can be wrong."

RAND has intense respect for intuition as well, a point well made in its research on the Delphi technique, and in its more recent embrace of what some leadership experts call naturalistic decision making. Unlike rational decision making, which is built around a careful comparison of all options against all futures, naturalistic decision making accepts the notion that individuals often make very good decisions based on little more than hunch.

But what seems like hunch to some can actually be the product of years of experience to others. Instead of treating biases and shortcuts as things to control or eliminate, naturalistic decision making celebrates hunches as well-grounded expressions of experience. "Scientists form hypotheses—often just glorified hunches—whose proof they pursue vigorously," according to RAND's Jonathan Kulick and Paul Davis. "If the evidence is lacking or disconfirming, they typically adapt the hypothesis and tack a revised course, without dwelling on the prior mismatch between theory and data."

Firefighters, airplane pilots, emergency room staff, and a host of other decision makers do the same thing, albeit much, much faster. In most circumstances, there is no such thing as an optimal solution—leaders do not have enough time to define all their goals in quantitative teams; situations are rarely stable; the decision almost always involve more than just picking between options; probability estimates are rarely accurate; and even with computers, the scenarios can never be exhaustive. Even as leaders search for a command concept, or business plan, that is robust, they must be able to adapt, and often quickly.

Hunch is not enough for a good decision, however. Even as RAND researchers work to understand the naturalistic decisions that organizational leaders make, they are also trying to understand how to help leaders both build and apply the right intuition. Call it hunch, judgment, instinct, or intuition, but it all involves a set of understandings that can be informed and shaped through recruitment, training, and real-world experience. The challenge, according to a recent RAND study, is to meld the research-based knowledge with storytelling to create a three-step process for making choices:

1. Outline the links between cause and effect, options and consequences, and how decisions can affect the flow from choice to action.

2. Sharpen the sense of dilemmas and subtleties embedded in the course of action implied in the cause-and-effect sequence.

3. Communicate the package of options and impacts by increasing the vividness of the conversation, turning abstractions such as probabilities into something that listeners can "feel" viscerally.

As the RAND research team argues, the blend of storytelling and analysis does not require an appeal to base emotions such as fear or hubris, nor folksy stories about "Grandpa and his hound dogs." "They may, however, require making options seem real and their consequences important. Better decisions may sometimes come from thinking about hundreds of innocent people being killed rather than about 'collateral damage.' "

Much of this advice sits well within the contemporary knowledge base on leadership development. RAND's work has moved well beyond the *great man theories* of the 1940s, which emphasized traits and personality, and the *contingency theories* of the 1950s, which emphasized the match between leaders and situations, into the cognitive and strategic leadership approaches associated with competence, experience, and change management.

Whether naturalistic or rational, decisions are not self-implementing. As RAND has also learned over the years, organizations need to develop leadership skills that encourage alignment around a clear plan of action. Toward this end, RAND's current work is less concerned with finding the secret trait of great leadership than with making sure that leaders have the core competencies that allow them to step into command on a moment's notice. Robust organizations do so by growing the right stuff themselves, preparing leaders in futures tense, thinking in images, and understanding the adversary.

Leading to Mission

1.   Grow the right stuff yourself

2.   Lead in futures tense

3.   Communicate through images

4.   Anticipate the adversary

5.   Ignore the irrelevant

Grow the Right Stuff Yourself

As with motivation, no amount of information can substitute for having smart, able commanders to consume it. "They say you can delegate authority," says Leland Joe, "but you can never delegate responsibility. The point here is that in war, people get killed. You always want to have someone who is responsible in the chain of command.... If you're going to lose a life, it should be for a reason."

Toward this end, RAND has also done a fair amount of research, much of it classified, on managing the careers of leaders from their first day on the job. Led by Albert Robbert, the research is designed to enrich the pool of potential leaders ready for advancement at all levels of the hierarchy. Since the armed services have to work with what the recruiters send them, the emphasis is on advancing the right people at the right time up through the hierarchy. Simply asked, what do commanders need to be effective?

Robbert answers that effectiveness is a blend of both hard (functional) and soft (motivational) skills: "There's a tendency to glorify leadership and denigrate management. I'm almost certain that it's wrong-headed. You want the core leadership to come from the operators—in the Air Force, they are the pilots; in the Army, they are from combat arms; in the Navy, they come from the ship drivers and airplane drivers." Because they know war, they may not know management. "They would be better served if they were to recognize that they're employing instinctive management skills that have gotten them through, that they would be more effective as leaders if they had better honed their management skills along the way."

Robbert says the trick is to make sure an organization develops a large enough pool of candidates with both hard and soft competencies to make sure the armed services have enough candidates to provide good selectivity for each post that opens up. This leads inevitably to skill and gap analysis, which the private sector is pursuing through various standardized tests. "I think you'll find that the private sector is much more willing to invest in assessment, so they have a much better sense of their gaps, particularly on what we call the soft side." As for the Air Force, Robbert assumes that the various leadership and professional schools supply the soft side. In addition, "the selection processes tend to promote people that are strong on those competencies even if you do nothing. But the Air Force is not doing nothing."

Even though much of this work is classified, RAND does have some ideas in the public domain. In 1994, for example, RAND pulled together a 17-member team to examine the military's career management system. The team examined a variety of alternatives to the military's traditional *up-or-out system*, in which officers are either promoted up or forced out. One involved simply stretching the period in which an officer had to be promoted; another allowed for in-and-out, meaning lateral entry into the traditional up-and-out system; still another encouraged up-and-stay by providing a longer period before the up-and-out decision; and a final offered up-or-out for the first 10 years of career, then up-and-stay for the rest.

Recognizing that *mission* is the key to selecting a career system, RAND noted that "the benefits of uniformity should be balanced by a capacity for flexibility." Instead of continuing with a one-size-fits-all up-or-out policy, the military might consider a system that permits different models for different needs. Up-and-out early in career produces high turnover and the new energy that can go with it, which is highly desirable for combat arms, while up-and-stay produces officers with greater experience and knowledge, which is highly desirable for better command and control. The point is that career should fit organizational needs, not vice versa.

Lead in Futures Tense

Growing the right stuff also means learning the right stuff. Leaders can hardly help their organizations shape the future if they have only learned how to repeat the past. If organizational agility depends on recruiting and training the workforce in futures tense, alignment depends on recruiting and training leaders in futures tense, too.

Consider RAND's study of how the Army trains its own leadership corps. According to RAND's David Johnson, relatively few Army officers have the training to participate in the kind of multinational operations of today. Relatively few have experience with joint operations, and even fewer have experience in multinational settings. Army officers are trained to lead U.S. troops in U.S. battles, not joint or multinational forces in coalition settings. "Clearly, as in the past, senior Army leaders must remain proficient at the core competency of America's Army—fight and winning wars," Johnson writes. "Nevertheless, if the past is any prologue to the future, senior Army leaders could also at any time be expected to deal with the complexities of stability and support operations, peacetime engagement, deployments in support of unplanned contingencies, or a host of other missions. Additionally, Army forces will almost certainly be employed as part of a joint or combined joint task force—that will often be ad hoc." Put these missions together with the rising probabilities of urban combat, and the question is whether the Army is preparing its leaders to operate in the right environment.

RAND researchers see the mismatch between skills and mission in other sectors, too. For an example, we return to RAND's study of organizations with global missions, which was shepherded by Tora Bikson and Gregory Treverton. According to the research, all three sectors—government, nonprofit, and business—are looking for leaders with skills and experiences that extend well beyond the four corners of contemporary curricula.

As the RAND team notes, "the outlook for future leadership in international organization is very mixed.... The bad news is that, at present, these organizations lack the multidimensional competence in their human resources that future leadership cadres will need to carry out their global missions effectively. The good news is that contemporary demographic and cohort factors combine to create an unprecedented opportunity for organizations with a global reach to repopulate their upper ranks."

The nation's leading corporations accepted the new reality in the 1990s, and began looking for leaders with a mix of old and new competencies, including "a revolutionary way of understanding the structure of the world economy and the position of U.S. firms within it," along with "the skills and attitudes necessary to translate that understanding into new ways of performing business missions that are more responsive to local opportunities and threats." Whether government and nonprofits will catch up is anyone's guess.

Regardless of sector, however, RAND appears convinced that September 11, 2001, intensified an already developing demand for a new kind of international leader who understands the impact of globalization in different settings and under heightened stress. Organizations are desperate for leaders with general cognitive strengths such as problem-solving and analytical ability, strong interpersonal and relationship skills, tolerance for ambiguity and adaptability, and personal traits such as character, self-reliance, and dependability. Specialized skills are less and less in demand, if only because "what has been learned in the past is subject to obsolescence." Operating knowledge can be continually acquired as long as the learning skills and openness to ideas exist.

Communicate through Images

RAND researchers believe that information and delegation matter greatly to high performance. They worry about getting bombs on target in 10 minutes instead of 72 hours, moving troops in and out of battle in days instead of months, and giving teachers, doctors, patients, police, first responders, and maintenance workers enough information to do their jobs.

Hence, they also believe that the leader's work is not to fight the wars, but to create the conditions for others to do so effectively. This means making sure commanders, whether generals or CEOs, have the information they need to create and disseminate accurate images of both present and future tense reality. According to a 1989 RAND report that remains highly relevant to this day, commanders need "a dynamic *image* of the battlefield" that will shape "what *action* needs to be taken. This image, which is the commander's mental model of the battlefield, and its contextual surroundings, including military, political, and psychological considerations....The *meaning* of any information gained by the commander is driven by the image that frames it, and the value of that information is determined by the manner in which it fits into the image."[19]

This is why, for example, staff members must share their commander's image if they are to understand and supply his or her information needs.

Instead of sharing information or shouting orders, commanders must saturate their organizations with well-informed images. As RAND's research team concludes, the failure to communicate is the primary cause of inaccurate or inappropriate information. "When the commander's intent is ambiguous, unspecified, incorrectly specified, or incorrectly interpreted, then the wrong information can be conveyed. Inappropriate content may also result from the difficulty of expressing uncertainty. Because there is no standard way to communicate uncertainty, common estimates of uncertainty in a given situation can be difficult to share."

In this regard, the air war over Serbia was a wake-up call for both the Army and the Air Force. The Army had problems deciding how to use its Apache attack helicopters to apply additional pressure on Slobodan Milosevic as the ethnic cleansing of Kosovo accelerated, while the Air Force had enormous difficulty hitting moving targets throughout the engagement.

In retrospect, the U.S. desperately needed new tactics for merging intelligence, reconnaissance, and experience with capabilities. Writing of the difficulty engaging adversaries that use camouflage, deception, and "shoot-and-scoot" tactics, a RAND study recommended just such a new approach in a 2002 report titled *Enhancing Dynamic Command and Control of Air Operations Against Time-Critical Targets*. Assuming that adversaries will become even more agile in the future, the study team urges the Air Force to develop a "robust collaborative environment" that includes "automated tools: on-demand, high-data-rate communications; a robust network and server architecture with responsive operating protocols; an expert network manager; and an expert and empowered information manager."

Better command and control also involves understanding just what commanders need. RAND researchers tend to view the command-and-control system as a web of information that draws upon a variety of sources, including human beings, computers, documents, intelligence, devil's advocates, images of the enemy, and collective intuition and experience. As in logistics, commanders simply cannot know everything they need to know.

In echoes of RAND's 1989 study, the 2002 team concludes that the problem is not so much a lack of information, but "getting the right information in the right form to the right place at the right time, to be used in the right way. Each of these elements—content, format, location, timing, and use—is *necessary* to good command and control." According to their analysis of command posts around the world, these RAND researchers suggest that the traditional view of command communication as a linear flow of information up and decisions down is no longer valid. Rather, well-functioning command posts allow commanders to probe for understanding as well as needed information.

It is important to note that leadership is not restricted just to the senior commanders. It also involves every member of the organization down to the foxhole. In the environmental management cases described above, corporate leaders clearly recognized that they needed to delegate responsibility downward to organizational champions who would execute the general strategy and adapt as necessary. Most of the success stories also involved cross-cutting teams that took leadership for actual implementation.

The same conclusion emerges from the New American Schools project, where teams of teachers, parents, and even students helped design and implement successful whole-school reforms, often in spite of a lack of alignment at the top, and from Pittsburgh's Early Childhood Initiative. Indeed, both efforts might have been much more successful if leadership had been fully delegated down to the frontline instead of being divided among competing stakeholders at the top.

Anticipate the Adversary

RAND has also done a great deal of work on how enemy leaders think and behave, including groundbreaking work on the political psychology of the Soviet leadership. Led by the early giants of the field, Nathan Leites and Alexander George, this work covered a broad range of topics, from how the Soviets fight wars to Kremlin moods.

This early work is reflected in Stephen Hosmer's bluntly titled 2001 book, *Why Milosevic Decided to Settle When He Did.* Although his work is less psychoanalytic in tone than Leites or George, the book asks a critically important question about how tactics shape enemy behavior, and is well-linked to George's earlier work on the psychological effects of U.S. air operations in World War II and Korea.

As Hosmer frames his book, Milosevic's decision to settle on June 3, 1999, after 78 days of bombing, actually raises two questions: First, why did he not settle earlier, say, after the first few days of bombing, as the U.S. and its North Atlantic Treaty Organization (NATO) allies had hoped, and second, why did he not hold out longer, as the U.S. and NATO had feared?

On the first question, Hosmer believes that Milosevic assumed the bombing would be limited and that he could get better terms by holding firm. As he writes, "even if the bombing proved more costly than expected, Milosevic apparently assumed that sufficient countervailing pressures would eventually come to bear on NATO to cause the allies to terminate the bombing."

On the second question, Hosmer believes that Milosevic eventually realized that his leverage was gone. As such, the bombing produced a political climate conducive to concessions. Although the attacks on military targets did not provide a major source of pressure, in part because the Air Force had so much difficulty hitting moving and hidden targets, the bombing of *dual-use infrastructure* such as bridges, electrical plants, communications, and other industrial facilities caused significant damage to the Serbian economy. "The bombing was also imposing psychological and physical hardships on the ruling elite," Hosmer concludes. "The trauma caused by frequent and prolonged air raid warnings and the deprivations caused by the electric power blackouts in Belgrade undoubtedly affected the families of many persons connected to the regime. The air attacks were also destroying assets owned by the ruling elite."

RAND's early work also figures prominently in David Ronfeldt's exploratory work on the *hubris-nemesis complex* in leaders like Adolf Hitler and Saddam Hussein. "It is often said that leaders like these are megalomaniacal, power-hungry, confrontational, vengeful, messianic, grandiose, crazy, etc. The concept of the hubris-nemesis complex offers a way to view such attributes comprehensively. Such concepts—notably about charisma and narcissism—already exist for this purpose."

Although Ronfeldt uses Fidel Castro as his example, the complex is just as easily illustrated by Saddam Hussein, whose belief in himself as a warrior with a historic mission, demand for absolute power, loyalty, and attention, and fierce sense of struggle fits the complex almost perfectly. As Ronfeldt argues, a hubris-nemesis leader behaves very differently in crisis from other types of leaders: "They may have high risk-taking tendencies in a crisis, and they may be unusually demanding, confrontational, unyielding, and posturing in negotiation. A method should help determine what to expect from them, under what circumstances." To the extent possible, therefore, Ronfeldt urges that democratic nations try to identify these leaders early in their career, and try to control them or keep them from rising to power.

Even as RAND researchers encourage organizations to know their adversaries, they also believe that organizations should never become leader-dependent—leaders come and go, get killed, deliver, or depart. Organizations cannot afford to let everything ride on the mythic, heroic leader. Although RAND researchers do have their heroes, they believe in delegation in part because wars of all kinds get fought by the troops.

Ignore the Irrelevant

Robust organizations focus on all aspects of workforce planning, while ignoring the irrelevant along the way. They know that engaging the talent base is impossible if they exclude expertise on the basis of race, gender, disability, or sexual orientation. Alignment is impossible, therefore, if organizations concentrate on issues that have absolutely no bearing on actual performance.

This is certainly the message of RAND's study of gays in the military. Working under intense time pressure, RAND convened nearly 60 researchers to ask whether lifting the ban on gays in the military would somehow weaken America's military performance.

RAND answered the question through an exhaustive review that covered 50 years of research. Starting with the assumptions that gays (1) are not inherently less capable of performing military tasks than others, (2) already serve in the U.S. military, always have, and almost certainly always will, and (3) would be held to standards of conduct, appearance, demeanor, and performance at least as stringent as the standards for their straight peers, RAND turned to the relationship between sexual preference and group cohesion.

It is important to note that RAND did not accept the notion that cohesion is always a good thing. Cohesion can produce the kind of *groupthink* that led the Kennedy administration to launch the disastrous 1962 Bay of Pigs invasion of Cuba, for example, and produce rate-busting agreements and excessive socializing (read "partying") that reduces performance. Hypercohesion can also produce resentment toward external control, as well as hubris about capacity.

More important for those who argue that teams are the answer to all that ails organizations, RAND reports that "task cohesion generally accounts for only a small portion of the total variance in performance.... Even if the results of combat exercises generalize to actual combat, it is clear that a variety of nonpsychological factors are crucial to battlefield performance, and can be decisive: supplies and logistical support, the quality and quantity of information, the weather, geographical constraints, and pure dumb luck."

As for the impact of sexual preference on either task or social cohesion, the RAND study does not mince words: "it is not necessary to like someone to work with them, so long as members share a commitment to the group's objectives." Even if members of a unit were hostile to someone, as some almost certainly are, RAND noted three factors that would likely hold the team together.

First, team leaders play a critically important role in holding teams together—whether straight or gay, they either have the skills and respect of their units or not. Second, military norms, regulations, and disciplinary tools all matter to team cohesion—team members must be rewarded and sanctioned on the basis of performance, and performance only. Third, and most important perhaps, external threats have a strong effect on team cohesion regardless of personality, sexual preference, or cultural differences—teams that do not work in the military get dead.

The basic point is hard to miss. Organizations and their leaders should pay attention to how units and individuals perform their jobs. Although competition and war can create an acute sensitivity to teamwork and consistency, no amount of outside pressure will matter if an organization and its units are not committed to the mission. And they cannot be committed to the mission (e.g., recruiting young soldiers, improving health care, teaching kids) if they do not know what the mission is and how they will know they have succeeded if they actually do.

CONCLUSION

Much as they try to minimize regret and hedge against threats, robust organizations do not always succeed. In theory being robust should lead to more successful missions, if only because the missions should hedge and shape. In theory, too, robust plans must allow for adaptation as the future changes.

However, there are times when the mission is simply undoable. New products are hard to design and sell, agile adversaries are hard to locate and defeat, students come to school with both assets and deficits, police officers often work under great stress, targets are illusive, measurement is often difficult, and the world keeps changing for everyone. The essence of high performance, therefore, involves a willingness to change, which in turn requires the alertness, agility, adaptability, and alignment to do so.

Change management is a special skill in itself, however. As the next chapter will show, The RAND knowledge base holds a series of simple recommendations regarding change, starting with instructions on how to select the right change in the first place. Organizations have never been under greater pressure to do something, anything, to change, but often fail because they pick the wrong solution for the wrong problem for the wrong time. Although RAND has learned a great deal about how to increase the odds that change will actually occur, its researchers would almost certainly agree that the first step is to pick the right velocity and vector for the change itself. Any change will do for organizations that do not know where they are going.

NOTES

1 F. J. Gruenberger, "The History of the JOHNNIAC," RM-5654-PR, RAND, October 1968, p. 4.

2 Charles Wolf, "Doom or Boom?" *Wall Street Journal*, December 2, 2002, p. A16.

3 James A. Dewar cites E. O. Teisberg, "Strategic Response to Uncertainty," Harvard Business School Case 9-391-192, Harvard Business School, 1993, on this point in *Assumption-Based Planning: A Tool for Reducing Avoidable Surprise*, New York:Cambridge, 2002, p. 12.

4 Davis's analysis of surprise is from his chapter in Johnson, Libicki, and Treverton, *New Challenges, New Tools for Defense Decisionmaking*, cited in the bibliography at the end of this book.

5 The study is titled *Past Revolutions, Future Transformations*, and is cited in the bibliography

6 See Paul C. Light, *Still Artful Work: The Continuing Politics of Social Security Reform*, New York:McGraw Hill, 1995.

7 John Birkler and John Schank, "The Carrier Shortage," *The Atlantic Monthly*, July/August 2003, p. 88.

8 For a summary of the Center's work, visit www.rand.org/pardee/projects/reason.html.

9 Abstracted from Steven W. Popper, "The Third Ape's Problem: A Parable of Reasoning Under Deep Uncertainty," RAND P-8080, 2004.

10 For further reading on this point, Lempert recommends Daniel Kahneman's Nobel Prize-winning work on how people make judgments under uncertainty.

11 Hosek's analysis can be found in Johnson, Libicki, and Treverton, *New Challenges, New Tools for Defense Decisionmaking*, cited in the bibliography.

12 Tom Ricks, "Intelligence Problems in Iraq Are Detailed," *The Washington Post*, October 25, 2003, p. A1.

13 Peter Senge, et al., *The Fifth Discipline Fieldbook: Strategies and Tools for Building a Learning Organization*, New York:Doubleday, 1994.

14 Camm cites Brenda Klafter, "Pollution Prevention Benchmarking: AT&T and Intel Work Together with the Best," *Total Quality Environmental Management*, Autumn 1992, pp. 27–34, on this topic.

15 See Faith Arner and Adam Aston, "How Xerox Got up to Speed," *BusinessWeek*, May 3, 2004, p. 103, accessed at http://www.nexis.com, July 10, 2004.

16 This description of good research comes from Robert Klitgaard's lecture notes on what constitutes exemplary RAND research, March 6, 2000, author's files.

17 Bernard Rostker, "Analysis and Decision Making in the Department of Defense: Reflect on RAND," Comments for the One-RAND Colloquium, April 6, 2001, p. 7.

18 H. Norman Schwarzkopf and Peter Petre, *It Doesn't Take a Hero*, New York: Bantam, 1992, p. 453.

19 The report was written by James P. Kahan, D. Robert Worley, and Cathleen Stasz.

CHAPTER 5

LESSONS ON
MANAGING CHANGE

Like most, but not all, think tanks, RAND has always been interested in discovering the "right" answer to the research question at hand. Although it always hoped that decision makers would take its advice, it tended to leave the implementation to others.

In recent years, however, RAND and its researchers have become much more active in influencing actual decisions, whether through congressional testimony, press releases, opinion pieces, magazine articles, a much more active Internet presence, and direct consulting. Always rated as one of the nation's most reputable think tanks, RAND is becoming one of its most visible. Along the way, RAND has learned a great deal about how organizations change.

As RAND also learned through its own transformation, organizations do not become robust by merely wishing it so. They must also make the investments needed to achieve and sustain alertness, agility, adaptability, and alignment. Given their current structure and operations, some organizations will require deep change to become robust, while others may need only occasional fine-tuning to keep their edge. But whatever they need to do, their efforts will almost certainly fail if they do not pick the right velocity and vector for improvement.

Ford Motors and IBM both understood the lesson as they began implementing a new generation of environmental management standards in 1996. On the one hand, both organizations had plenty of experience with the continuous improvement required to meet the International Organization for Standardization's environmental standards. On the other hand, each had more than 20 years of experience with environmental management, and understood the step-by-step process for defining a clear environmental policy, creating compliance and monitoring systems, and detecting and correcting failures quickly. In short they knew that success would depend on steady progress toward a very clear goal.[1]

Given their previous experience with quality management, Ford and IBM pursued registration one facility at a time, accelerating their implementation strategies as they learned how to meet the standards. Ford started its effort at five North American plants in 1996, and accelerated to 50 more in 1997, and all 140 in 1998, while IBM started at five plants in 1996 and accelerated to all 28 the next year.

As Frank Camm's history of the two efforts shows, implementation required a deep commitment to experimentation and participation. Ford started the process at its Oakville, Ontario, assembly plant, where an earlier certification effort had significantly reduced the use of cleaning solvents in its paint shop, and soon moved onto Lima, Ohio, where the 10-month implementation effort was led by a cross-functional team that invited all 2100 employees to help identify targets for improvement. Building upon Lima's earlier success in implementing total quality management, the plant used its Intranet to promote change, document progress, and disseminate lessons learned. As Camm notes, the payoffs of the $220,000 in training costs and 5600 hours of meetings were immediate. Within a year of launching its new environmental management system, the plant was not only registered under the international standards, but had reduced water usage by 200,000 gallons per day, eliminated production of boiler ash, which had been the plants biggest source of solid waste, and increased the use of returnable packaging on its newest engine product, the V-8 used in the Lincoln LS8. Other plants followed one by one until all were registered by 1999.

Having been intimately involved in drafting the new environmental standards, IBM followed a somewhat different course. Like Ford, IBM started out with five pilots, developing needed corporate expertise along the way. But unlike Ford, IBM soon decided to seek a single registration for the rest of its 33 facilities, including headquarters. Although each facility went through its own environmental audit, the single registration sent a clear signal that IBM wanted environmental management to become a unique corporate asset.

Neither Ford nor IBM could have pursued their respective versions of such rapid, incremental change if they had not addressed what Camm believes are the key ingredients of successful implementation, including senior leadership support, a motivated and engaged workforce, continuous communication in all directions, and simple perseverance. Although leadership support is essential for overcoming inertia at the start of the process and employee engagement is critical throughout, Camm puts a special emphasis on time, especially if the organization adopts a continuous improvement approach. "Specific changes affecting small parts of an organization—say, a few hundred people—may take as much as two years to work through," he writes. "Implementing a specific change throughout an organization with tens of thousands of employees can easily take five years or more. Implementation of a new approach to environmental management typically involves a series of specific changes that can extend the period of change beyond a decade."

As Camm's work suggests, getting robust involves a two-step process for actually improving performance. First an organization must decide what kind of change will produce the greatest improvement in a given attribute of robustness. Second it must adopt a strategy for implementing the change. In short the organization must select the vector for change and manage the velocity of implementation. Even with these choices in hand, Camm's colleagues in RAND's education program note that successful change involves an inherently difficult process: "No matter what the target of reform or the design construct, the scale-up process is necessarily iterative and complex and requires the support of multiple actors." One reason so much change fails to take hold is that change is just plain hard.[2]

Thus, even before making these choices, an organization must ask whether change is actually possible. It is a question well worth asking before an organization mounts a campaign for improvement.

CAN ORGANIZATIONS CHANGE?

Marc Robbins and the Velocity Management team clearly believe that organizations can become more robust. "The nice thing about military bureaucracies is that they tend to be inertial, for good or bad." At least for logistics reform, inertia was good:

> Once it got going, there was no stopping it.... I think most people's view was that the system didn't work as designed, but they didn't really think anything could change, because nothing ever does. Fort Bragg proved it could happen, and suddenly we started having these big meetings where Fort Bragg would say "We did good. We did real good." All the generals would say, "Good for you, good for you! Hey, Fort Campbell sitting there, what are you guys doing? You see yourselves as competitors with Fort Bragg, what are you doing?" So Fort Campbell has to do it, then Ford Drum, then Fort Stewart. Fort Stewart has an armored

division. If that armored division can do it, then Fort Hood with two armored divisions can do it. Pretty soon it spreads like that.

The change process began with a simple agreement that the Army logistics process was broken. Although moving mountains of material is a perfectly logical hedge against the volatility of war, there are limits to a mass-based approach to logistics. "Mass brings with it chronic problems in responsiveness, reliability, and efficiency," the RAND Velocity Management team writes. "Having massive stockpiles on hand has not guaranteed that combat forces will get what they need when they need it.... In the early 1990s it took a month, on average, for an Army mechanic to receive an ordered part if it was not available on his installation." Mass begets mass, which begets confusion.

As John Dumond says, "that's the problem of having big piles." The Army faced the problem during the peacekeeping mission in Bosnia. As one Army official told Dumond in the mid-1990s, "We're proving once again that we can overwhelm the theater with piles of stuff. We have no problem sending big piles in; that's not the problem. The problem is what we do with it once it arrives."

According to the Velocity Management team, the Army had to move from defining logistics as piles of stuff to a set of processes for delivering products and services, shift its metrics from days of supply to time, quality, and cost, and switch its focus from compliance and budget execution to customer satisfaction and performance improvement. "At the outset of the Velocity Management initiative," according to *Velocity Management*, "Army logisticians commonly asked, 'When will this initiative end?' Initially, they did not conceive of it as a new paradigm for managing the logistics system. As a new way of doing business, Velocity Management has no planned end point."

Velocity Management has yielded a deep inventory of lessons on managing change, including the need for a clear vision; assured successful, institutionalized improvement; early victories; and at least some dollars for training and technologies. Another key is what the team calls continuous innovation: "Reform began with the order fulfillment process, then progressed to related processes such as the repair process, inventory management, and logistics financial management."

Most important perhaps, the Army built a coalition for change that has survived the ordinary turnover that marks military careers. It did so in part by building a succession chain that would ensure that the effort would outlast the departure of any given officer or officers. "General officers enter the coalition while in one position," the Velocity Management team writes, "then often move to other positions in the coalition as the Army rotates them through assignments to increase their knowledge and experience."

The Velocity Management initiative has clearly had an impact on the Army's logistics process, changing everything from metrics to truck routes along the way. Where the Army once used *days of supply* as its basic metric of speed, it now uses order and ship times. As Dumond remembers, "If you have a measure like days of supply and you think better means more, then you want to pile the stuff in. But it is better to have an order and ship time of seven days. This means that you'll get what you need in seven days. 'Days of supply' says you value piles. 'Order and ship time' means you value speed."

The change was unmistakable in the war in Afghanistan. "We still had people who were willing to send in big piles," Dumond remembers. "The war-fighters said, 'Stop! I don't need all that. I don't have room for all that here.' That's a giant step forward. We have people who now believe the process is in place to get the stuff in when they need it."

The Army was not alone in seeking change. The Air Force also streamlined its supply chain by adopting what it labeled as *lean logistics*. As Robert Tripp acknowledges, "just like the old British Navy, the Air Force needs logistic islands that are largely forward-based with heavy processes and resources, so that it doesn't have to move everything from home." Most of what gets moved is not aircraft or pilots, but tents, bombs, and even steam shovels. "It's like building a little city," says Tripp. "What the Air Force is doing is picking up production processes and laying them down in very rapid order. And it turns out that, as in soccer, most of the important moves are away from the ball. Everyone looks at the airplanes over there, but the important moves are happening over here with the munitions and the tents."

Logistics is particularly important in keeping the Air Force fresh enough to maintain its strength, especially during the past 15 years of non-stop action. Despite the wear-and-tear on its equipment, the Air Force has steadily improved its agility. "Bombs were falling over Afghanistan on October 7," only 25 days after the attacks on New York City and Washington, Tripp notes. "The forces were deployed and sustained, and Kabul fell on December 1. It was pretty rapid deployment of air power to very austere locations." Asked if the Air Force had enough stuff, Tripp says, "Sure, there was not a sortie missed. But the question is what battles the Air Force could have fought in addition to Afghanistan. That's a better question."

This belief in evidence-based change underpins much of RAND's work. "The values of Total Quality Management have been dominant at RAND for as long as I've been here," says Frank Camm of RAND's defense logistics work. "It wasn't called that, because we didn't know what TQM was. The notions of taking a systems view; of demanding the application of objective analysis where possible and as quantitative as possible; of taking ideas to the field, testing them, bringing them back, and being accountable for the effects of your recommendations have been part of the RAND culture for as long as I've been here."

Defined as such the quality movement has supporters in other RAND programs, most notably in health care. As Cretin explains, successful quality programs are not about having fishbone diagrams, flowcharts, and process control. Rather, it comes as a basic commitment to experimentation and understanding failure. "One of the great regional efforts around improving quality of care has been in Minneapolis," she says. "They have now gone on for 10 years and they've developed a repertoire of 30 or 35 guidelines that affect most of the day-to-day stuff and outpatient practice. They keep them up-to-date and they have a schedule for updating them, but what they really do is they get all the practices engaged in trying to work together collaboratively and share ideas about what works and have this supportive community of making health care in Minneapolis as good as it can be."

What works in Minnesota does not necessarily work elsewhere, however, in part because Minnesota has long been committed to innovation and change, and in part, Cretin suggests, because Minnesota is, well, "nice." As Cretin notes, "They've never come out and said, 'What we're doing here is quality improvement according to anybody's model, and it's going to turn us around.' They just have this attitude that 'we all want to do better at this and we're trying to learn how to do that together. Here's an idea, let's try this and here's another idea, let's try that. If that doesn't work, let's revisit it.' "

Two points emerge from RAND's research about changing organizations. First, there are clear risks in *not* acting. As Robert Lempert makes the case for robust adaptive decision making, "It's easy enough to show all the places where not doing anything gets you into trouble.... Robust adaptive decision making is most useful when there are futures you're ignoring because you don't think you can deal with them. So you just put the blinders on. You just keep cruising. If you can discover ways that organizations can deal with the future that they haven't thought about so they can actually accept it, that's where I think we're making a big contribution."

Second, changing organizations takes time and patience, not to mention a great deal of coaching. "When we get a new weapon, which is like a new business practice, it's very complex," says Nancy Moore. "We wouldn't give a pilot a new airplane and just say, 'Here, go fly it.' Would we? Not only 'Go fly it,' but "Go to war and kill someone.' No, we would give them training. When we felt they were ready, we would send them into conflict. When we start an initiative, and the generals want results yesterday, it's like putting a pilot into a plane that they've never flown."

The fact is that organizations often coup-proof themselves against change. Asked what he would do to change an organization like the Army, Leland Joe answers the question with a question: "Basically, what I would ask is, 'What can I do? What are my degrees of freedom? You can't get rid of everybody, but sometimes you can get rid of somebody, and sometimes you have restraints where you just have to make do with what you've got. Sometimes you want to hire smart people, but you can't because you don't have the money. High-performance units will examine their constraints and adjust by a combination of finding new people, training those they have, and acquiring new equipment. The mix of solutions depends on the specific situation."

Or, as Quinlivan suggests, "First get rid of the stupid things, then make a line that you're going to grade people on what you say they're really going to do." As Quinlivan remembers his time in Vietnam, there are just some places where incompetence simply will not suffice:

> When I was in Vietnam, one of the last things I had to do was stand at a promotion board to get promoted to E-5. If I'd stayed in, by now I'd be E-6. You go up to this board. At the time, there was a drug problem in the Army in Vietnam. You may have heard.
>
> I came in from a fire direction center in the field. I was a shift leader in a fire direction center. They ask you what you do if there's somebody in your section who has a drug problem that you have to supervise. I know what they want me to do. They want me to echo back the posters and say that I counsel them, that this could ruin their lives, that they ought to turn themselves in to this program and get clean, that this is very important.
>
> I'd get the heads nodding up and down, then I said, "But of course, the first thing I'd do is get them the hell out of the fire direction center, because we kill people either way, right?" Nobody wanted to hear me say that this was important. We were in the critical path. Every time I would pick up that telephone and tell the guns which way to point, they were going to point that way.
>
> Make it so that if the guy fails on the critical path, the guy is gone. There are guys who can't do that job. You can get another one. That helps. Then train him.

The problem is that most organizations impose sharp limits on what they spend on readiness and training. "How much money gets used in a battalion really matters, how many parts, how many get called for, whether you broke the damn thing when you took it out last time," says Quinlivan. "If you really, really want them to do what they've got to do, you can't have people saying, 'Take the third platoon. Park it over there. Don't move it for two months. We can't afford it.' You don't want to just send these little things down to balance the budget and have these guys walking around picking up daisies instead of driving this thing. You've got so many things you're being scored on that you say, 'Hey, don't use the tank. It's kind of pricey.'"

THE VELOCITY AND VECTOR OF CHANGE

Pick an organization, any organization, and chances are that it is doing something, often many things, to strengthen its performance in an increasingly turbulent environment. According to Bain & Company's 2003 survey of organizational change, which was the most recently available reference point as this book went to press, the typical company used 16 different management tools to improve its performance in 2003, up from 10 in 2002.[3]

The larger the company, the more frantic the pace. Companies with revenues under $600 million used an average of 15 tools in 2002, while companies over $2 billion used 17. The most popular tool was strategic planning (89 percent), followed by benchmarking (84 percent), mission and vision statements (84 percent), customer segmentation (79 percent), outsourcing (78 percent), customer surveys (78 percent), and codes of ethics (78 percent).

Bain argues that at least some of the increased activity reflects an effort to stay on course during uncertain times. After all, the three most popular tools in 2002 involved what Bain's Darrell Rigby calls "tried and true compass-setting tools," strategic planning, benchmarking, and mission and vision statements. Eighty percent of companies used all three tools in 2002, up from 70 percent in 2000. Moreover, there was ample economic pressure during the recession to justify action, not to mention increased scrutiny in the wake of Enron and WorldCom.

But Rigby also viewed the flurry as a mix of hope and fear. "Senior executives had reservations about short-term prospects for their own markets and the global economy," writes Rigby. "But they also voiced strong confidence in their ability to manage during prolonged economic uncertainty. Surprisingly, given the pressure to control expenses, their choice of tools shows a clear bias toward growth over cost cutting."[4]

He also writes that change is oversold as the answer to all that ails organizations. "The term 'management tool' now encompasses a broad spectrum of approaches to management—from simple planning software to complex organizational designed to revised business philosophies. Many of these tools offer conflicting advice. One may call for keeping all your customers, while another advises you to focus only on the most profitable. But all of these tools have one thing in common: they promise to make their users more successful. Today, beleaguered managers—struggling to demonstrate that they can adapt to rapid change in an increasingly challenging world—are turning to management tools in unprecedented numbers."[5]

The Fear of Standing Still

The only problem is that the change often fails to deliver. Organizations spend billions in time and energy on getting better only to find that the latest reform has passed over and through them with little or no effect. It is safe to say that the problem in organizational life today is not too little change, but too much.

Organizations might face better odds if the options pointed in the same direction. However, organizations confront a vast inventory of recommendations for improvement. Although there are many ways to sort the inventory, I have found it easiest to sort the recommendations by velocity and vector, meaning the pace and destination of organizational change.

Velocity involves a mix of duration (short- or longer-term), motivation (thinking or feeling), and intensity (incremental or radical). Although many organizations progress from one velocity to another, high velocity tends to reside in calls for immediate, feeling-driven, sometimes radical action, while low velocity tends to involve longer-term, thinking-driven, incremental change.

In turn vector involves a mix of targets (the whole organization or a specific process), participants (the workforce or leadership), and goals (steady growth or breakthroughs). Broad change efforts tend to focus on the whole organization, the entire workforce, and steady growth, while focused change tends to involve a specific process or two, leadership, and a hope for breakthroughs.

Organizations can and often do pursue more than one change effort at a time, often mixing velocities and vectors across business units. Moreover, there is no one right combination of velocity and vector that appears to assure success. Indeed, one reason change has such a disappointing record is that organizations often put high- and lower-velocity, and broad- and narrower-vector options together in the same change initiative.

At least by my reading of the knowledge base and RAND's own transformation, and it is my reading and mine alone, RAND appears to have a preference about both velocity and vector. On velocity, for example, they tend to favor longer-term, thinking-based, incremental change over the radical, disruptive change currently in vogue. Although they do see occasions where radical change is essential, particularly when threats are high, they generally believe that organizations should avoid fads whenever possible.

On vector, they also tend to favor process change over whole-organization reform, employee-centered change over leader-driven change, and a goal of steady growth over the pursuit of breakthrough innovation. Again there are occasions where breakthroughs are essential, but not if it involves a *bet-the-company philosophy* that puts longer-term performance at risk. Whatever the product or process, most revolutions start with a single battle and can last years before victory. DuPont's comeback lasted more than a decade, and Volvo waited even longer before it entered the SUV fray.

A Preferred Velocity and Vector

▶ Velocity

- Focus on the long term
- Start with thinking
- Be pragmatic (unless the future says otherwise)

▶ Vector

- Change processes, then organizations
- Change the workforce first
- Focus on growth and breakthroughs will follow

Velocity

Organizations face at least three choices in setting the velocity of organizational change. First, they can focus on short-term implementation or embrace longer-term progress. Second, they can make the case for change based on thinking or feeling. Third, they can seek more pragmatic, quasi-incremental improvement or radical impact. As the following exhibit, "Velocities for Change," shows, short-term, feeling-based, radical change creates the greatest sense of organizational urgency.

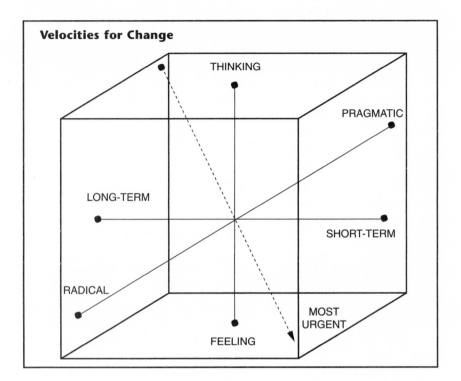

Velocities for Change

THINKING

PRAGMATIC

LONG-TERM

SHORT-TERM

RADICAL

MOST
URGENT

FEELING

The choices are not always mutually exclusive. Total quality management often starts with a thinking-based effort to achieve immediate results in one or two processes, followed by incremental expansion across the entire organization, while reengineering often starts with an urgent, feeling-based call for radical action, followed by years of incremental adjustment.

So noted, my sense is that RAND prefers organizational change that focuses on long-term, thinking-based, quasi-incremental improvement. Although RAND has made many recommendations for radical reform, especially regarding the war on terrorism, its conclusions are often accompanied by recognizing that change takes time, requires careful measurement and adjustment, and happens in small steps, only occasionally punctuated by great disruption.

Duration RAND is actually somewhat conflicted on the choice between long-term, continuous change and short-term change. On the one hand, many RAND researchers argue that organizations must be able to adapt quickly if they are to achieve and sustain high performance. "The need for government organizations of all kinds to change and change faster is very great," says Nancy Moore. "I don't think it's going to go away, even though there is the threat of terrorism and stuff. It won't go away. They've got to change and change fast."

Yet RAND researchers also know that organizational change takes time and patience, a point confirmed by its 10-year effort to improve Army logistics. As the nine authors of *Velocity Management* write, "Transformation of large systems and complex processes takes time—many years—despite dramatic and continuous improvements early in the implementation period."[6] The need for perseverance is especially important in the military, but not because it has a rigid hierarchy and command structure. As the team notes, the problem is that officers change assignments about every two years as a matter of normal career development. Even if they favored it, creative destruction would not outlast a single two-year cycle. Hence, the need for a coalition of Army generals who could provide the institutional memory to keep the effort going—when one leader left, there has always been another to take his or her place. As much as Defense Department planners talk about a revolution in military affairs, it is a revolution that will be long in the making.

This commitment to long-term change can be seen in the military's strategic distribution management initiative, which is taking velocity management organization-wide. Operated under the joint ownership of the U.S. Transportation Command and the Defense Logistics Agency, the initiative is designed to address what RAND calls the "mal-positioning" of military stock here and there across the world; the initiative is designed to streamline distribution and minimize stops, queues, and touches.

There are plenty of potential horror stories about the need for continuous improvement. A container of cargo can sit for weeks waiting for the ship it was assigned to, even as other ships head for the same destination ahead of the booking, while a pallet of consolidated materials can sit for days at a transit hub such as Ramstein, Germany, waiting for the aircraft it was booked on, even though a truck could deliver it to its European customer in a day. Like FedEx or Worldwide Express, the Defense distribution system must be able to satisfy its customers on every delivery. But unlike private shippers, the defense system can experience severe and unpredictable, up-and-down movements in demand, and must go anywhere the customer wants, even Afghanistan.

Starting with a database that shows the end-to-end delivery time for every package, the military has set a series of process goals for its various customers. In Europe, for example, the new system is being streamlined to deliver at least 85 percent of a customer's shipment from the closest distribution point. At the launch of the system in 2000, only 51 percent of orders met the goal; in 2001 the percentage rose to 56 percent; by March 2002 the percentage was up to 65 percent. Most of the change was accomplished by simply moving stock from one distribution center to another and increasing the use of scheduled deliveries.

As RAND cautions, it will take time for the system to change. Like the Six Sigma system pioneered by Motorola and General Electric, the strategic distribution model must become part of the military's normal operating culture, not just a one-time experiment.

Motivation It is hardly surprising that RAND and its researchers prefer thinking to feeling as a primary motivation for change. That is how they were trained, they like to be treated as professionals themselves, and how they study problems.

RAND clearly believes in using analysis to set national goals, even when the analysis leads to sharp disagreements with current policy. If it cannot be measured, it cannot be defended, a point well made in RAND's controversial work on controlling cocaine. With funding from the White House Office of National Drug Control Policy, the U.S. Army, and the Ford Foundation, RAND has been following the war on drugs for the past 20 years. Despite the political popularity of "supply-side" policies such as interdiction and imprisonment, RAND's research clearly demonstrates that treatment was the most effective option for winning the war on drugs. In 1993, for example, its seminal statement on the war concluded that treatment is much more effective than the much more expensive effort to destroy coca crops and stop trafficking.

> One might wonder how this squares with the (dubious) conventional wisdom that, with treatment, "nothing works." There are two explanations. First, evaluations of treatment typically measure the proportion of people who no longer use drugs at some point after completing treatment; they tend to underappreciate the benefits of keeping people off drugs while they are in treatment—roughly one fifth of the consumption reduction generated by treatment accrues during treatment. Second, about three fifths of the users who start treatment stay in their program less than three months. Because such incomplete treatments do not substantially reduce consumption, they make

treatment look weak by traditional criteria. However, they do not cost much, so they do not dilute the cost-effectiveness of completed treatments.

The conclusion was built upon 10 years of peer-reviewed work that covered the history of the cocaine trade; produced an economic model of how cocaine is produced and marketed; examined the drug legalization debate; profiled the Colombian drug industry; analyzed drug use in the United States; assessed the U.S. military's role in drug control; mapped the organization of drug markets; and reviewed government's rather dismal success in controlling vices of all kinds. As the studies piled up, RAND reached the inevitable conclusion that the war on drugs could best be won by reducing demand, not supply.

RAND does not dismiss feeling as a part of change, especially when it involves communication. As Nancy Moore and her colleagues write of best practices in purchasing and supply management, communication is essential to any change effort: "We repeatedly heard that there is no such thing as too much communication when it comes to change. Not only do messages need to be repeated, they also need to come in different modes because different people process and access information differently.... Leaders need to use every available forum to support the change implementation."

Yet, even when they embrace new communication tools such as story-telling or applaud leading from the gut, they see an underlying analytic process. "When people say they're going with their gut, they are actually saying something more complex," says Steven Popper. "They've thought through a number of ways this thing can play out; they've thought of a couple of solutions. And they've played those solutions out taking a shower, playing golf, and stuff like that. The decision is the result of a process that is very similar to robust adaptive decision making, which breaks up the hunch and makes it into something that is visible and tractable, but may exist only at the subconscious level."

Intensity RAND is not unwilling to embrace radical, disruptive change, a point well made by its early work on everything from ballistic missiles to the earliest version of the Internet. However, most of its recommendations tend to support more pragmatic, even incremental change. More often than not, RAND recommends that organizations start the change process with experiments rather than immediate adoption; more often than not, it recommends evaluation of progress carefully before taking the next step; more often than not, it focuses on basic issues of readiness to adapt than the adaptation itself.

At least some of this *go-slow approach* resides in RAND's own culture, which gives researchers the opportunity to follow a lead for years, even decades. RAND rarely solves a problem with a single breakthrough study. Rather it wears down an issue study after study, year after year. As RAND notes on its website, "To add value, research should draw conclusions and inferences beyond the point already achieved within the professional community and reflected in the existing literature. Added value is at the heart of quality and, in fact, is sometimes even confused with it."

RAND's work on educational testing is a good example. Launched in the early 1990s when RAND responded to a U.S. National Science Foundation request for proposals, the research program asked whether there were any reasonable alternatives to the standardized tests that California and other states were using to measure educational progress and allocate real dollars.

The RAND researchers who won the $1.8 million grant had little interest in proving that testing is *the* answer to all that ails schools. As one of the investigators told the RAND student who wrote the case study for Klitgaard and Wolf's course, "Wild claims were being made for performance assessments. Steve and I took a traditional RAND skeptic's view of things: We wanted to subject the claims to more rigorous analysis."

The research took many twists and turns over the years, resulting in dozens of publications and intense debate. But the first task was to determine whether an open-ended test was more reliable than the standardized multiple-choice tests then, and still, in vogue. The program eventually ended up almost exactly where it began: Testing is very difficult and expensive to do well and promises far more than it can deliver in measuring how much students are actually learning.

Even when RAND recommends whole-organization change, it tends to favor a more pragmatic approach in both designing and implementing the change. Thus, RAND's recent study of the Naval Sea Systems Command (NAVSEA) began with the development of an entirely new methodology for helping the giant organization make the painful choices needed to do more with less far into the future.[7]

As RAND's 12-person study team notes, NAVSEA is one of the world's most important businesses. In 2002 it employed 45,000 people in 319 different occupations, and managed 108 products, 49 business processes, 1200 activities, 70 technologies, 195 facilities, and 7 major business units, including a refueling unit that handles the nation's nuclear-powered carriers and submarines.

RAND's team used a variety of techniques for addressing NAVSEA's request, starting with assumption-based planning to help the Navy think in futures tense. It then used market and portfolio analysis to identify future customer demand, and rank NAVSEA's products by relative importance and market impact. In doing so, RAND's team was able to identify products that could be considered candidates for new or continued investment versus those that were candidates for evaluation and potential elimination. Surface communications, sonar systems, and submarine periscopes all fell into the new or expand category, while electrochemical propulsions systems, microwave weapons, and semiconductor research moved onto the maintain or evaluate list. With these and other measures of product impact in hand, RAND's team then asked how NAVSEA's organizational structure should change to accommodate the new priorities.

The RAND team eventually concluded their analysis with three basic questions about NAVSEA's future: Which business units and products should remain in the corporate portfolio? Which business units and products can be easily purchased outside the organization without sacrificing quality and customer needs? And which business units and products are so central that they should stay within NAVSEA? These are not the kinds of questions that RAND or NAVSEA can answer alone—Congress and the president have something to say about what the Navy buys and from whom.

Notwithstanding the political realities, RAND's team recognized that organizations are not made and remade overnight, especially when most of their products are at sea somewhere around the globe. Rather, they get reshaped through careful analysis and painstaking reform. Reshaping NAVSEA is no doubt an audacious goal, but it is one that RAND would say needs to be undertaken one process at a time as part of a long-term strategy.

Vector

Organizations also face at least three choices in picking the vector of change. First they can focus on organization-wide reform or target a specific process or two. Second they can invite the entire workforce to participate in change or focus their energies on the leadership. Third they can adopt changes to spur steady growth or ignite breakthroughs. As the following exhibit, "Vectors for Change" shows, organization-wide, whole-workforce, and breakthrough-oriented change is the most diffuse.

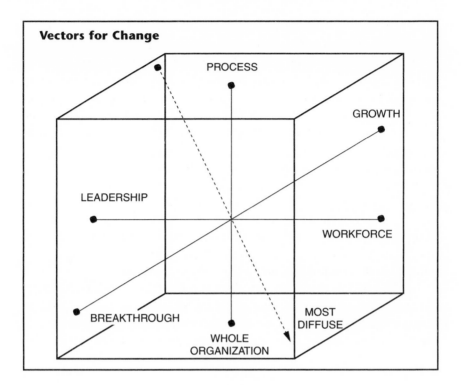

Vectors for Change

Once again the choices are not necessarily exclusive. Total quality management often starts with a single process, then expands steadily outward to cover the entire organization, while the search for innovation often starts with a senior-level commitment of resources, but extends down through the entire workforce.

My sense is that RAND prefers organizational change that focuses on processes, workforce improvement, and steady growth, rather than whole-organization, leader-centered, and breakthrough oriented reform. Again there are times when RAND has called for massive organizational change in aging industries such as mining and refining. But as with velocity, such calls are almost always guarded by an acknowledgment that reform cannot happen instantly, nor is breakthrough thinking possible without a steady infrastructure.

Target RAND has done its share of research on whole organization reform, including the study of the New American Schools' break-the-mold effort discussed earlier in this book. But when it comes time to setting the vector for change, process comes first.

Just because RAND tends to focus on process rather than whole-organization reform does not mean the processes are small. According to RAND's recent report on the midlife refueling of the nuclear-powered carrier, the *U.S.S. Nimitz*, refueling may well be "the most challenging engineering and industrial task undertaken anywhere by any organization." Even as the nuclear reactor is refueled, the entire ship must be repaired and modernized, including everything from the ship's combat and war-fighting systems to its water, electrical power, aircraft refueling system, ventilation, and air conditioning, all of which must last 23 years, more or less.

There is no doubt that the $2.2-billion refueling was a success. As RAND's study team notes, the Navy and the Newport News Shipbuilding performed admirably during the last year of the overhaul, adding on more than a million hours of last-minute work, while making significant improvements in support of just-in-time decision making.

Nevertheless, the execution process was far from perfect. Not only did the refueling come in roughly $1 billion and more than 4 million hours above budget, it showed significant weaknesses in all but one of the team's criteria for successful program management. Lines of authority were sometimes unclear and confusing, and changed at different points in the refueling; Navy management of the project was hampered by the lack of timely, accurate, and relevant data; the two parties used different systems to manage cost and schedule; there was no evidence of a risk-management program of any kind; the project goal was unclear, and necessary work was left out of the initial plan; cost estimates were clearly inaccurate; funding was unstable; and the Navy went through two project managers, four deputy managers, and four assistant program managers during the life of the effort. Although everyone involved wanted to deliver a quality ship on time and within budget, the Navy did not have the staff to bring its 50 years of experience to provide an independent check on the cost and schedule estimates, and progress-related information was often late and inaccurate. (See RAND's briefing slide on the nine criteria for successful program management.)

This is not to argue that the *Nimitz* went back to sea in poor condition. Nor is it remotely possible to define all the work needed for the success of a specific, active ship, if only because some parts of a ship are inaccessible while it is still at sea, or cannot be inspected until it is dismantled.

But RAND's analysis clearly indicates a need for improvement, not the least of which is better planning, contract design, and workload forecasting.

Assessing Program Management

1. Clear and effective lines of authority have been established

2. Communication is encouraged

3. Methods for cost, schedule, and change control are used

4. A risk-management process is used

5. Requirements for work are clear and sound

6. Cost estimates are well defined and justified

7. Incentives are apparent and appropriate

8. Funding is adequate and stable, and control and support are established

9. The management team is selected for credibility and stability, and is of adequate size

Even with these changes, execution will remain difficult unless the Navy and its contractors get much better at determining all *potential* tasks that might come up during the refueling process. At the same time, the Navy and its contractors must improve data and estimating capabilities, creating an open-book environment in which both know enough about what is happening in each organization to plan accordingly.

Newport News Shipbuilding has improved since the *Nimitz* left port. Now owned by Northrop Grumman, the company completed a $100 million overhaul of its information systems in 2002, importing SAP enterprise software for business planning, and Dassault Systemes CAD-CAM software for project design. It also streamlined its old 21-step supply chain by collapsing 8.5 million often unique part numbers into 3.5 standardized part names. "There are not a lot of opportunities for organic growth," a senior manager told *Fortune* in 2002. "We're not going to get a phone call saying 'We want you to build 30 aircraft carriers, and we want you to build them now.'" The only way for Newport News Shipbuilding to survive and prosper as a whole is to improve every process under its control.[8]

Participants   RAND and its researchers clearly believe that a talented, highly skilled workforce is a core asset for organizational performance under any conditions, but it is particularly important for organizations that face uncertain futures. Although they do worry about leadership, they tend to believe that organizational improvement involves all employees, not just the cadre at the top.

The military used to have little need for specialization, for example. Most soldiers were in the infantry, most sailors were on ships. But as the world changed, so did the structure of the workforce. Today's military requires a vast inventory of skills, some of which require intense training and on-the-job experience. Although the immediate future of the armed services has already been determined by recent recruitment, the workforce must be able to adapt. Hence the increasing focus on recruiting in the college-bound market.[9]

Workforces do not change by accident, of course. They change in response to incentives. RAND's own internal labor market makes the case. "We have a very loose internal market where you're trying to compete with other projects for the really good people," Beth Asch explains. "And similarly, as somebody who is in demand, you have the ability to pick and choose…. To compete you've got to make sure your project is not only policy relevant to the sponsor but also attractive to high-quality researchers who might work on the project. That means making sure there's an opportunity to do interesting and creative work that draws on the researcher's skills. As a person who is formulating and leading projects, I feel that's a real discipline because if I want good people, I've got to get good projects. And conversely, I feel I owe the project sponsor a well-done effort, and the only way to ensure a good product is to get good people to work on it."

The question is which comes first, of course: the internal labor system or the talent? Should organizations focus on finding and motivating talented employees or building internal labor markets and reward systems that attract and energize talent? RAND would likely answer that the internal market creates external interest—drawing talent to the institution because of the opportunity to work on creative, interesting projects, rather than vice versa.

RAND and its researchers have written extensively about two specific areas where organizations must change, and change soon. First, organizations must deal with the changing nature of work itself. As RAND's Lynn A. Karoly and Constantijn Panis write in *The 21st Century at Work*, the U.S.

labor force is not growing fast enough to keep up with demand. Having grown 2.6 percent each year during the 1970s, the labor force grew by 1.1 percent a year during the 1990s, and will fall to 0.4 percent a year during the 2010s, and just 0.3 percent a year during the 2020s. Absent some spectacular surprise in immigration policy that would permit millions of highly trained foreign-born workers across the border, future economic growth will depend more on increased productivity than people.

Karoly and Panis are particularly persuasive in discussing the impact of technology on work. Productivity has finally caught up to technology as industries have incorporated computer chips and software into every aspect of production. Although it is impossible to assign returns of investment to all breakthroughs, bar codes alone have created immeasurable gains in organizational performance, whether in retail services, transportation, banking, or human tissue management.

More importantly for robustness, technology has created greater opportunities for the delegation and information sharing so integral to high-performance work systems, which in turn leads to greater investment in training, more opportunities to create and track strong, clear incentives for performance, and more accuracy in measuring results. As RAND writes, information technologies also "facilitate the move toward more decentralized forms of business organization, both the vertical disintegration of firms evident by increased specialization and the organization work within firms.... Shifts in business organization in turn have implications for compensation structures, including wages and employee benefits." Some sectors may soon rely almost entirely on "e-lancers" who drift from employer to employer in a recruitment process that operates more like a movie casting call than a traditional contract.

RAND and its researchers also worry about how to bring employees together in effective teams, a concern well illustrated by its report on the U.S. National Transportation Safety Board (NSTB). Although the NTSB is the best aviation investigator in the world, it has been stretched to the breaking point by a series of highly complicated accidents, most notably the explosion of TWA Flight 800, which was eventually traced back to fumes in an empty fuel tank, and the crash of USAir Flight 427, which was caused by a bizarre rudder malfunction in the last minutes of an otherwise routine flight.

RAND's report *Safety in the Skies* was produced by its Institute for Civil Justice and stands as the most thorough examination of NTSB in its 30-year history.[10] It also opens the window on an investigation process that the public follows closely. Noting that aviation accidents are often viewed as nothing short of national catastrophes, RAND's five-person team also reports that an NTSB "statement of cause" regarding what went wrong can be nothing short of catastrophic for the airline or aircraft manufacturer.

Unfortunately, the NTSB's system for investigating accidents is threatened at two levels. First, the NTSB relies on investigative teams to determine the causes of accidents. These teams of parties often include manufacturers (e.g., Boeing in TWA 800 and USAir 427), operators (e.g., the Air Line Pilots Association), and representatives from different parts of the Federal Aviation Administration (e.g., air traffic control). The resulting potential for conflict of interest can undermine public confidence in the results, while slowing the investigation as potential litigants struggle to understand the fact.

More importantly, NTSB does not have the resources to keep up with the rising complexity of its mission. As RAND's team writes, "Given modern aircraft design, manufacture, and operation, the NTSB's investigative techniques are in some respects archaic, raising doubts that complex accidents will be expeditiously, or even conclusively, resolved."

More resources will do little, however, without the systems to manage information and investigate accidents. The NTSB most certainly does not want for highly motivated professional employees. "In its review, RAND found an agency that is wholly dependent on the professionalism of its staff for success," the team concludes. "So far, the staff has been able to deliver, but this strategy cannot ensure the NTSB's long-term independence or continued technical excellence. In significant ways, the NTSB is already at or near the breaking point."

According to RAND's team, NTSB's strength is its human capital. But it is capital poorly managed and developed. The agency has no way to accurately measure how human resources are applied to a given accident investigation, for example, and cannot tell whether it has the right expertise for the changing nature of the industry.

Goals RAND recognizes that organizations often need revolutionary thinking, technological breakthroughs, and innovation to survive. But given a choice between steady growth and breakthrough as the destination for change, I am convinced RAND would urge steady growth.

Take education reform as a first example. Tempting though it might be to declare victory after a year or two of higher scores, RAND's education researchers look for sustained achievement far into the future.

This is certainly the case in a report subtitled *What We Know and What We Need to Know about Vouchers and Charter Schools*. As the four-person RAND team states, "It would be fair to say that none of the important empirical questions have been answered definitively. Even the strongest evidence is based on programs that have been operating for only a short time with a small number of participants, serious questions about generalizability remain."[11]

After summarizing the available evidence, RAND concludes that the list of unknowns far outweighs the list of knowns. No one knows, for example, why African-American students do better with vouchers and in charter schools, nor does anyone know how such programs sort students across schools. Are vouchers just another device for moving pee-wee hockey, basketball, and football players to the better programs? Do parents really know enough to use vouchers and charters effectively? And just what makes voucher systems and charter schools different from traditional systems and schools? These researchers would almost certainly favor analysis over exhortation, and continuous improvement over disruption.

Take health care as a second example. According to RAND, new medical technologies are often touted as the answer to all that ails us. Unfortunately, as the study team notes, some technologies simply do not work, while others cost much more than they yield. Finding some way to winnow technologies would send a socially valuable message to inventors and innovators: "Technologies that serve the social good are likely to be rewarded in the marketplace; other technologies are not." The cautionary note is clear:

> Striking an appropriate balance between benefits and costs is very difficult, and the stakes are high. Use of unproven technologies involves risks of injuries to patients, lost patient benefits from failing to use a different technology, and wasted resources. But, of course, all successful technologies were initially unproven, and limiting or delaying the use of new technologies also involves risks: lost benefits to patients who could have been treated more effectively and taking the profit out of innovation, thus reducing incentives to innovate....

RAND and its researchers would almost certainly recommend continuous change and careful measurement over the disruptive embrace of promising technologies. They might also caution that exhortation is a poor instrument for achieving lasting change in the health industry.

Once again, where an organization stands on the course of change depends in large measure on where it sits. The Defense Department might be due for radical change, or at least that is what Secretary Donald Rumsfeld argued after September 11, while the mining industry might need continuous improvement as its workforce adjusts to new challenges. In a similar vein, schools might need more continuity, analysis, and leadership, and a lot less innovation, just as Enron, WorldCom, the U.S. Immigration and Naturalization Service, and the Red Cross, might have benefited from a swift, hard kick to rearrange their operating cultures.

The Long-Haul Philosophy

Whatever an organization decides regarding velocity and vector, RAND clearly believes in preparing for the long haul. Part of this belief comes from RAND's own history in systems analysis. "When you think about it," says Moore, "an organization is a system of structure, processes, practices/policies, personnel, cultures or subcultures, constraints/barriers, and incentives. Thus, it is not surprising that when RAND thinks about change, it does so from a 'systems of systems,' or 'organizational ecosystem' perspective. When you look at change from this perspective with all its many dimensions, you realize how truly hard change can be, particularly significant or transformational change. And given the high level of complexity and the likelihood that some relationships are not known or poorly understood, it is not surprising that we recommend a cautious approach that begins with careful tests and evaluations to try and uncover possible hidden interdependencies that can kill a change or lead to unintended outcomes."[12]

As RAND's work on environmental management suggests, even radical change can take a very long time. "Specific changes affecting small parts of an organization—say, a few hundred people—may take two years to work through. Implementing a specific change throughout an organization with tens of thousands of employees...can easily take five years or more. Implementing a new approach to environmental management typically involves a series of specific changes that can easily extend the period beyond a decade."

Moreover organizational change itself must be subject to change. Locking in an organization to an immutable plan is a near-certain guarantee of failure. Whatever an organization decides to do, whether based on my winnowing process or my deeper reading of the RAND knowledge base, it needs to have an ordered approach to change.

Consider RAND's report on the agile Air Force. "Combat support is either an enabler or a constrainer of combat power," Robert Tripp explains. "It has a big influence on how fast the Air Force can project power, how fast it can employ power, how long it can sustain power. And so, the Air Force expedition aerial force concepts of a very rapid deployment, employment, seamless shift to sustain, and so forth—are depending upon combat support.... It's all about how combat support processes and resources can be moved around to enable the operational tricks."

RAND's 2002 report is actually the eighth in what promises to be a long series on how to change Air Force combat support from the current *AS-IS system* into the hoped for *TO-BE approach*.

From an AS-IS perspective, the Air Force combat support system lags well behind future needs. Drawing lessons from past air wars, including Operation Enduring Freedom in Afghanistan, the eight-member RAND team concludes that combat support was poorly integrated into operational planning. In Operation Noble Anvil over Serbia, for example, combat support was slow to catch up with the changing mission. As a team of RAND researchers writes, the combat support system was slow to redirect material, adjust maintenance priorities, and change distribution routes and modes in part because Air Force personnel were inexperienced, and in part because the combat support infrastructure simply did not have enough support itself.

It would be easy to argue for immediate change—after all, what could be more important to saving lives than ensuring that the Air Force has enough stuff to fight and win wars? However, moving from AS-IS to TO-BE is anything but easy. According to the RAND team, it will take large-scale organizational change, as well as a revolution in thinking about the relationship between combat support and combat success. But that revolution will not happen overnight. It will take planning, perseverance, and visible commitment at all levels of the organization.

RAND is clearly committed to staying with the Air Force reforms through the long haul, suggesting the importance of research as part of the change process. "We've been working on this one theme for six years," says Tripp of the effort, "but we've had incremental adoption and experience with the ideas through war games or for incremental institutionalization of components." Speaking to RAND's role in supporting the effort, Tripp maintains that "there's no big bang with us, so we have something on the table, internally managed, to make sure that we're influencing something while we're generating large ideas, hopefully. So, every year, we've had a product the Air Force connects on." Asked whether six years is long or short, Tripp answers that "One can say six years is a fairly lengthy time. Okay, maybe, but the Air Force is still the most powerful Air Force in the world. It's pretty damned quick. Maybe the leadership should be conservative on what they change and don't change."

SIX STEPS FOR MANAGING CHANGE

The RAND knowledge base contains a long list of studies that address change management—not just the need for change or the change itself, but the process for securing full implementation.

Interestingly one of RAND's most important studies on change management involves the kind of whole-organization reform it rarely recommends. Commissioned by the U.S. Environmental Protection Agency, the study examined innovation and change management at six organizations, three public and three private. Comparing recent improvements at the U.S. Customs Service, DuPont, U.S. Food and Drug Administration, Marriott, Procter & Gamble, and the U.S. Veterans Health Administration, the RAND research team concluded that no single action is sufficient to ignite organization-wide innovation.

Rather it takes an ensemble of actions to create a supportive organizational infrastructure, including strong individual incentives for innovation, a clearly identifiable management process for generating, evaluating, and funding new ideas, and an internal environment that encourages risk taking. As the study concludes, "Innovative organizations have leaders who establish a clear and compelling vision, create alignment of the entire organization around that vision, and personally lead organizational change." These organizations also create an environment in which innovation can flourish, institutionalizing good ideas along the way, and adopting many of the attributes of a robust organization.

Once again wishing will not make it happen. As the RAND study suggests, organizations need a change process built around two basic steps. They must first prepare for change by making the case, creating a vision of the hoped-for future, building senior leadership support, and creating an action plan. They must then execute the change by creating a formal process and measurement, testing and evaluating pilots, and adapting the change as appropriate. At both stages, however, they must provide organizational support through communication, training, resources, and incentives. Then they start all over in a constant prepare-execute-support process that assures ongoing commitment. (See Nancy Moore's briefing slide on change management, which the RAND team used in the Environmental Protection Agency study.[13])

The findings are not unlike other RAND studies of process-oriented change, including its work on proactive environmental management, logistics reform, and strategic purchasing. According to one recent study, supply-chain management was an unknown field 30 years ago, for example. Most manufacturers made their own parts and relied on purchasing

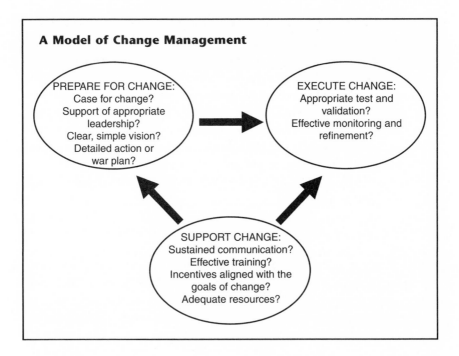

A Model of Change Management

PREPARE FOR CHANGE:
Case for change?
Support of appropriate
leadership?
Clear, simple vision?
Detailed action or
war plan?

EXECUTE CHANGE:
Appropriate test and
validation?
Effective monitoring and
refinement?

SUPPORT CHANGE:
Sustained communication?
Effective training?
Incentives aligned with the
goals of change?
Adequate resources?

departments to do the rest. "That scene has changed dramatically," RAND's study team reports. "Although few companies are as strategic as they need to be, and few apply best practices to a maximum benefit, almost every company today understands the link between supply management principles and strategic goals."

The question is just what good companies do. According to RAND's research, effective firms have shifted from a tactical to a strategic, or goal-oriented, approach to supply management, meaning that they have aligned their supply-chain with their broader goals. This means simplifying less-important, lower-risk, lower-value purchases, while focusing more attention on the more-important, higher-risk, higher-value purchases that make or break the firm. Over time, this focus creates the kind of deep, strategic partnerships with suppliers that promote greater quality and savings.

This strategic approach does not come easily to most organizations, however. At the planning stage, the question is whether the case for change is clear: "If not, the senior leadership cannot effectively support or sell the change." The next question is whether the vision can be understood in five minutes or less: "If not, the conflicts that inevitably arise during implementation are likely to move the change away from the original corporate goals or eviscerate the plan entirely." If so, the next question is whether the action plan identifies barriers, assigns responsibilities, and provides a framework for execution: "If not, details critical to success can easily fall through the cracks, allowing the change effort to lose critical momentum or veer off course before anyone notices."

At the implementation stage, the question is whether employees have any reason to change. "An organization can use any combination of monetary inducements, awards, career actions, and other incentives that is compatible with its corporate culture to reward or punish its employees. But if no personal benefits flow from changing their behavior on the job, or the risk of adverse consequences increases, employees see little personal connection to the success of the change."

Finally, at the execution stage, the question is whether the organization is testing new practices: "Serious failures or inadequate validation of the benefits can easily threaten any further implementation of the change." RAND also asks whether ongoing monitoring provides information for needed refinement: "If not, a change effort may slip off track or, more subtly, realize only a portion of the benefits available from change."

Ultimately, the failure to address these questions at the beginning of the process creates a reasonable expectation that the change will fail. Although some failures can be rescued with heroic efforts, it is far better to build the scaffolding of change before, not during or after, the effort begins.

These lessons are echoed and enriched in other RAND work on organizational change, including a host of studies cited earlier in this book. If there is such a thing as a RAND model for managing change, it would include at least six steps: create a sense of urgency, remove the barriers, find and equip the champions, build support inside and outside the organization, prove success with early wins and valid metrics, and always experiment.

Rand Lessons on Managing Change

1. Create a sense of urgency

2. Remove the barriers to success

3. Recruit the champions

4. Build internal momentum

5. Prove that change works

6. Keep experimenting

Create a Sense of Urgency

RAND and its researchers are absolutely convinced that analysis is essential for showing the need for change. For the Velocity Management effort, this meant showing the Army how bad it looked. "I can remember briefing this one general who didn't like what we were doing," John Dumond remembers. After the meeting one of his colonels said, "We held up a mirror and said, 'Look how ugly your system's performance looks.' And this general didn't like his system looking ugly. The general was upset because we were showing them how badly they performed." Dumond sees the case for change as much more than holding up a mirror to the organization, however.

> We started off with this view of a vision of what could be. I think that was a portion of it. We had to show them how ugly they were. It's really easy. One of the things that disheartens me often when I see some RAND workers is when we go in and tell them that they did a lousy job and that they look ugly. To me, that's not adequate. We get paid too much for that.
>
> We have to come in and tell them that this is the way you look, but this is the way you could look, and the way you get from here to there. If I were to deploy to any part of the world, how would I get from where I am to there and back? What do I have to think about and do differently?
>
> So instead of having a mass-based system, I have a velocity-based system. What does that mean? That means you have to have processes that are ready. How good is your process to do what it needs to do? I'm measuring the readiness of your process. Your process sucks when you have 30 days, give or take 100, but if you can get a process that's reliable and gets you something in seven days, that's great improvement.

RAND researchers are hardly the first to argue for urgency as a lever for change. John Kotter made the case quite clearly in *The Heart of Change*.[14] The book actually has a small following at RAND, especially among the researchers who have become involved in hands-on implementation projects. Like Kotter, the RAND team came away from their research believing that leadership is the first step to successful change. As Frank Camm explains:

> It's got to come from the top. You've got to have leadership commitment for the entire period of the change. How do you get that? You actually frame the change in a form that the leadership

can understand and appreciate. In the case of outsourcing, rather than saying, "The goal here is to review 15 percent of the billets and the inventory of eligible jobs by the end of '03," say something like, "We want to maintain our capability while reducing the number of billets in this activity by 5 percent by the end of this year." Leadership doesn't care about that first statement. It's meaningless to them. That second statement is something leadership can relate to. You phrase the change itself in terms that are meaningful to the leadership.

Where RAND might argue a bit with Kotter is on the need for analysis in making the case. "It's analysis, and it's communication," Nancy Moore says. "You've got to have the analysis; that's necessary. The communication is also incredibly necessary, just how you communicate and the different ways and channels you use. It's getting those people to realize that sense of urgency and to want to change, then getting them to understand how to change, because the next problem is that they don't know how to do it. They really don't know."

Moore also happens to be one of RAND's most voracious readers. Her office is piled with business best sellers, not to mention the latest in logistics management. *The Heart of Change* lays on top of *Mechanics of Fluids*, while *Execution* is next to *The Purchasing and Supply Yearbook*. Moore is about as ecumenical as they get. "I read slowly; I'm an engineer, and I plod and highlight. I read the media, too. I may not be selecting appropriately; I have no idea."

Asked what she has learned from the hundreds of books she reads and highlights, Moore is sharp and direct: "If I were God for a day and had an organization, the first thing I would do is build a case about why you should change. Then you've got to educate leaders and find a way to do it. It isn't easy. That's one of the things I excel at—developing relationships with leaders and guiding them through these things." Moore's reading list is part of her strategy. "I get them to read books that have little points. I read to learn, and when I find a lesson in an article or a point, I share the article with the leaders. They see the point and read the article, and internalize it. They won't do that by just listening to me. You change their thinking. You have to get them to understand that they need and want to change. That's hard to do. It's through relationships." (See Moore's briefing slide on communication.)

Debra Knopman echoes the conclusion, drawing in part upon her study of DuPont, Marriott, and Procter & Gamble. "Leaders need to be sending a clear and consistent set of signals, whether it is in the execution of business processes or in relationships with customers. Employees need to be hearing one core message—not fragments of a new message mixed with the old, but a new message that applies to the entire organization."

Once the case is made, Knopman notes that the leadership also had to "excuse the cliché, empower the people on the frontlines to make the decisions. They needed to know they were being supported from the top. And sometimes that is said, but not always backed up. In Marriott's case, it meant pushing things down to the regional level, and then down from there to each franchise."

Communication and Change

▶ Communication must continue throughout the change process

- Top down: case for change, vision, goals, on-going guidance

- Bottom up: current status, incremental successes

- Side to side: lessons learned, rumor control

▶ There's no such thing as too much communication

- Speeches, meetings, electronic bulletin boards, newsletters

▶ Senior leadership must "walk the talk"

- Actions must always be consistent with goals

Remove the Barriers to Success

Perhaps it is RAND's history of dealing with big organizations in general. Perhaps it is their research on the military, health care, and school systems, all of which have different forms of tenure. But whatever the reason, RAND researchers are persistent about the need to clear the underbrush of bureaucracy as an early step toward successful change.

Barriers come in many shapes and sizes, however. Moore talks about "barriers of the mind," for example:

NANCY MOORE: Oh, removing barriers are important, but a lot of them are barriers of the mind more than they are actual barriers. They're barriers of the mind in the people that say they can't do things. In fact, this one general who cosponsors our project will say, "There's no law that says we can't do this stuff. We can do it. It may be a little harder, but we can do it." It's more barriers of the mind that we just can't do it.

PAUL LIGHT: Do you want to wax poetic about that? Is that just a natural resistance to change?

NANCY MOORE: It's that, and when you're so busy trying to do the day-to-day stuff and don't have time to sit back and reflect or learn, you just don't know that things have changed sometimes.

PAUL LIGHT: Around you, outside?

NANCY MOORE: Around you, outside, or even that you could always have done it in the first place, but it was just the way it was always done. You're so busy that the easiest way is just to continue business as usual.

PAUL LIGHT: Is that the boiled frog syndrome?

NANCY MOORE: I don't think it's the boiled frog, because it doesn't hurt them.

Moore suggests that the first step in change is to determine the source of low performance. "What are some of the causes of low performance?" she asks. "Do they get the objective done, but in an ugly and expensive way? You have to think about their strategic goals and where they're missing them. The focus goes from there." Shan Cretin agrees: "There's a wonderful quote from John Kenneth Galbraith that says given the choice between changing our minds or proving that there is no need to do so, most of us will immediately get busy on the proof. You're coming in to tell me I've got to change. My first response is that you're wrong."

Other RAND researchers focus on clearing out the deadwood, reducing micromanagement, and cutting red tape—all the usual suspects of organizational malaise. "First get rid of the stupid things, then make a line that you're going to grade people on to what you say they're really going to do," James Quinlivan recommends. "Right now you can actually screw up your command, and still survive. If you go out to one of the training centers and don't do well, everyone says that it's just training, 'we want people to learn, yadda, yadda, yadda.' But if you screw that thing up bad, somebody in your chain of command is going to say something. That's good, in my view. If you can't train your unit to the point that you demonstrate that you know what you're doing out there, then they ought to can you."

Recruit the Champions

RAND researchers may not think much of charismatic leadership, but they do believe leaders are important to successful change. The first challenge is finding a champion. "It's very difficult if the leadership is not on board, because the top person has his or her finger on the resources," says Moore. "Most change, especially transformational change, requires some resources of different kinds. For example, people's time; you can't burn them out. It requires them getting courses and finding ways to learn, maybe some consultants or advisors to come in and hold their hand, maybe some help with some analysis to make a broader case or maybe some communication. If you don't have someone who has their hands on the purse or the resources, it's extremely difficult. It's not impossible, but it makes it a lot harder."

The second challenge is to deploy the champions throughout the organization. Consider RAND's brief case study of how Hewlett-Packard distributed its leadership on environmental management:

> HP's environmental stewardship program in effect built an entire corporate environmental policy around champions strategically placed through a highly decentralized and entrepreneurial organization. Each business and product line had a steward. This placed 75 to 100 environmental champions in normal business processes—research and development, marketing, manufacturing, procurement, distribution, and especially design—around the world. Stewards established policies and tools supporting environmental policy implementation for the business overall. They communicated to raise awareness; tracked, assessed, and related market and legislative trends to HP strategic decisions; advocated new procedures to reflect environmental priorities in corporate decisions; and deployed metrics and other tools to support decision making. In each product line, stewards effectively linked environmental issues to design teams.

The third challenge is to provide the tools to succeed. This might mean building easily understandable indicators that leaders can use to cajole, discipline, and reward colleagues. "I think it's a combination of having the right measures to drive the right performance and having the right audience who is willing to look at it," says Dumond. "If someone says, 'My performance is terrible because you have a stupid policy,' the guys sit around the table and say, 'Whose policy is that?' 'Oh, it's mine. Okay, we'll take a look at it and see what we can do.' I think you have to have the measures, because it really does get people motivated to change. I think you have to have a structure that enables the change to occur at the top level."

The final challenge is to recruit new champions. This is exactly what kept Velocity Management going over the years. "I learned something from the Army," says Dumond. "They are a consensus-building group of generals. The power of that is that they continue this agreement. Any time a new general comes in, they've got 20 other generals who tell him this is where we're going. We have colonels who are now one-, two-, or three-stars that have been raised in this environment that this is our agreed-upon approach. Once you get the agreement, it seems to move quite well."

Build Internal Momentum

As Moore says, no one can command an organization to change. Rather leaders must build coalitions for change one unit, even one individual, at a time. "You can't just go to the generals, you've got to kiss frogs," says Tripp. "You've got to deal with the chief master sergeants and the lieutenants and the colonels to get the ideas through, because those generals are going to come back down hill and say, 'Does any of this make sense to the enlisted corps? Does this make sense, does it make sense to the officers?'"

A first step in building support is simple honesty. Birkler minces few words on the issue: "You've got to understand what you're about. And that's part of having a vision of where you want to go. And then you need to move the organization in that direction and not to pull any punches." Asked about inevitable resistance, Birkler recommends, "I think you make it clear to everybody that this is the direction you're going to move. You know, actions speak louder than words and start doing those things. And the people who are not part of the plan are left behind or asked to leave." (See Nancy Moore's slide on the characteristics of a powerful guiding coalition.)

The Characteristics of a Powerful Guiding Coalition

- ◗ Includes senior members representing all key stakeholders with enough power to lead the change

  - Operates outside the normal hierarchy

- ◗ Develops knowledge of and support for changes

> ▶ Diagnoses organizational needs to implement change

> ▶ Plans and designs the action/war plan

> • Creates specific change initiatives/pilots/tests

> • Maintains communication

> • Institutionalizes continuous improvement

A second step is to provide a clear plan of attack. Robert Lempert believes that the planning process itself can produce needed momentum. "One of the ideas is that you lay out a whole range of plausible future and ways of valuing the future so that people are confronted with something they can relate to and given some alternatives," Lempert says of robust adaptive decision making. "It lets people buy into the analysis more easily. Once they buy into the analysis, they can say 'What about this?' and 'What about that?'"

Robust adaptive decision making and other computer-aided decision systems also help organizations focus on the facts. "Basically, when you had these meetings, people would get up and perform," Lempert says of planning at a major automobile maker. "They would bring all the data and say they were for this; the next person would get up, give a performance, and say they were for that. Everybody would cheer. The people running the process were very worried about making decisions on the information, not who told the best story."

A third step is to celebrate the small wins. "Most people won't go on the long march unless they see compelling evidence within six to eighteen months," Kotter writes in *Leading Change*. "Without short-term wins, too many employees give up or actively join the resistance."

Kotter also warns against declaring victory too soon, while neglecting to anchor changes firmly in the corporate culture. "Real transformation takes time," he writes of the first error. "After a few years of hard work people can be tempted to declare victory with the first major performance improvement. While celebrating a win is fine, any suggestion that the job is mostly done is generally a terrible mistake. Until changes sink down deeply into the culture, which for an entire company can take three to ten years, new approaches are fragile and subject to regression." As for the second error, "One bad succession decision at the top of an organization can undermine a decade of hard work."[15]

Prove that Change Works

It is impossible to overstate the importance of metrics for successful change. Metrics help create the baselines against which to measure progress, small and large. In Velocity Management, for example, most Army logistics staffs believed that delays were anyone's fault but their own. "It did not occur to them that the installation's own ordering and receiving activities might be major contributors," write the authors of *Velocity Management*. "Yet investigation revealed that ordering could be substantially delayed by manager reviews of individual requisitions and various financial management issues."

There were also significant problems once supplies arrived at a particular base. At the beginning of the change effort, for example, FedEx shipments were routinely dropped at a single distribution point on a base and sorted into batches to be delivered later that day or the next with the rest of the mail and packages. So much for the EXTREMELY URGENT label on the FedEx packages.

Luckily, the data showed that the Army could get big results through simple changes. Installations redesigned delivery routes, and even decided to let FedEx trucks deliver directly to the customer. "They changed work schedules so that supply teams could meet scheduled trucks at specific points and unload deliveries very quickly, much like the 'pit crews' of stock car racing," the Velocity Management team writes.

The results were instantly visible in order and ship times, as well as customer satisfaction, not to mention plain common sense. "When we first started this," Dumond remembers, "we had people saying to us that we couldn't get it there faster and cheaper. It's just impossible; there's no such thing as faster and cheaper. We can't afford to put everything on airplanes.' Our guys said, 'You know, you're absolutely right. We'll put it on a truck.' It turns out that you can drive a truck 500 miles a day, and it's faster than Fed Ex and a lot cheaper."

Keep Experimenting

If there is one sure thing about organizational change, it is that something will go wrong somewhere along the way. It might be a small mistake such as a tank engine being sent to an aircraft facility, or a big mistake such as a surgical technique that does more harm than good, but there will always be errors. "Large organizational changes are complicated and never go exactly as planned," RAND's study of best practices in supply management concluded. "Execution is an intricate dance that supports ongoing learning even as real, operational requirements persist and demand some resolution. It seeks and recognizes each incremental success, detects failures before they get out of hand and learns from them, and keeps everyone in the coalition aligned with their joint strategic goals, even as execution itself reveals new, unexpected conflicts among their individual interests."

The question is not whether trial and error will produce error, however, but what organizations do in response. Do they treat every defect as a treasure or nuke the offending unit? Do they develop workarounds for the inevitable casualties, as Leland Joe might argue, or strive for near perfection?

As Shan Cretin told me just before she left RAND, one answer is to avoid dogmatism. "The one thing that bugs me about total quality management is that everybody's got their own little dogma. It's the Juran model, and if you don't do the 12 steps in this order with the Juran name all over it, you will fail. It's the Deming model, and if you don't follow the Deming 14 points, you will fail. Or it's the Toyota production system, and if you don't use this terminology and way of looking at the world, you will fail."

Cretin's background as a mechanical engineer and operations researcher gives her some confidence that the underlying concepts of quality improvement can produce higher performance, especially if organizations embrace the emphasis on experimentation. "The people who are doing this work are experts about the things that are getting in their way. They really work to articulate the problem, then design the sorts of experiments that will help get them to a better place. They have other ideas that I think are just practical and common sense, but in all of the quality improvement literature, you see this basic commitment to experimentation, that every defect is a treasure and you learn from failures and mistakes, and you figure out what went wrong."

Jacob Klerman provides another answer: "Rossi's Law states that the expected impact of an innovation is zero. And the statistician in me will tell you, that if the expected effect is zero, half of the effects are negative.... The point is not that there are some programs that are working and some programs that aren't. The point is that you have to test your programs."

As Klerman tells the story of Riverside County, California, the key to successful change lies at least in part in abandoning unsuccessful change.

> The director of research got up at a meeting and started talking about a program they had set up to match welfare recipients with caseworkers to counsel them intensively so that they could keep their jobs. "We looked at the results of the study and people that were in the experiment were doing much better," he told his audience. "They kept their jobs. They increased their earnings. And not only that, but we talked to the caseworkers and they said they were going great guns. And they were really helping people. And they really felt fulfilled."

And he paused at that point in that meeting and somebody asked a question: "So you went national with the program, right? You went live with the program." And he said, "Actually, no. We looked at the random-assignment evaluation and determined the program was useless. And we closed the program down." And he closed the program down.

They're willing to ask; they're willing to wait until the results come in. They are willing to make the hard decisions.

For most RAND researchers, this willingness to start over is essential to organizational impact. Changing from one dumb program to another is just as bad, and probably more expensive, than just staying put. Moreover effective organizations have to know when to pull the plug on a given initiative. Sometimes the best thing an organization can do is stop innovating, for example, especially if the innovation undermines the things it is already doing well.

Moreover as Moore and her colleagues note, there are many places where change can come undone:

- Without a strong case for change (pressure and urgency), there is likely to be no change.
- Without senior leadership support, there is likely to be little change.
- Without a future vision, there is likely to be confusion over where the change effort is going.
- Without an action or war plan, there are likely to be false starts as efforts are launched, but not coordinated.
- Without sustained communication, there is likely to be a loss of momentum, which can either drag out the change effort or lead to its abandonment.
- Without the required training and skills, stakeholders and participants will have anxiety over execution and are more likely to resist or make more mistakes, which lead to poor outcomes.
- Without incentives to permanently change, there are likely to be temporary islands of change that will revert back to the old ways when the local sponsors move on.
- Without the time and budget resources to execute the change, there is likely to be frustration and slow progress because the change has to be implemented by personnel in their spare time.
- Without test and validation of new practices, the implementation is likely to have unintended consequences.

- Last, without a formal monitoring and refining process, which catches problems and shares lessons learned, change implementation is likely to lead to dead ends and repeated mistakes.

High velocity without any vector at all is a nearly perfect guarantee of eventual disaster. But even with vector, change is both difficult and error prone. The trick is to catch mistakes in time to prevent an entire power outage.

Avoiding the Quick Fix

Much of this chapter has been about avoiding the quick fix. Despite the old adage that desperate times call for desperate actions, RAND research suggests that desperation almost always leads toward failure and frustration.

My favorite piece on the subject is Dominic Brewer's analysis of the *administrative blob* in education reform. The term was first coined by Reagan Administration Education Secretary William Bennett, and refers to the notion that administrative costs are too high. As Brewer explains, "The assertion that there is 'too much' administration has been accompanied by a somewhat more refined argument, namely that public schools are too centralized and rule bound. This bureaucratic structure has led, it is claimed, to decision making unresponsive to the demands of parents and needs of students."

It turns out, however, that the blob is more of a mini-blob than cause of concern. As Brewer shows, those who would gamble on downsizing as the solution to resource shortages will likely lose: "While there appears to have been some growth in school districts' use of non-instructional inputs over the last decades or so, this has largely been in the form of paraprofessional support staff rather than administration, at least in New York." According to his statistical analysis, spending for central administration often, but not always, has a negative effect on educational productivity, while building-level administration often, but not always, has a positive effect.

RAND researchers tell a second cautionary tale about public access to health information. According to the five-person team that wrote RAND's *Dying to Know*, publishing of data about health performance is not a new phenomenon. Patients have been dying to know for several centuries.[16]

However, as the team notes, the "theoretical foundation in support of the use of performance data to make judgments about quality is based on sparse and generally weak empirical data." As much as advocates might argue that access to information will encourage consumers to choose high-quality providers, constrain costs, and/or alter provider behavior, it is not clear that publicity is more effective for improving quality than privacy.

What is clear is that public disclosure represents what RAND describes as a "major culture challenge" for professionals and health-care organizations. If not done well, disclosure could produce exactly the wrong result: "There is a danger that public disclosure may be perceived as threatening professional autonomy and therefore work against the creation of an environment where systematic evaluation and improvement can flourish." As RAND continues, "Change will take time and the quality of the performance data will be an important determinant of the acceptability of the public information and its ability to promote change. The state of the art of performance indicators and the information technology to support them need to be continuously refined."[17]

Even when RAND calls for great transformations, it almost always recommends continuous effort toward the goal. This is not to suggest that RAND prefers the conventional wisdom, however. But imagination is not enough for success. Continuity may not be in fashion as organizations reject one leader after another in the search for magic, but it is definitely one option in RAND's preferred vector for change.

CONCLUSION

After spending four years and countless hours exploring the RAND knowledge base, I have come to embrace three broad lessons for organizations that want to begin the journey toward higher performance.

First, there is no doubt that organizations can become more robust. The RAND knowledge base contains a long list of organizations that have gotten better over time, not the least of which are the Army, Navy, and Air Force. The U.S. has never been better able to project power in a turbulent environment. The challenge is to do so at the right time in the right places.

Second, robust organizations are far from perfect. Even if a practically perfect organization did exist, RAND researchers would argue that it could always get better, whether through better metrics, more experimentation, or deeper communication. RAND researchers would also caution against the search for the heroic, tap-dancing, charismatic leader as the cure for all that makes an organization vulnerable. RAND has worked with every kind of leader imaginable, including some that would most certainly fit the *hubris-nemesis profile*. It is not the leader's characteristics that matter most to success. Rather it is the leader's commitment to the mission.

Third, becoming robust requires evidence-based decisions at every step of the change process. Organizations must know where they are in the present to shape where they want to go in the future. Although intuition and judgment clearly have a place in setting course, measurement is essential for staying on course. Organizations have to take leaps of faith if they are to innovate and adapt, but they should make an effort to learn just how big the leaps will be.

Ultimately building a robust organization is not rocket science. Rather it requires a blend of common sense, organizational self-awareness, greater rigor, and perseverance. Becoming more alert requires a willingness to confront the possibility that there is not one future, but many; becoming more agile requires an eagerness to delegate and participate, lean out and engage; becoming more adaptive requires a readiness to confront the prevailing wisdom through trial *and* error, not trial *for* error; and becoming more aligned requires a commitment to saturate the organization with the information and purpose to become greater than the sum of its parts.

Getting robust involves more than just the right process for change, however. It must also involve a clear focus on the vulnerabilities that undermine the four pillars of high performance described in this book, exploring the plausible futures ahead, creating the capabilities to hedge against vulnerabilities and exploit opportunities, erecting signposts that might reveal a critical moment for action, developing an inventory of measures that tell the truth about the realities ahead, and accepting the potential for surprise. But RAND would almost certainly start the process by asking whether the organization needs to change at all. The capacity to change may be an asset, but the decision to change is not a requirement.

There is no point in asking the question if the organization is not going to be honest about the answer, however. This is where RAND's own belief in evidence-based knowledge has such appeal. Setting the course to high performance involves more than yet another strategic plan or organizational assessment. Organizations must also be honest with themselves, which requires trust, rigor, and a faith in the possible. Otherwise, they are doomed to irrelevance, if not bankruptcy court, takeover, or dissolution. It is no longer get innovative or get dead, as Tom Peters once advised, but get robust or get dead[18]

NOTES

1   An introduction to the ISO 14001 standards can be found at http://www.iso.org/ iso/en/prods-services/otherpubs/iso14000/index.html. Camm's report, *Environmental Management in Proactive Commercial Firms*, can be found in the bibliography at the end of this book.

2   The conclusion comes from a 750-page analysis of efforts to expand educational reforms by Thomas K. Glennan, Jr., Susan J. Bodily, Jolene R. Galegher, and Kerri A. Kerr, and is cited in the bibliography.

3 Darrel Rigby, "Management Tools Survey 2003: Usage Up as Companies Strive to Make Headway in Tough Times," *Strategy & Leadership*, vol. 31, no. 6, 2003, pp. 4-11.

4 Rigby, "Management Tools Survey 2003," p. 4.

5 Darrell Rigby, *The Bottom Line on Management*, research brief, Bain & Company, 2003, p. 2.; the article can be found on the Bain & Company web site at www.bain.com.

6 The authors are John Dumond, Marygail K. Brauner, Rick Eden, John R. Folkeson, Ken Girardini, Donna J. Keyser, Eric Peltz, Ellen M. Pint, and Mark Wang.

7 The study was conducted by Elwyn D. Harris, Michael Hynes, Harry Thie, Bob Emmerichs, Malcolm MacKinnon, Denis Rushworth, Brian Nichiporuk, John E. Peters, Maurice Eisenstein, Jennifer Sloan, Charles Lindenblatt, and Charles Cannon, and is cited in the bibliography.

8 Philip Siekman, "Build to Order: One Aircraft Carrier," *Fortune*, July 22, 2002, p. 180; accessed at http://www.nexis.com, July 16, 2004.

9 See Harry J. Thie's chapter titled "Planning the Future Military Workforce," in Johnson, Libicki, and Treverton, *New Challenges, New Tools for Defense Decisionmaking*, cited in the bibliography.

10 The report was authored by Liam Sarsfield, William L. Stanley, Cynthia C. Lebow, Emile Ettedgui, and Garth Henning, and is cited in the bibliography.

11 The report was written by Brian P. Gill, P. Michael Timpane, Karen E. Ross, and Dominic J. Brewer.

12 Moore cites Peter Senge, *The Fifth Discipline: The Art and Practice of the Learning Organization*, New York:Doubleday, 1990, in making her point.

13 The slide is drawn from Moore's report, which was co authored with Laura Baldwin, Frank Camm, and Cynthia Cook.

14 John P. Kotter, *The Heart of Change*, New York:Cambridge, 2002.

15 Kotter, *Leading Change*, pp. 11-14.

16 The report was written by Martin Marshall, Paul G. Shekelle, Sheila T. Leatherman, Robert H. Brook, and John Wyn Owen, and is cited in the bibliography.

17 Robert J. Kriegel and Louis Patler, *If It Ain't Broke, Break It*, New York:Warner Books, 1992.

18 Tom J. Peters, "Get Innovative or Get Dead," *California Management Review*, vol. 33, no. 4, 1990, p. 9.

BIBLIOGRAPHY

The RAND research literature that underpins this book can be divided into four categories: (1) managing organizations, (2) strengthening performance, (3) designing organizations, and (4) implementing and managing change. The following list of papers and books is meant as a sampling of the RAND literature, with particular emphasis on the publications referenced in this book. However, all of the research cited in this book is easily accessible on RAND's searchable publication website. Readers can search more than 50 years of research by author, title, or subject, with almost all the results downloadable online. Parts of this book also draw upon draft papers written for a March 2004 RAND conference on building a high-performance public service.

ORGANIZATIONAL MANAGEMENT
Command and Control

Bonds and, Nelson, "Taking Command—Improving Command and Control," IP-8057 (2001).

Builder, Bankes, and Nordin, *Command Concepts: A Theory Derived from the Practice of Command and Control* (1999).

Hura, et al., *Enhancing Dynamic Command and Control of Air Operations Against Time Critical Targets* (2002).

Kahan, et al., *Understanding Commanders' Information Needs* (2000).

Nardulli, et al., *Disjointed War: Military Operations in Kosovo, 1999* (2002).

Compensation

Asch, "Assessing the Adequacy of the Military's Compensation and Personnel Systems," DRR-1907-OSD (1998).

Asch and Hosek, J., *Military Compensation: Trends and Policy Options*, (1999).

Asch and Warner, *Separation and Retirement Incentives in the Federal Civil Service* (1999).

Fair, Asch, and Kilburn, *An Assessment of Recent Proposals to Improve the Montgomery GI Bill* (2000).

Gibbs, "Pay Competitiveness & Quality of Civil Service Scientists and Engineers in DoD Laboratories," DRR-2094-OSD (1999).

Leadership

Bikson, Treverton, Moini, and Lindstrom, *New Challenges for International Leadership: Lessons from Organizations with Global Missions* (2003).

George, *The "Operational Code": A Neglected Approach to the Study of Political Leaders and Decision-Making* (1967).

Johnson, *Preparing Potential Army Leaders for the Future* (2002).

Kahan, et al., *Understanding Commanders' Information Needs* (1989).

Kulick and Davis, *Modeling Adversaries and Related Cognitive Biases* (2003).

Leites, *Kremlin Moods* (1964).

Ronfeldt, *Beware the Hubris-Nemesis Complex: A Concept for Leadership Analysis* (1994).

Measurement

Beckett, et al., *Accountability for After-School Care: Devising Standards and Measuring Adherence to Them* (2001).

Buddin, *Building a Personnel Support Agenda: Goals, Analysis Framework, and Data Requirements* (1998).

Hunter, *The Environmental Implications of Population Dynamics* (2000).

Orvis, et al., *Effect of Personnel Quality on the Performance of Patriot Air Defense System Operators* (1992).

Winkler, et al., *Effect of Aptitude on the Performance of Army Communications Operators* (1992).

Motivation and Incentives

Dertouzos, "Management Options for Increasing Recruiter Productivity," draft report (2001).

Gates, et al., *Who Is Leading Our Schools: An Overview of School Administrators and Their Careers* (2003).

Oken and Asch, "Encouraging Recruiter Achievement: A Recent History of Recruiter Incentive Programs," MR-845-OSD/A (1997).

Recruitment

Asch, Du, and Schonlau, *Policy Options for Military Recruiting in the College Market: Results Form a National Survey* (2004).

Asch and Hosek, J., *Looking to the Future: What Does Transformation Mean for Military Manpower and Personnel Policy?* (2004).

Asch, Kilburn, and Klerman, "Attracting College-Bound Youth into the Military: Toward the Development of New Recruiting Policy Options," MR-984-OSD (1999).

Dertouzos and Garber, *Is Military Advertising Effective? An Estimation Methodology and Applications to Recruiting in the 1980s and 90s* (2003).

Fricker, Jr. and Fair, *Going to the Mines to Look for Diamonds: Experimenting with Military Recruiting Stations in Malls* (2003).

Hosek, J., et al., *Attracting the Best: How the Military Competes for Information Technology Personnel* (2004).

Kilburn and Klerman, "Enlistment Decisions in the 1990s," MR 955-OSD-A (1999).

Orvis, "What Should the Army Do About Its Recruiting Problem?" AB-415-A (2000).

Orvis and Asch, "Military Recruiting: Trends, Outlook, and Implications," MR-902-A/OSD (2000).

Orvis, et al., "Future Personnel Resource Management: Initial Report," AB-210-1-A (1998).

Team-Building

Berlowitz, et al., "Quality Improvement Implementation in the Nursing Home," *Health Services Research*, 2003, vol. 38, 1.

Finegold, et al., "Closing the Knowledge Gap for Transit Maintenance Employees: A Systems Approach," DRU-1472-TCRP (1996).

Joe, et al., "Characteristics of High Performance Units, Implications for Force XXI," DRR-1225-1-A (1996).

Robbert, et al., "Differentiation in Military Human Resource Management," DRR-981-A (1995).

Rostker and, Harris, Sexual Orientation and U.S. Military Personnel Policy: Options and Assessment (1993).

Rubenstein, et al., "Understanding Team-Based Quality Improvement for Depression in Primary Care," *Health Services Research*, 2002, vol. 37, no. 4.

Training

Bigelow, et al., *Models of Operational Training in Fighter Squadrons* (2003).

Ettedgui, Oaks, and Bondanella, *The Use of Microworld Simulations to Train Theater-Level CSS Staffs: Training Development Considerations* (1999).

Gill and Hove, *The Benedum Collaborative Model of Teacher Education: A Preliminary Evaluation* (2000).

Glenn, et al. *Training the 21ˢᵗ Century Police Officer: Redefining Police Professionalism for the Los Angeles Police Department* (2003).

Kirby, et al., *Reforming Teacher Education: A First Year Progress Report on Teachers for a New Era* (2004).

Leonard, et al., *Enhancing Stability and Professional Development Using Distance Learning* (2001).

Levy, et al., *Exploring the Use of Microworld Models to Train Army Logistics Management Skills* (2001).

Rostker, et al., "An Assessment of Training and Human Resources at American Red Cross Blood Services," PM-231-ARC (1994).

Schank, et al., *Consolidating Active and Reserve Component Training Infrastructure* (1999).

Winkler, et al., *The Total Army School System: Recommendations for Future Policy* (1999).

Winkler and Steinberg, *Restructuring Military Education and Training: Lessons from RAND Research* (1997).

Workforce Planning

Asch, "Ensuring Successful Personnel Management in the Department of Homeland Security," IP-235-NSRD (2002).

Asch, Du, and Law, *Policy Options for Recruiting in the College Market* (2004).

Bikson and Law, "Toward the Borderless Career: Corporate Hiring in the '90s," RP-443 (1995).

Emmerichs, Marcum, and Robbert, *An Executive Perspective on Workforce Planning* (2004).

Emmerichs, Marcum, and Robbert, *An Operational Process for Workforce Planning* (2004).

Finegold, Robbins, et al., *Closing the Knowledge Gap for Transit Maintenance Employees: A Systems Approach* (1996).

Gritton, et al., *Ground Forces for a Rapidly Employable Joint Task Force: First-Week Capabilities for Short-Warning Conflicts* (2000).

Karoly and Panis, *The 21st Century at Work: Forces Shaping the Future Workforce and Workplace in the United States* (2004).

Orvis, et al., *Future Personnel Resource Management: Initial Report* (1998).

Taylor, et al., *The Air Force Pilot Shortage: A Crisis for Operational Units?* (2000).

Thie and Brown, *Future Career Management Systems for U.S. Military Officers* (1994).

STRENGTHENING PERFORMANCE

Acquisitions

Birkler, Schank, et al., *Options for Funding Aircraft Carriers* (2002).

Camm, *Expanding Production of Defense Services* (1996).

Camm, Blickstein, and Venzor, *Recent Large Service Acquisitions in the Department of Defense* (2004).

Drezner and Krop, "The Use of Baselining in Acquisition Program Management," MR-876-OSD (1997).

Keating, *Government Contracting Options: A Model and Application* (1996).

Lorell, et al., *Cheaper, Faster, Better? Commercial Approaches to Weapons Acquisitions* (2000).

Moore, et al., "Implementing Best Purchasing and Supply Management Practices: Lessons from Innovative Commercial Firms," DB-334-AF (2002).

Sarsfield, *The Cosmos on a Shoestring: Small Spacecraft for Space and Earth Science* (1998).

Citizen Communication

Botterman, Bikson, et al., *Public Information Provision in the Digital Age: Implementation and Effects of the U.S. Freedom of Information Act* (2000).

Marshall, et al., *Dying to Know: Public Release of Information About Quality of Health Care* (2000).

Neu, Anderson, and Bikson, *Sending Your Government a Message: E-Mail Communication Between Citizens and Government* (1999).

Information Management and Technology Trends

Anton, Silberglitt, and Schneider, *The Global Technology Revolution: Bio/Nano/Materials Trends and Their Synergies with Information Technology by 2015* (2001).

Arquilla and Ronfeldt, *The Advent of Netwar* (1996).

Arquilla and Ronfeldt, *Swarming and the Future of Conflict* (2000).

Galway and Robbins, "Leveraging Information for Better Transit Maintenance," DRU-1158-1-TCRP (1996).

Hachigian and Wu, *The Information Revolution in Asia* (2003).

Hundley, Anderson, Bikson, and Neu, *The Global Course of the Information Revolution* (2003).

Joe, "Impact of Information Technologies on Organizations: Implications for the Army," DRR-858-A (1994).

Ronfeldt, et al., *The Zapatista Netwar in Mexico* (1998).

Logistics

Dumond, et al., *Velocity Management: The Business Paradigm that Has Transformed U.S. Army Logistics* (2001).

Edwards and Eden, "Velocity Management and the Revolution in Military Logistics," RP-752 (1999).

Ramey, *Lean Logistics: High-Velocity Logistics Infrastructure and the C-5 Galaxy* (1999).

Robbins, "Measuring the Performance of USMC Logistics Processes," AB-123-USMC (1996).

Robbins, "The Need to Measure Repair Cycle Time: Performance Measurement in the Army's Velocity Management Initiative," DDR-981-4 (1995).

Robbins, Boren, and Leuschner, *The Strategic Distribution System in Support of Operation Enduring Freedom* (2004).

Vick, et al., *The Stryker Brigade Combat Team* (2002).

Wang, *Accelerated Logistics: Strengthening the Army's Supply Chain* (2000).

Manufacturing

Arena, Schank, and Abbott, *The Shipbuilding & Force Structure Analysis Tool: A User's Guide* (2004).

Birkler, Drezner, et al., *Competition and Innovation in the U.S. Fixed-Wing Military Aircraft Industry* (2003).

Birkler, et al., *The U.S. Aircraft Carrier Industrial Base: Force, Structure, Cost, Schedule, and Technology Issues for CVN 77* (1998).

Cook and Graser, *Military Airframe Acquisition Costs: The Effects of Lean Manufacturing* (2001).

Lorrell, *The U.S. Combat Aircraft Industry, 1909–2000: Structure, Competition, Innovation* (2003).

Schank, et al., *CVX Propulsion System Decision: Industrial Base Implications of Nuclear and Non-Nuclear Options* (1999).

Measurement and Evaluation

Defense

Darilek, et al., *Measures of Effectiveness for the Information-Age Army* (2001).

Girardini and Miller, "Metrics for the Army's Stockage Determination Processes," AB-106-A (1996).

Hillestad, "How to Better Reflect the Value of Air and Space Power in Joint Force Assessments," AB-280-AF (1998).

Karasik, *Toxic Warfare* (2002).

Lambeth, "Learning from the Gulf War," P-7850 (1993).

Lambeth, "Lessons from the War in Kosovo," RP-1017 (2002).

Matsumura, et al., *Lightning Over Water: Sharpening America's Light Forces for Rapid Reaction Missions* (RAND, 2000).

McNaughter, et al., "Agility by a Different Measure: Creating a More Flexible U.S. Army," IP-195 (2000).

Mosher, et al., *Beyond the Nuclear Shadow: A Phased Approach for Improving Nuclear Safety and U.S.-Russian Relations* (2003).

Oliker, *Russia's Chechen Wars, 1994–2000* (2001).

Rosenau, *Special Operations Forces and Elusive Enemy Ground Targets: Lessons from Vietnam and the Persian Gulf War* (2001).

Steeb, et al., "Turning Light Forces into Heavy Hitters," RB-2101 (1996).

Environment

Lempert, et al., "Performance Measures for the Federal Investment in Environmental and Natural Resources Research and Development," DRU-1179-CTI (1995).

MacDonald, et al., *Alternatives for Landmine Detection* (2003).

Health

Brower and Chalk, *The Global Threat of New and Reemerging Infectious Diseases* (2003).

Garber, et al., *Managed Care and the Evaluation and Adoption of Emerging Medical Technologies* (2000).

Jackson, Pitkin, and Kington, *Evidence-Based Decision Making for Community Health Programs* (2000).

Kerr, et al., *Quality of Care for General Medical Conditions: A Review of the Literature and Quality Indicators* (2000).

Marshall, et al., *Dying to Know: Public Release of Information About Quality of Health Care* (2000).

McGlynn, et al., *Health Information Systems: Design Issues and Analytic Applications* (1998).

Ridgely, Borum, and Petrila, *The Effectiveness of Involuntary Outpatient Treatment: Empirical Evidence and the Experience of Eight States* (2001).

Education

Gill, et al., *Rhetoric Versus Reality: What We Know and What We Need to Know about Vouchers and Charter Schools* (2001).

Gill, *The Governance of the City University of New York: A System at Odds with Itself* (2000).

Grissmer, et al., *Improving Student Achievement: What NAEP State Test Scores Tell Us* (2000).

Klein and Hamilton, *Large-Scale Testing: Current Practices and New Directions* (1999).

Stetcher and Klein, eds., *Performance Assessment in Science: Hands-On Tasks and Scoring Guides* (1996).

Criminal Justice

Caulkins, et al., *An Ounce of Prevention, A Pound of Uncertainty: The Cost-Effectiveness of School-Based Drug Prevention Programs* (1999).

Greenwood, *Diverting Children from a Life of Crime: Measuring Costs and Benefits* (1998).

Greenwood, et al., *The California Wellness Foundation's Violence Prevention Initiative* (2001).

Karoly, et al., *Investing in Our Children: What We Know and Don't Know about the Costs and Benefits of Early Childhood Interventions* (2003).

Lane, et al., *South Oxnard Challenge Project* (2002).

The Arts

McCarthy, et al., *The Performing Arts in a New Era* (2001).

McCarthy and Jinnett, *A New Framework for Building Participation in the Arts* (2001).

McCarthy and Ondaatje, *From Celluloid to Cyberspace: The Media Arts and the Changing Arts World* (2002).

Planning
Assumption-Based Planning

Anton, et al, *The Vulnerability Assessment & Mitigation Methodology* (2003).

Dewar, et al., Assumption-Based Planning: A Planning Tool for Very Uncertain Times (1993).

Dewar, et al., "Assumption-Based Planning and Force XXI," DRR-1348-A (1996).

Dewar, *Assumption-Based Planning: A Tool for Reducing Avoidable Surprises* (2002).

Lacroix and Blickstein, *Forks in the Road for the U.S. Navy* (2003).

Robust Adaptive Decision Making

Lempert, et al., "When We Don't Know the Costs or the Benefits: Adaptive Strategies for Abating Climate Change" (RP-557), 1996.

Lempert, Popper, and Bankes, "Confronting Surprise," *Social Science Computer Review*, Vol. 20, No. 4, Winter, pp. 420-440 (2002).

Lempert, Popper, and Bankes, *Shaping the Next One Hundred Years: New Methods for Quantitative Long-Term Policy Analysis* (2003).

Lempert and Schlesinger, "Adaptive Strategies for Climate Change," *Innovative Energy Strategies for CO2 Stabilization* (Cambridge University Press, 2001).

Meade, Lempert, et al., *Assessing the Benefits and Costs of a Science Submarine* (2001).

Exploratory Modeling/Analysis

Bankes and Gillogly, *Exploratory Modeling: Search through Spaces of Computational Experiments* (1996).

Brooks, Bennett, and Bankes, "An Application of Exploratory Analysis: The Weapon Mix Problem," *Military Operations Research*, (1999).

Davis and Finch, *Defense Planning for the Post-Cold War Era: Giving Meaning to Flexibility, Adaptiveness, and Robustness of Capability* (1993).

Dewar, et al., *Expandability of the 21st Century Army* (2000).

Uncertainties/Capabilities/Effects-Based Planning

Davis, *Analytic Architecture for Capabilities-Based Planning, Mission-System Analysis, and Transformation* (2002).

Davis, *Effects-Based Operations* (2001).

Davis, *Exploratory Analysis Enabled by Multiresolution, Multiperspective Modeling* (2000).

Davis, *New Challenges for Defense Planning: Rethinking How Much is Enough* (1992).

Davis, "Protecting the Great Transition," in New Challenges for Defense Planning: Rethinking How Much Is Enough (1994).

Davis and Hillestad, *Exploratory Analysis for Strategy Problems with Massive Uncertainty* (unpublished draft, 2001).

Davis and Khalilzad, *A Composite Approach to Air Force Planning* (1996).

Johnson, Libicki, and Treverton, *New Challenges, New Tools for Defense Decision Making* (2003).

Walker, "Uncertainty: The Challenge for Policy Analysis in the 21st Century," P-8051 (2000).

Program Evaluation

Gray, et al., *Combining Service and Learning in Higher Education: Evaluation of the Learn and Serve America, Higher Education Program* (1999).

Hosmer, *Operations Against Enemy Leaders* (2001).

Kakalik, et al., "Just, Speedy, and Inexpensive? An Evaluation of Judicial Case Management Under the Civil Justice Reform Act," RP-861-ICJ (2000).

Klerman, et al., "Welfare Reform in California: Design of the Impact Analysis," MR-1266.0-CDSS (2000).

Libicki and Pfleeger, *Collecting the Dots: Problem Formulation and Solution Elements* (2004).

ORGANIZATIONAL DESIGN

Consolidation/Flattening/Coordination

Byman, et al., *Strengthening the Partnership: Improving Military Coordination with Relief Agencies and Allies in Humanitarian Operations* (2000).

Fukuyama and Shulsky, "The 'Virtual Corporation' and Army Organization," DRR-1483-A (1996).

Johnson, Poehlman, and Buenneke, "Space Roles, Missions, and Functions: The Challenge of Organizational Reform," PM-382-CRMAF (1995).

Peterson, et al., *New Forces at Work in Mining: Industry Views of Critical Issues* (2001).

Peterson and Mahnovski, *New Forces at Work in Refining: Industry Views of Critical Business and Operations Trends* (2003.)

Outsourcing

Chapman, *The Machine That Could: PNGV, A Government-Industry Partnership* (1998).

Gates and Robbert, *Personnel Savings in Competitively Sourced DoD Activities: Are They Real? Will They Last?* (2000).

Held, et al., *Seeking Nontraditional Approaches to Collaborating and Partnering with Industry* (2002).

Horn, et al., "Conducting Collaboration Research and Nontraditional Suppliers," RP-790 (1997).

Kaganoff, "Collaboration, Technology, and Outsourcing Initiatives in Higher Education," MR-973-EDU (1998).

Robbert, Gates, and Elliott, *Outsourcing of DoD Commercial Activities: Impacts on Civil Service Employees* (1997).

Process Redesign

Birkler, et al., *An Acquisition Strategy, Process, and Organization for Innovative Systems* (2000).

Drezner and Camm, *Using Process Redesign to Improve DoD's Environmental Security Program* (1999).

Lebow, Sarsfield, et al., *Safety in the Skies: Personnel and Parties in NTSB Aviation Accident Investigations* (1999).

Leftwich, Tripp, et al., *An Operational Architecture for Combat Support, Execution, Planning, and Control* (2002).

Schank, et al., *Refueling and Complex Overhaul of the USS Nimitz: Lessons for the Future* (2002).

Steecher and Kirby, *Organizational Improvement and Accountability: Lessons for Education from Other Sectors* (2004).

Reshaping/Downsizing

Asch, et al., *Separation and Retirement Incentives in the Federal Civil Service* (1999).

Asch and Warner, "Defense Downsizing: An Examination of the Effects of Voluntary Separation Incentives," DRR-1562-OSD (1996).

Brewer, "Does More School District Administration Lower Educational Productivity?" RP-546 (1996).

Bronstedt and Stecher, *Class Size in California, 1996-98: Early Findings Signal Promise and Concerns* (CSR Research Consortium, 1999), *Class Size Reduction in California: Summary of the 1998-1999 Evaluation Findings* (CSR Research Consortium, 2000).

Klitgaard, "Cleaning Up and Invigorating the Civil Service," RP-697 (1998).

Reichardt, *The Cost of Class Size Reduction: Advice for Policy Makers* (2000).

ORGANIZATIONAL CHANGE

Designing Change

Eiseman, et al., *Case Studies of Existing Human Tissue Repositories* (2003).

Gill, et al., *A "Noble Bet" in Early Care and Education: Lessons from One Community's Experience* (2003).

Gompert, "Preparing Military Forces for Integrated Operations in the Face of Uncertainty," IP-250 (2003).

Gompert, Oliker, and Timilsina, "Clean, Lean, and Able: A Strategy for Defense Development," OP-101-RC (2004).

Harris, Hynes, et al., *Transitioning NAVSEA to the Future: Strategy, Business, and Organization* (2002).

Hess, et al., *The Closing and Reuse of the Philadelphia Naval Shipyard* (RAND 2001).

Hosek, S., and Cecchine, *Reorganizing the Military Health System: Should There Be a Joint Command?* (2001).

Jenkins, *Countering al Qaeda* (2002).

Lesser, et al., *Countering the New Terrorism* (1999).

McNaughter, et al., "Agility by a Difference Measure," IP-195 (2000).

Peltz, et al., *Speed and Power: Toward an Expeditionary Army* (2003).

Quinlivan, "Coup-Proofing: Its Practice and Consequences in the Middle East," RP-844 (1999).

Ronfeldt, "Tribes, Institutions, Markets, Networks: A Framework About Societal Evolution," P-7967 (1996).

Zimmer, et al., *Charter School Operations and Performance: Evidence from California* (2003).

Managing Change

Implementation Analysis

Berends, *Assessing the Progress of New American Schools* (1999).

Berends, Bodilly, and Kirby, *Facing the Challenges of Whole-School Reform: New American Schools After a Decade* (2002).

Bodilly, "Lessons from New American Schools Development Corporation's Demonstration Phase," MR-729-NASDC (1996).

Loo, et al., *Cannabis Policy, Implementation and Outcomes* (2003).

Moore, et al., *Implementing Best Purchasing and Supply Management Practices* (2002).

Rydell and Everingham, *Controlling Cocaine: Supply vs. Demand Programs* (1994).

Zellman, et al., *Welfare Reform in California: State and Local Implementation of CalWORKS in the First Year* (1999).

Change Management

Berends, *Challenges of Conflict School Reforms: Effects of New American Schools in a High-Poverty District* (2002).

Camm, *Environmental Management in Proactive Commercial Firm: Lesson for Central Logistics Activities in the Department of Defense* (1999).

Camm, *Environmental Management in Proactive Commercial Firms: Lessons for Central Logistics Activities in the Department of Defense* (2001).

Camm, et al., *Implementing Proactive Environment Management: Lessons Learned from Best Commercial Practice* (2001).

Dertouzos, et al., *Facilitating Effective Reform in Army Acquisition* (1998).

Gompert and Lachow, "Transforming U.S. Forces: Lessons from the Wider Revolution," IP-193 (2000).

Hundley, *Past Revolutions: Future Transformations: What Can the History of Revolutions in Military Affairs Tell Us About Transforming the U.S. Military?* (1999).

Lachman, Camm, and Resetar, *Integrated Facility Environmental Management Approaches: Lessons from Industry for Department of Defense Facilities* (2001).

Moore, "Leadership Challenges to Accelerating the DoD Logistics Transformation," PM-1138-OSD (2000).

Schmidt, *Changing Bureaucratic Behavior: Acquisition Reform in the United States Army* (2000).

Schmidt, *Friend or Foe: Bureaucratic Behavior and Acquisition Reform in the U.S. Army* (1998).

Tripp, et al., *Supporting Expeditionary Aerospace Forces: An Integrated Strategic Agile Combat Support Planning Framework* (1999).

Tripp, et al., *Supporting Expeditionary Aerospace Forces: New Agile Combat Support Postures* (2000).

ORGANIZATIONAL LEARNING/INNOVATION MANAGEMENT

Camm, *Environmental Management in Proactive Commercial Firms: Lessons for Central Logistics Activities in the Department of Defense* (2001).

Dobbins, et al., *America's Role in Nation-Building: From Germany to Iraq* (2003).

Garber, Ridgeley, et al., Managed Care and the Evaluation and Adoption of Emerging Medical Technologies, (2000).

Isaacson, et al., "Predicting Military Innovation," DB-242 (1999).

Keltner, Eden, "RAND Research in support of Organizational Innovation," DRU-1645-RC (1997).

Knopman, et al. Systems Innovation within Public and Private Organizations: Case Studies and Options for EPA (2003).

Lorell and Levaux, The Cutting Edge: A Half Century of U.S. Fighter Aircraft R&D (2000).

Resetar, *Technology Forces at Work: Profiles of Environmental Research and Development at DuPont, Intel, Monsanto, and Xerox* (1999).

INDEX

A

Accenture, 153–154
ACOVE (Assessing Care of Vulnerable Elders) project, 84–85
Adaptability, 170–189
  aggregating expertise, 176–178
  creating freedom to imagine, 172–176
  creating freedom to learn, 171–172
  embracing command concept, 186–189
  at Intel Corporation, 15–16
  at Marriott, 95
  in petroleum industry, 3–4
  as pillar of robustness, 109–113
  in planning, 36
  and unbalancing the scorecard, 178–186
Adidas, 28
Administrative blob, 241
Advanced Research Projects Agency (ARPA), 44
Adversaries, anticipating, 196–197
Afghanistan war, 207
Aggregation of expertise, 176–178
Agile combat support, 105–106
Agile manufacturing systems, 28
Agility, 149–170
  at Kvaerner, 13, 14
  at Marriott, 95
  as pillar of robustness, 104–109
  providing authority to act, 165–167
  recruiting in futures tense, 151–153
  and revolution in materials/manufacturing, 28
  setting just-beyond-possible goals, 161–165
  thinking lean, 167–170
  training for, 153–161
Aidid, Mohammed Farrah, 144
AIG, 153–154
Aircraft industry, 79–81

Aker Maritime, 13
Al Qaeda, 99
Alertness, 131–149
  challenging assumptions, 136–138
  expecting surprise, 134–136
  focusing on effects, 147–149
  at Marriott, 94–95
  as pillar of robustness, 100–104
  reducing regret, 138–147
  thinking in futures tense, 131–134
Alignment, 189–199
  anticipating adversaries, 196–197
  communicating through images, 194–196
  ignoring the irrelevant, 197–199
  leading in futures tense, 193–194
  managing careers of leaders, 191–193
  at Marriott, 95–96
  as pillar of robustness, 113–116
Allied Signal, 168
Alternative futures, 131–134
American Telephone & Telegraph (AT&T), 44, 159
Ardais Corporation, 45, 46
Army 21 project, 3
ARPA (Advanced Research Projects Agency), 44
ARPANET, 44
Arquilla, John, 32, 33, 99–100, 135
AS-IS system, 227
Asch, Beth, 150, 222
Assessing Care of Vulnerable Elders (ACOVE) project, 84–85
Assumption-based planning, 35, 97–98, 137–138
Assumptions:
  challenging, 136–138
  failure of, 100
  load–bearing, 13
  in robust organizations, 98

Assumptions (*Cont.*):
  testing of, 34–36
  vulnerability of, 145–146
AstraZeneca, 21
Asymmetrical innovation, 135
The Atlantic Monthly, 137
AT&T (American Telephone &
  Telegraph), 44, 159
Authority to act, 165–167
Aviation industry, 223–224
Avoiding the unintended, 142–145

B
Balanced scorecard, 178
Bank America Corporation, 153–154
Bankes, Steven, 7, 24, 97, 134–135
Baran, Paul, 43–44
Barney, Heather, 115–116
Barrett, Craig, 16
Barriers to success, 233–234
Beltway sniper, 181
Bennett, William, 241
Berra, Yogi, 131
Big hairy audacious goals, 87
Bikson, Tora, 50, 193
Biotechnology, revolution in, 27, 111–112
Birkler, John, 78, 80, 100–101, 136–137, 236
BMW, 109
Boeing, 79, 81, 127, 168
Boiling peace, 22
Bolivia, 135
Bomb-making, 31
Booz Allen Hamilton, 44–45
BP Amoco, 153–154
Break-the-mold reform (schools), 17
Brewer, Dominic, 172, 177, 241
Brunner, Gordon, 20
Builder, Carl, 187
Built-not-to-last organizations, 66
Built-to-flip organizations, 66
Built to Last (James Collins and Jerry
  Porras), 87, 94
Burtless, Gary, 30
Bush, George H. W., 17
Byng, John, 85–86

C
Cadillac, 109
California:
  charter schools, 166
  Riverside County, 239–240
California Wellness Foundation, 148, 149
CALL (Center for Army Lessons
  Learned), 157
Camm, Frank, 22–24, 51, 68–69, 78,
  81–82, 104, 113–114, 159–160, 163,
  164, 178, 204–205, 207–208,
  231–232

Capabilities-based planning, 35
Career management, 191–193
Castro, Fidel, 197
CATIA (Computer-Aided Three-
  Dimension Interactive Application)
  system, 72
Center for Army Lessons Learned
  (CALL), 157
Centralized organizational structure,
  73–77
Chaco War, 135
Challenging assumptions, 136–138
Champions, recruiting, 234–236
Change:
  and communication, 233
  current tone of, 26
  events signaling, 100
  evidence-based, 207–208
  possibility for, 205–210
  proving worth of, 238
  signposts of, 133, 145–146
  state-of-the-world, 23, 24
  and terminations, 44–45
  willingness to embrace, 28
  in workforce demands, 153–154
Change management, 203–243
  and ability of organizations to change,
    205–210
  avoiding quick fixes, 241–242
  building internal momentum, 236–237
  creating sense of urgency, 231–233
  at DuPont, 11–12
  experimentation in, 238–241
  and fear of standing still, 211–212
  long-haul philosophy for, 226–227
  model for, 229
  and performance improvement tools,
    210–211
  and proving that change works, 238
  recruiting champions, 234–236
  removing barriers to success, 233–234
  steps in, 228–230
  and vector for change, 211, 212,
    218–221
  and velocity for change, 211–218
Chapman, Robert, 18, 19
Charisma, performance and, 77–78
Charter schools, 166–167, 225
Chechen military campaign (Russia),
  14–15
Chrysler, 18–19
Churchill, Winston, 8
Cisco, 153–154
Clark, Wesley, 69
Clinical depression, 86
Clorox, 21
Coal industry, 110
Coartlauld Coatings, 84

Cold War:
   uncertainty in, 22–23, 26
   and vulnerability of assumptions, 145
Collaboration:
   and revolution in materials/
      manufacturing, 28
   for Ventura County juvenile
      delinquency, 76–77
Collins, James, 66, 87, 89, 94, 127
Colombia:
   drug industry in, 216
   rebels' use of toxic weapons, 32
Command concept, 186–189
Communication:
   and change, 233
   netwars, 33–34
   through images, 194–196
Competition, performance and, 80–82
Computer-Aided Three-Dimension
   Interactive Application (CATIA)
      system, 72
Computer-assisted decision-making
   system, 7–8
Computer chip manufacture, 15–16
Computers, early construction of,
   129–130
Contingency theories, 191
Core characteristics for high
   performance, 46–47
Corporateness, cultivation of, 159–161
Coup-proofing, 66–67, 209
Cretin, Shan, 57–58, 183–185, 208, 234,
   239
Crime prevention program, 112–113
Cross-functional teams, 176–178
Customs Service, 22
Cyber soldiers, 151, 152

D
DaimlerChrysler, 85
Davis, Paul, 1–2, 25, 35, 36, 38, 50–52,
   134, 147, 148, 190
Decentralized organizational structure,
   73–77, 223
Decision making:
   computer-assisted system for, 7–8
   naturalistic, 189–190
   robust adaptive decision making, 35,
      37, 140–142, 208, 237
Decision-quality information, 186
Deep uncertainty, 24, 25
Deerberg Systems, 84
Defense Communications Agency, 44
Defense Logistics Agency, 214
Define-measure-improve continuous
   improvement system, 9
Delegation:
   and giving authority to act, 165–167

Delegation (Cont.):
   and performance, 85–86
   of responsibility, 191
   and technology, 223
Delphi technique, 185–186
Depression, 86
Dertouzos, James, 50–51, 66, 114,
   161–162, 165
Dewar, James, 24, 26, 35, 97–98, 100,
   124, 133, 134, 137, 138, 145–146,
   185–186
Dogmatism, 239
Dow Chemical, 159
Drugs, war on, 215–216
Duke University, 45
Dumond, John, 9–10, 51, 108, 206, 231,
   235, 236, 238
DuPont:
   as benchmark, 125–126
   environmental management at, 163
   in high performance study, 47, 48
   inflexibility in, 10–12
   innovation and change management
      at, 228
   organizational structure of, 74
   pollution prevention at, 159
   proactive management at, 162
Dying to Know, 241

E
Eagle Alliance, 80
Early Childhood Initiative (Pittsburgh),
   114–115, 196
Eastman Chemical Company, 100
Education reform:
   administrative blob in, 241
   goals for, 224–225
Educational testing research, 217
The Effect of Personnel Quality on the
   Performance of Patriot Air Defense
   Operators, 150
Effectiveness:
   definitions of, 87
   and efficiency, 71–72
   skills blend for, 192
Effects, focusing on, 147–149
Efficiency, performance and, 71–72
Enemy leaders:
   anticipating thinking of, 196–197
   attempted removal of, 143–145
Environmental management, 162–164
   change management in, 226
   metrics for, 178–179
   organizational structure for, 73–74
Environmentally-friendly cars, 18–19
Everingham, Susan, 77, 165, 182–183
Evidence-based change, 207–208
Experimentation, 238–241

Expertise, aggregation of, 176–178
Exploratory analysis, 35
Explore-then-adapt model, 131

F
Fault tolerant organizations, 146
FDA (*see* U.S. Food and Drug
    Administration)
Fertilizer (as weapon), 31
The Fifth Discipline Fieldbook (Peter
    Senge), 158
Flat organizations, 73–76
Ford Motor Company:
    change management at, 203–204
    and new generation vehicles,
        18–19
    proactive management at, 162
Fortune, 12, 20, 96
Four pillars of high performance (*see*
    Robustness)
FOX Pollution Packers, 84
France, Germany's invasion of, 6
Freedom:
    to imagine, 172–176
    to learn, 171–172
Fukuyama, Francis, 74–76, 84
Futures tense:
    leading in, 193–194
    measurement in, 180–181
    recruiting in, 151–153
    thinking in, 130–134
    training in, 155

G
Galbraith, John Kenneth, 234
Gates, Susan, 70, 177
Gays in the military, 198–199
General Electric Capital, 170
General Mills, 153–154
General Motors, 18–19
Genetic engineering, 27
Genomics Collaborative, Inc., 45, 46
Germaischer Lloyd, 83
Germany, invasion of France by, 6
Global commerce, revolution in,
    30–31
Global Course of the Information Revolution,
    29
Global Positioning System, 110
Globalphobia, 30
Goals:
    big hairy audacious goals, 87
    for change, 224–226
    just-beyond-possible, 161–165
Gompert, David, 31
Gonzalez, Gabriella, 161
Good to Great (James Collins), 89
Gordon, John, 132

Government:
    control over information by, 29
    coup-proofing, 67
    partnership with automakers, 19–20
Great man theories, 191
Groundbreaker program, 80
Groupthink, 198
Guiding coalitions, 236–237
Gulf War of 1991, 155–156
    command concept in, 188
    supply lines during, 8, 9

H
Hafner, Katie, 43, 44
Hamel, Gary, 98
Hamilton, Laura, 161
Hanks, Christopher, 71
"Hardening" organizations, 97
Harvard University, 111
H.B. Fuller, 159
Health care:
    alignment in, 113
    decentralization in, 73
    goals for change in, 225
    information and quality of, 83
    metrics in, 103–104, 183
    for older adults, 84–85
    public access to information, 241–242
    quality movement in, 208
    team-based, 177–178
The Heart of Change (John Kotter), 231,
    232
Hewlett-Packard, 102–103, 153–154,
    162, 235
Hierarchy, performance and, 73–77
High performance, 43–90
    and charisma, 77–78
    and competition, 80–82
    core organizational principles for,
        46–47
    and delegation, 85–86
    and design of organizations, 47–48
    and efficiency, 71–72
    and hierarchy, 73–77
    identifying characteristics associated
        with, 52–64
    and information availability, 82–85
    and intentional poor performance,
        66–68
    Internet survey of organizations, 48–52
    lessons on, 64–65
    and management quality, 78–80
    measuring, 72
    "minimal viability" for, 78–80
    and mission of organization, 87–89
    and neatness/orderliness, 68–70
    and New American Schools initiative,
        17–18

High performance (*Cont.*):
  pillars of, 64 (*See also* Robustness)
  winnowing strategy in study of, 52–65
Hitler, Adolf, 197
Hoffman, Bruce, 31, 177
Honda, 18
Hosek, James, 151, 164–166
Hosmer, Stephen, 88–89, 143–145, 196–197
Host Marriott, 94
Housing industry, 173–174
Hubris-nemesis complex, 197
Human tissue banks, 45–46
Hunches, 189–190
Hundley, Richard, 136, 174–176
Hussein, Saddam, 88–89, 156, 197
Hypercohesion, 198

I
IBM, 85, 127
  change management at, 203–204
  proactive management at, 162
  supplier base of, 168
Ignorance:
  characteristics associated with, 63
  vulnerability from, 4–8
Images, communication through,
    194–196
Imagination, freedom of, 172–176
Incentives:
  for environmental management,
    163–164
  workforce change due to, 222
Incoherence, organizational, 16
Inconsistency:
  characteristics associated with, 63
  vulnerability from, 4, 16–22
India, 29, 30
Indifference:
  characteristics associated with, 63
  vulnerability from, 4, 12–16
Inertia, 205–206
Inflexibility:
  characteristics associated with, 63
  vulnerability from, 4, 8–12
Information:
  collecting/using right information,
    181–182
  for command-and-control, 195
  decision-quality, 186
  from images, 194–195
  in Mexican netwar, 33–34
  performance and availability of, 82–85
  revolution in, 29–30
  and structure of terrorist organizations,
    99
  technology and sharing of, 223
  too much, 182–183
Infrastructure of high performance, 63–64

Innovation:
  in aircraft industry, 80
  asymmetrical, 135
  and change management, 228
  and competition, 81
  at DuPont, 10–11
  and freedom of imagination, 183
  in housing industry, 173–174
  incentives for, 135
  at Intel, 15–16
  at Marriott, 96
  in mature process industries, 3
  at Procter & Gamble, 20
  reasons for stopping, 240–241
  in ship design, 83–84
  by Sodexho, 69
Intel Corporation, 15–16, 159
  environmental management at, 163
  supplier base of, 168
Intelligent shoes, 28
Intensity of change, 216–218
Internal momentum, building, 236–237
Internet, Baran's imagination of, 43–44
Intuition, 185–186
Iraq War, 24
Irreducible trade-offs, 142
Irrelevant, ignoring the, 197–199
Isaacson, Jeffrey, 135, 136

J
Jenkins, Brian, 99
Joe, Leland, 71–72, 83, 108–109, 165,
    173, 182, 191, 209, 239
John Deere, 82, 167–168
JOHNNIAC, 129
Johnson, David, 193
Jotun, 84
Juvenile delinquency program, 76–77

K
Karasik, Theodore, 31
Karoly, Lynn A., 222–223
Kindergarten class size, 143
Kinko's, 65
Kirby, Sheila Nataraj, 115–116
Klerman, Jacob, 239–240
Klitgaard, Robert, 172
Knopman, Debra, 232–233
Kosovo war, 69–70, 88, 186–187, 195
Kotter, John, 231, 232, 237
Kulick, Jonathan, 190
Kurds, toxic weapons of, 32
Kvaerner, 13–14

L
Labor force (*see* Workforce)
Lachman, Beth, 163
Lafley, A. G., 20, 21

Lambeth, William, 155–156
LAPD (*see* Los Angeles Police Department)
Layne, Christopher, 135
Leaders:
    charismatic, 77–78
    coup-proofing, 66
    development of, 191–193
    hubris-nemesis complex in, 197
Leadership:
    for alignment around mission, 191
    developing competencies for, 192
    in futures tense, 193–194
    recruiting champions, 234–236
    and revolution in materials/
        manufacturing, 28
Leading Change (John Kotter), 237
Lean manufacturing, alignment in, 115
Lean thinking, 167–170
Learning:
    creating freedom for, 171–172
    from experience, 155–157
    reducing cost of, 157–159
Lempert, Robert, 7, 24, 37, 97, 124,
        134–135, 138–142, 208, 237
Lessons, learning, 155–157
Libicki, Martin, 181, 182
Libya, 145
Light, Paul, 234
Litan, Robert, 30
Living things, revolution in, 27
Load-bearing assumptions, 13
Lockerbie air tragedy, 145
Lockheed-Martin, 79, 81
Logistics:
    in Air Force, 106–107
    of Army supply systems, 8–10, 207
    inertia and reform of, 205–206
    lean, 207
Long-haul change philosophy, 226–227
Longer-range policy analysis, 35
Lorell, Mark, 61, 81
Los Angeles Police Department (LAPD),
        67–68, 157
Lyon, Matthew, 43, 44

M
MacArthur, Douglas, 187
The Machine that Could, 19
Mahnovski, Sergej, 3
Management:
    of change (*see* Change management)
    performance and quality of, 78–80
    supply-chain, 228–229
    tools for, 210–211
Manufacturing, revolution in, 27–28
Marriott:
    Associates First program, 159
    as benchmark, 125–126

Marriott (*Cont.*):
    in high performance study, 47, 48
    innovation and change management
        at, 228
    learning systems at, 158
    robustness at, 94–96
Marriott, Bill, 94, 95
Marriott International, 94
Masa Yards Group, 13, 14
Materials, revolution in, 27–28
May, Ernest, 6
McDonnell-Douglas, 127
McGlynn, Beth, 83, 103–104, 113, 165
McKillop, Tom, 21
Measurement:
    in futures tense, 180–181
    in health care, 103–104
    of high performance, 72
    new metrics for, 178–186
    of performance, 101
    selecting metrics for, 103
Media arts, agility in, 104–105
Mercedes, 109
Merck, 153–154, 168
Metals industry, 110
Mexico, 33–34
Microsoft, 85, 153–154
Microworld simulators, 158–159
Military aircraft industry, 79–80
Milosevic, Slobodan, 69–70, 88,
        195–197
Mind, barriers of, 233–234
"Minimal viability," 78–80
Mining industry, 110–111
Minneapolis health care, 208
Mission:
    and high performance, 87–89
    and identification of success, 66
    and leadership, 191
    mismatch of skills and, 193–194
    in robust organizations, 130
Mission-system capability, 147
Moe, Terry, 66
Momentum, internal, 236–237
Monsanto, 111–112
Monsanto's Law, 112
Montgomery, Bernard, 188
Moore, Nancy, 208, 213–214, 216, 226,
        232–236, 240
Motivation, velocity for change and,
        215–216
Motor Trend, 7, 8, 20
Motorola, 9

N
Nanotechnology, 28
National Cancer Institute, 45
National Medal of Technology, 12

NATO (North Atlantic Treaty Organization), 69–70, 196
Naturalistic decision making, 189–190
Naval Sea Systems Command (NAVSEA), 217–218
Neatness, performance and, 68–70
Netwars, 33–34, 99
New American Schools initiative, 17–18, 196, 219
Newport News Shipbuilding, 220, 221
Nichiporuk, Brian, 132
Nimitz, Chester, 187
No Child Left Behind Act, 18
No-surprises future, 134
Norsk Hydro, 84
North Atlantic Treaty Organization (NATO), 69–70, 196
Northrop Grumman, 79, 81, 221
NTSB (U.S. National Transportation Safety Board), 223–224
Nuclear reactor refueling, 220, 221

O
Ohno, Taiichi, 115
Oliker, Olga, 14–15
Olin Corporation, 74, 162, 179
Orderliness, performance and, 68–70
Organizational design, 2
 for high performance, 47–48, 64–65
 and level of uncertainty, 25
 and wild cards in information revolution, 29–30
Organizational effectiveness, 87
Organizational incoherence, 16
Organizational structure, performance and, 73–77
Outsourcing (of NSA IT jobs), 80

P
Pakistan, 30
Panis, Constantijn, 222–223
Paraguay, 135
Pardee Graduate School, 172
Partners in Care program, 86
Partnerships:
 advantages of, 81–82
 automaker-government, 19–20
 industry, 20–21
 as source of viability, 80
 in treating depression, 86
Pearl Harbor attack, 5–6
Penske, 9
Performance:
 improvement tools for, 210–211
 intentionally poor, 66–68
 measuring, 101
 two-step process for improving, 205
 (*See also* High performance)

Performing arts, 180–181
Peterson, D. J., 3
Petroleum industry:
 adaptability of, 3–4
 uncertainty in, 3
 vulnerabilities of, 4
Pfizer, Inc., 84–85, 153–154
Philadelphia Naval Shipyard, 13
Pillars of high performance, 64
 (*See also* Robustness)
Planning:
 adaptability in, 36
 for alternative futures, 131–132
 assumption-based, 97–98, 137–138
 case for change in, 229
 strategic, 35
 traditional methods of, 7
 for uncertainty, 34
Plausible realities, scenario space of, 7
Pleege, Shari, 181, 182
Pollution prevention, 159–160
Poor performance, 66–68
Popper, Steven, 6, 7, 24, 26, 37, 97, 134–135, 139–140, 216
Porras, Jerry, 87, 94, 127
Portfolio careers, 159
Predict-then-act model, 36–37, 131
Predictions, failure of, 134
Predictive relationships with performance, 59–63
Prevailing wisdom, challenging, 130
Proactive environmental management, 162–164
Procter & Gamble, 20–21, 153–154
 as benchmark, 125–126
 environmental site audits, 104
 in high performance study, 47, 48
 innovation and change management at, 228
 pollution control, 160–161
 proactive management at, 162
Program management, 220–221

Q
Qaddafi, Muammar, 145
Qatar, 122
Quality of management, performance and, 78–80
Quantum dots, 28
Quick fixes, avoiding, 241–242
Quinlivan, James, 16–17, 66–67, 70, 101–102, 153, 165, 183, 209–210, 234

R
RAND:
 cross-functional teams at, 176–178

RAND (*Cont.*):
  high performance study by (*see* High
    performance)
  transformation of, 116–123
  (*See also specific topics*)
Recruiting:
  of champions, 234–236
  in futures tense, 151–153
Reducing regret, 138–147
  by avoiding the unintended, 142–145
  by reducing vulnerability, 145–247
  by starting robust, then adapting,
    140–142
Refueling, reactor, 220, 221
Resetar, Susan, 163
Resiliency, 98
Revolution(s), 26–27
  conceptual breakthroughs associated
    with, 135
  in global commerce, 30–31
  in information, 29–30
  in living things, 27
  in materials and manufacturing,
    27–28
  in revolutions, 31–32
  in strategy, 32–34
Rich, Michael, 116–118, 120–121
Rigby, Darrell, 210–211
River War (Britain), 8
Riverside County, California,
    239–240
Robbins, Marc, 77–78, 86, 107–108,
    205–206
Robert, Albert, 78, 191, 192
Robust adaptive decision making, 35, 37,
    140–142, 208, 237
Robustness, 93–127
  and adaptability, 109–113
  and agility, 104–109
  and alertness, 100–104
  and alignment, 113–116
  benchmarks of, 122–126
  defining, 97–99
  four pillars of, 99–100
  at Marriott, 94–96
  operating with, 130–131 (*See also
    specific topics, e.g.*: Agility)
  planning and levels of, 37–38
  at RAND, 116–122
  resiliency vs., 98
Roll, Robert, 38–39, 105, 189
Rolling Stones, 106
Ronfeldt, David, 32, 33, 99–100, 197
Rossi's Law, 239
Rostker, Bernard, 176–177
Rumsfeld, Donald, 226
Russian military, indifference in, 14–15

S
Safety in the Skies, 223–224
Saturn plant (Spring Hill), 101–102
Scenario space:
  creating, 138
  of plausible realities, 7
  of possible futures, 117–118
Scenarios:
  Delphi technique in creating, 185–186
  exploration of, 36–38
Schank, John, 137
Schelling, Thomas, 5
Schiphol airport, 34
Schlumberger, 153–154
Schwarzkopf, H. Norman, 188
Scorecard, balanced, 178 (*See also*
    Unbalancing the scorecard)
Self-driving cars, 110
Semiotics, 133
Senge, Peter, 158
September 11, 2001:
  and demand for international
    leadership, 194
  warnings of, 181
Serbian war, 195, 227
Sexual preference, impact of, 198–199
Shaping actions, 146
Shaping the Next One Hundred Years
    (Robert Lempert, Steven Popper, and
    Steven Bankes), 24, 97
Ship design, 83–84
Shoes, intelligent, 28
Shulsky, Abram, 74–76, 84
Siemens, 85
Simplicity of metrics, 184–185
Simulators, microworld, 158–159
Singularity, 38
The Six Sigma Way, 23
Skills:
  for effectiveness, 192
  mismatch of mission and, 193–194
Smart materials, 28
Social Security funding, 136
Sodexho, 68–69
Somalia:
  attack on Mohammed Farrah Aidid,
    144
  peace-keeping in, 107
South Oxnard Challenge Project,
    76–77
Sri Lankan rebels, toxic weapons of, 32
State-of-the-world uncertainty, 23–25
    (*See also* Revolution(s))
Statistical uncertainty, 22–24
Stecher, Brian, 161
Stone and aggregates industry, 110
Storytelling, analysis and, 190–191

Strategic alliances, 168
Strategic distribution management
    initiative, 214–215
Strategic planning, 35
Strategy, 2
    for Army agility, 107
    revolution in, 32–34
    swarming as, 32–33
    and systems design, 93
strategy+business, 44
Success, barriers to, 233–234
Sun Microsystems, 153–154
Supply-chain management, 228–229
Supply lines, Army, 8–10, 207
Supply-side factors, 162
Surprise, expecting, 134–136
Swarming, 32–33
Systems design, 93

T
Teams:
    agility in, 108–109
    creating effective, 223
    cross–functional, 176–178
Technology:
    agility from, 149
    impact on work, 223
    and revolution in information, 29
Technology treadmill, 15, 16
Terrorism:
    corporations expecting attack from, 32
    and evolution toward netwar, 99
    and "failed states," 29
    and revolution in revolutions, 31–32
    robustness of, 99, 100
Thinking lean, 167–170
Thomson, James, 117
Three-apes problem, 139
3M, 159
Tissue banks, 45–46
TO-BE approach, 227
Total Quality Management (TQM),
    207–208
Toxic warfare, 31
Toxic weapons, 31–32
Toyoda, Eiji, 115
Toyota Motor Company, 9, 18, 19, 109, 115
TQM (Total Quality Management),
    207–208
Trade-offs, irreducible, 142
Trafalgar House, 14
Training for agility, 153–161
    by cultivating corporateness, 159–161
    by drawing the right lessons, 155–157
    by reducing cost of learning, 157–159
Transit industry, 152–153
Treverton, Gregory, 23, 29, 37, 193

Tripp, Robert, 207, 226–227
TRW, 153–154
The 21ˢᵗ Century at Work (Lynn A. Karoly
    and Constantijn Panis), 222–223

U
Unbalancing the scorecard, 178–186
    by caution in use of metrics, 182–184
    by collecting the right dots, 181–182
    by inviting intuition, 185–186
    by keeping it simple, 184–185
    by measuring in futures tense, 180–181
Uncertainty, 1–2, 22–39
    changing character of, 22–25
    deep, 24, 25
    and exploration of scenarios, 36–38
    planning on, 34
    and revolution in global commerce,
        30–31
    and revolution in information, 29–30
    and revolution in living things, 27
    and revolution in materials and
        manufacturing, 27–28
    and revolution in revolutions, 31–32
    and revolution in strategy, 32–34
    and six revolutions, 26–34
    sources of, 25–26
    state-of-the-world, 23–25
    statistical, 22–24
    steps in dealing with, 25
    and testing of assumptions, 34–36
Uncertainty-sensitivity planning, 35, 37,
    97
Unicharm Corporation, 20–21
Unintended effects, avoiding, 142–145
United Parcel Service (UPS), 158
United Way, 114–115
Unocal, 153–154
UPS (United Parcel Service), 158
Urgency, creating sense of, 231–233
U.S. Air Force:
    agility in, 105–107, 226–227
    and Baran's imagination of Internet, 43,
        44
    developing leadership competencies,
        192
    fuel tank vulnerability study, 2
    Kosovo conflict, 186–187
    lean logistics in, 207
    Serbian war, 195
U.S. Army:
    agility in, 107–109
    alternative futures planning for, 132
    Army 21 project, 3
    Center for Army Lessons Learned, 157
    future opponents of, 169–170
    leadership corps training, 193

U.S. Army (*Cont.*):
lightning over water strategy, 169
recruiter motivation, 161–162
Serbian war, 195
supply systems, 8–10, 207
(*See also* Velocity Management program
(Army))
U.S. Customs Service:
as benchmark, 125–126
in high performance study, 47, 48
innovation and change management at,
228
U.S. Food and Drug Administration
(FDA), 22
as benchmark, 125–126
in high performance study, 47, 48
innovation and change management at,
228
U.S. Marine Corps mess halls, 68–69
U.S. military:
adaptability in, 111
attempts to remove enemy leaders,
143–145
career management system, 192–193
gays in, 198–199
health care organization in, 73
quality of personnel, 150
recruiting by, 151–152
strategic distribution management
initiative, 214–215
uncertain future of, 22
and Vietnam War, 87–88
U.S. National Security Agency, 80
U.S. National Transportation Safety
Board (NTSB), 223–224
U.S. Navy:
aircraft carriers in, 176
Naval Sea Systems Command
(NAVSEA), 217–218
nuclear reactor refueling, 220–221
U.S. Transportation Command, 214
U.S. Veterans Health Administration
(VHA), 22
as benchmark, 125–126
in high performance study, 47, 48
innovation and change management at,
228
U.S.S. Nimitz, 220, 221

V
Välikangas, Liisa, 98
VAM (Vulnerability Assessment &
Mitigation Methodology), 146
Vector for change, 211, 212, 218–221
goals, 224–226
participants, 222–224
preferred, 212
target, 219–221

Velocity for change, 211–218
duration, 213–215
intensity, 216–218
motivation, 215–216
preferred, 212
Velocity Management program (Army),
9, 108, 178, 205–207, 214, 231, 236,
238
Ventura County, 76–77
VHA (*see* U.S. Veterans Health
Administration)
Vietnam War, 87–89, 209
Violence Prevention Initiative (VPI),
148–149
Virtual organizations, 84, 100
Volvo, 7–8, 98, 140, 162
Von Neumann, John, 129
Vouchers, education, 225
VPI (Violence Prevention Initiative),
148–149
Vulnerability, 3–22
from ignorance, 5–8
from inconsistency, 16–22
from indifference, 12–16
from inflexibility, 8–12
reducing, 145–147
sources of, 4
to uncertainty, 37
Vulnerability Assessment & Mitigation
Methodology (VAM), 146

W
Wal-Mart, 9, 113
Walker, Warren, 34
Wall Street Journal, 10–12
Walt Disney World Resorts:
incentives at, 163
pollution control, 160
proactive management at, 162
War on drugs, 215–216
Warfare, swarming in, 33–34
Warning tree, 146–147
The Washington Post, 157
Watson, Thomas, Jr., 129
Weapons:
fertilizer as, 31
toxic, 31–32
*What We Know and What We Need to
Know about Vouchers and Charter
Schools*, 225
Where Wizards Stay Up Late (Katie
Hafner and Matthew Lyon),
43, 44
Whirlpool, 168
*Why Milosevic Decided to Settle When He
Did* (Stephen Hosmer), 196–197
Wohlstetter, Albert, 1–3, 93
Wohlstetter, Roberta, 5–6

Wolf, Charles, 131, 172
Workforce:
   agility in, 149–150
   change management for,
      222–226
   and globalization, 30–31
   ignoring irrelevant in, 197–199
   information revolution and reshaping
      of, 29
   training, 153–161
World War II, 187–188
Worldwide Express, 108

X
Xerox, 134
   environmental management at, 163
   lean thinking at, 170
   pollution prevention at, 159

Y
Yukos Oil, 13

Z
Zapatista rebels, 33–34

ABOUT THE AUTHOR

Paul C. Light is the Paulette Goddard Professor of Public Service at the Robert F. Wagner School of Public Service at New York University, and he holds the Dillon Chair at the Brookings Institution, where he established the Center for Public Service in 1999. The author of 19 books on business, public service, and education, he is a familiar voice on NPR's "Morning Edition" and a well–known public speaker on organizational life.